The Business of Cannabis

The Business of Cannabis

New Policies for the New Marijuana Industry

D. J. Summers

 PRAEGER™

An Imprint of ABC-CLIO, LLC

Santa Barbara, California • Denver, Colorado

Library of Congress Cataloging-in-Publication Data

Names: Summers, D. J., author.
Title: The business of cannabis : new policies for the new marijuana industry / D. J. Summers.
Description: 1 Edition. | Santa Barbara, California : Praeger, An Imprint of ABC-CLIO, LLC, [2018] | Includes bibliographical references and index.
Identifiers: LCCN 2017054055 (print) | LCCN 2018005548 (ebook) | ISBN 9781440857867 (hard copy : alk. paper) | ISBN 9781440857874 (ebook)
Subjects: LCSH: Marijuana industry—United States—Government policy.
Classification: LCC HD9019.M382 (ebook) | LCC HD9019.M382 U378 2018 (print) | DDC 338.1/73790973—dc23
LC record available at https://lccn.loc.gov/2017054055

ISBN: 978-1-4408-5786-7 (print)
        978-1-4408-5787-4 (ebook)

22 21 20 19 18   1 2 3 4 5

This book is also available as an eBook.

Praeger
An Imprint of ABC-CLIO, LLC

ABC-CLIO, LLC
130 Cremona Drive, P.O. Box 1911
Santa Barbara, California 93116-1911

www.abc-clio.com

This book is printed on acid-free paper ∞

Manufactured in the United States of America

Contents

Preface

I wanted this book to be a lens and a warning. Maybe I hit the mark, maybe I didn't.

I started covering the cannabis industry in Alaska in the summer of 2015. I did not decide to—in fact, I wasn't even in the state when it was decided I should cover it. When my co-worker picked me up from a short vacation to California, he told me he and the other editorial staff of my newspaper simply decided I would do it. He offered to flip me for the beat. I'm glad I didn't take him up on it.

I got to work building sources and attending regulatory board meetings and industry association meetings and nighttime parties at Anchorage's now-defunct smokeasy, Pot Luck Events, the de facto war room/night club of the advocates and business hopefuls flocking to the scene. Only weeks into covering the beat, I started noticing some faces falling. Many of those faces belonged to the advocates and vote-rustlers who jumped for joy when Alaska's cannabis legalizing Ballot Measure 2 passed. As they sat through board meetings and drained their energy trying to wade through the licensing process—trying to rectify what they wanted with what was—I couldn't help thinking, "Maybe they didn't know exactly what they were getting into."

Legalization advocates often come from the counterculture. I'm not the first journalist with a "careful what you wish for" message.

The political-industrial complex in the United States is just that—complex. When voters give the thumbs up to recreational weed, they vote for an outcome only, a legal gram in hand to roll and smoke. If they want something to do with the process—growing the gram or selling the Zig Zags to roll it—they are in for a rude awakening about the realities of commerce in this upstart industry.

We as a nation ought to talk about those realities, though, and ask whether they resemble what we really want. We should talk about how the system we have works in practice and whether it makes us not just better citizens, but better people. We have a big, grinding machine—what happens to a nug of White Widow when we throw it in, and do we like it?

If cannabis can ignite some interest in formerly uninterested people in the question, then this book is a win.

I wrote this book with the journalist's tool kit of reports, studies, and interviews, which is mostly to provide context and look for trends. Fortunately, two makes a pattern, and in the cannabis industry, there is always a pattern emerging to pore over.

The fact that all eyes are on cannabis helped the research. Even though there are plenty of studies on cannabis's medical impacts, the studies on market trends and economics are scarcer than for most other industries. There are many on policy and safety and tax impacts, however, and I made good use of them, as I did with the market trend and profitability reports many of the cannabis data firms produce in order to get policymakers' support.

What I couldn't get from studies, I got from news. I relied heavily on the excellent reporting being done around the country on the troubles the industry faces and what the Band-Aids are, in particular, the reporting of Debra Borchardt, Jacob Sullum, David Miyoga, and John Schroyer. Fortunately, pot is so existentially important to digital readers that no single national cannabis-centric event goes without dozens of reporters dog piling on it, like a Minor Threat mosh pit. In a way, cannabis testifies to the power of the press—when the press pays enough attention and the public enough attention. If only it were so with city council corruption—which is happening tonight, in your city council—or local charity, or any other issue citizens could pay attention to but can't smoke.

To fill in blanks and get context, I did as many interviews with industry leaders, political strategists, and officials as time allowed for. Time was indeed a factor, with Canada's recreational system set to start in the summer of 2018 and California to start licensing its recreational businesses in early 2018.

I have too many people to thank for getting me to book writing point, but a few in particular deserve a shout-out—I could not have done this without any of you.

First, thanks to my editor, Hilary Claggett, for working with a first-time author and especially for working with me on the deadline. To Stephanie Prokop for believing I could write a book and knowing I should at least try and then making me try, foot dragging and heel digging be damned. Her husband, Darren, for setting up an introduction with a publisher. My editor at the *Alaska Journal of Commerce*, Andrew Jensen, for teaching me to dig, to break numbers into narrative, and to look for the narrative people hide behind the numbers.

I owe untold gratitude to the friends who encouraged me along the way—three of Alaska's very finest reporters in particular: Elwood Brehmer, for not claiming the pot beat, because he could have and probably would have done a better job with it; Rashah McChesney, who told me to "just tell the story"—sorry, girl, I know it's heavy reading; and Elizabeth Earl, who made it a point to let me know when my motivations seemed less than journalistic. Thanks to the other friends who cheered me up with beer and let me crash their couches and barbecues for a chance to get away from the screen and mooch free food—Danielle Downs and her crew; the Robison family; Ben Jones and his new bride, Tara, for giving me a place to stay and to focus.

My brother Nate and his wife Allie, who told me to come stay with them, who gave me room and board and a truck, for no other reason than wanting to help. It did, and more than you can ever know. My sister Amber and her husband Jared, who are such a rock of cheer and vitality that visiting is like a reorientation to humanity. My brother Matt, who gave me the anti-authoritarian prism any journalist worth his salt needs.

For Mom, who never wanted me to settle for a job I only wanted to do for the money. Last but most important, for my Dad, who taught me to read, and to love to read, so well that it ended up spilling over into writing.

Check it out, Dad. I wrote a book.

Introduction

Cannabis is the consumer revolution of President Donald J. Trump's era.

In many ways, the late 2010s feel like a rerun, with the big difference of global populism and a populist American president.

Trump is the latest in a line of conservative presidents who have assumed office during periods of social upheaval, political divisiveness, threats of nuclear war and Islamic fundamentalism, immigration concerns, and a colossal upcoming younger generation of vocally liberal voters with penchants for street protests and weed.

Cannabis, it seems, is always somewhere in the mix.

Former president Richard Nixon created the Controlled Substances Act, which makes pot illegal, at the tail end of the 1960s civil rights activist age, first declaring a "War on Drugs" in 1971—a move a former Nixon advisor later claimed was specifically aimed to disrupt blacks and hippies. Former president Ronald Reagan ramped up spending and pushed for stiffer imprisonment penalties as the Iran Contra scandal began and the Cold War passed its final decade. Next, George H. W. Bush intensified the effort, promising CIA assistance and billions of dollars to halt international supply chains as the nation introduced itself to Saddam Hussein. Former president George W. Bush threw even more money to the cause against the backdrop of the War on Terror. The two Democratic presidents, Bill Clinton and Barack Obama, did little to reverse policies in their 16 combined years in the White House, though Obama's presidency marked the first time the federal government agreed to at least turn a blind eye to state-level reforms.

Trump not only inherited the War on Terror's continuation, but also the War on Drugs itself and all the cultural changes packaged alongside it. His presidency, though, brought a new flavor to the White House.

Trump's upset election in 2016 made the media world explode with think pieces about direct democracy and populism, which run the gamut, depending on the author's views. *The Washington Post* wrote Trump's populism was a "ruse" following the exit of advisor Steve Bannon from the White House in

August 2017, though it was the first to connect the dots in 2016 with a piece about the rise of global populism. Other *Post* pieces branded Trump with "authoritarian populism." If the Daily Beast publishes an article about Trump's populism being "phony," Bloomberg is there two weeks later to assure the world "Donald Trump Really Is a Populist."

Populism's popularity in the late 2010s has steam. Trump's victory pitted the popular vote against the Electoral College and an experienced Big Government politician against a Beltway outsider. The national ballot to remove Great Britain from the European Union succeeded. The media mostly characterizes populist agendas like the Brexit vote as uninformed and reactionary, but with cannabis, the anti-direct democracy furor flowing from newsrooms changes its tone. Populist tactics are effective, if cannabis is any lead. Brexit worked. The popular vote won the presidency. Cannabis ballots are passing.

Cannabis is a study in populist background.

For the entirety of human history, cannabis or its nonpsychoactive variant, hemp, was simply another plant. Hemp made clothes, rope, paper, and other products based on fibrous material on nearly every continent dating back to prehistory. The ancient world, including the Chinese, Egyptians, and Greeks, notes cannabis as a medicinal plant.

It was political leaders who banned it internationally. The 20th century's democratic nation-states were the first to ban it in treaties grown from the death of the 19th century's empires. Following World War I, the League of Nations, the United Nations' (UN) precursor, made a treaty aimed to discourage to use of cocaine and opium and their derivatives, mostly in use in each of the nations and regions formerly controlled by the British Empire. Several decades and treaties later, the Single Convention on Narcotic Drugs placed cannabis alongside them in 1961.

In the United States, the Marijuana Tax Act of 1937 (originally spelled "marihuana") made trafficking cannabis federally illegal without paying the prohibitive tax. At the time, cannabis was associated with incoming Mexican migrant workers fleeing the Mexican Revolution. Congress passed the Controlled Substances Act (CSA) in 1970, with cannabis in the most restrictive category, after the Supreme Court found the Marijuana Tax Act of 1937 unconstitutional. The CSA now keeps the United States in compliance with the UN's treaty.

Efforts to get a second look at cannabis and investigate its medical uses have all failed. The Drug Enforcement Agency and the Food and Drug Administration will not budge on loosening the difficult track to opening the testing pathways.

Now that states took their own route, cannabis serves as a perfect example of the populist's view of Washington, D.C., simultaneously overreaching yet unresponsive, intrusive yet unhelpful, demanding yet withholding. It installs environmental protections that it cannot enforce on cannabis. It calls for cannabis companies to have clean financials, but also denies the ability to track financial information. It wants highly tested consumable products, but will not give the cannabis industry guidance on what to test for or how to best test for it. It wants to encourage a nation of small businesses, but hamstrings small cannabis business from accessing the small business opportunities available to other industries.

The populist prism colors cannabis in a certain light, as a substance users seem quite willing to use of their own volition, without federal permission. Meanwhile, opponents want no part of it.

> As state legislators consider a proposal to give Marylanders a say in whether or not to legalize recreational marijuana in 2018, we hope the lawmakers will seriously consider the impact such a measure could have on the safety of our roadways. With an increasing number of impaired drivers 'high' on our highways, it is important that the state not contribute to this disturbing and dangerous trend.[1]

Ragina Cooper Averella, a worker for AAA, wrote that as an editorial in the *Baltimore Sun* on February 1, 2017, sparking what turned into a sustained anti-legalization lobbying effort from AAA across multiple states. Giving Marylanders "a say," in this light, is a "dangerous and disturbing trend."

Most opposition to cannabis legalization has the same take—that states moving a potentially harmful substance through direct democracy is a huge national risk. Instead, they try to put the conversation back on track to the Food and Drug Administration for more trials and studies about medical uses. Drug reformers' successes in the last five years, though, revolved entirely around giving Americans a direct "say."

Ballot initiatives drove nearly every legalization campaign for recreational weed—and none of them by a big margin. The only exception was in Vermont, where a legalization measure passed in bill form. Washington's ballot won with 56 percent, Alaska's by 53 percent, Colorado's by 55 percent, Oregon's by 56 percent, California's by 57 percent, Nevada's by 54 percent, Maine's by 50.26 percent, and Massachusetts's by 54 percent. In Washington, D.C., a district controlled by the federal government, the initiative passed by 70 percent.

Consumerism probably played as big a role as voter altruism. The voter turnout numbers correspond roughly to the amount of Americans who smoked cannabis in the last year.

What's good for industry is good for legalization campaigns, and vice versa. Behind pot legalization is a fresh, new industrial complex all its own. The states that have had the most success and received the most press are those with the commercial recreational model, rather than the more highly controlled medical options or less consumerist decriminalization options practiced by other states. Consumer choice, profit motive, and need for taxes accelerated the cannabis reform movement to its present American speed.

Behind that consumerism is, of course, the supply side. Illegal for nearly a century, legalization is dropping cannabis into something that will turn a formerly countercultural icon into commerce as usual. More than 80 years of prohibition means cannabis missed out on technological and industrial advances that would have given consumers more choice. With nearly every other agricultural product, consumers have an enormous variety of value-added products—potatoes become Lays, corn becomes Maker's Mark, yucca is processed to make aloe-packed skin care products. With cannabis, consumer demand in the regulated market is only starting to produce value-added products.

The cannabis industry is not growing, or at least not per se. It always existed, in basements and back alleys and border patrols; the cash coming in is simply visible now instead of locked in an underground, unquantifiable economy. To bring it into the light will be to change it in unpredictable ways, some of which are starting to show in states where it is legal.

If the United States is to ever enter the coming juggernaut of international cannabis, it has enormous changes to undergo.

Cannabis has missed out on an entire century's worth of human progress, and arguably the most rapidly advancing era known to human history, at that. Corn growers in the early 1900s can't have predicted how their crop would grow with rest of the world. Until it becomes fully legal, cannabis won't see the full scope of what the term *industry* really means, though it is catching on rapidly.

In the U.S. commercial world, cannabis will grow more complex than an ear of corn, which by itself doesn't matter commercially or politically as much as farmers insurance for the corn grower, agricultural political action committees (PACs) that hunt for corn subsidies, ethanol for automobiles, high fructose corn syrup to save the U.S. sweet-lovers from Cuban sugarcane embargoes, irrigation equipment manufacturers, stock prices on one of hundreds of byproducts or direct supply chains and distribution networks from Nebraska to Maine and all the trucking and shipping companies that go with them, seed patents, and John Deere tractors. International commerce doesn't care about ears of corn, either—it cares about export agreements, global shipping magnates, political stability, commodity futures, and food security for citizens and for key allies.

In 2017, the U.S. commercial landscape is still in flux. E-commerce has bitten enormous chunks from brick-and-mortar retailers. Silicon Valley tech developers devise more and more ways for physical products and human interaction to occupy digital space.

To catch up, cannabis has to undergo an immense political change as well. It must feed the political world as commerce does in the United States and cooperate with the political world to move through to its commercial aims.

Simply operating a business is not an option in the United States—politics are inevitable, especially with something like cannabis.

This book cannot overcome the distinct challenges of its subject material—namely, the only constant of cannabis is that the U.S. federal government declares it illegal. By publication date, much of this book will need updating.

Things have changed substantially just during the book's production. In January 2018, Trump's attorney general, Jeff Sessions, rescinded the Obama-era Cole Memorandum, a central piece of federal policy regarding state-level cannabis legalization. Despite widespread panic, most state's attorneys in pot-friendly states reassured the public and the cannabis industry that they will continue to leave legal businesses alone. However, as we'll see, a single policy can have massive impact in the cannabis world, and those effects could be on their way.

No single book could cover every facet of the world's favorite drug, either. Cannabis is a conversational Whack-a-Mole with hundreds of thousands of social, cultural, political, industrial, and religious moles to whack. Policy doesn't change in unison from a single point. Laws and regulations on cannabis change country by country, on every continent and in every hemisphere. Within the United States, they change state by state, county by county, city by city, and sometimes even neighborhood by neighborhood.

Along with being some of the most geographically scattershot laws in the world, the cannabis conversation is also the fastest moving and the most sensitive to change. The international and domestic tone and timbre and focus change on a monthly or even weekly basis, depending on the exact issue. Laws and regulations change endlessly, each one covered ad nauseam by straight media or by a new genre of pot-specific media. In the United States, entrepreneurs race into the cannabis spotlight faster even than media can shine it, spinning an endlessly more complicated web of industry trends and connections, each with their own political and commercial importance. An elected official can hijack a few days of news cycle simply by mentioning cannabis as a postscript to a subcommittee vote.

Describing the path is only the means to describing the destination, though. In the black market, cannabis was untracked and untraced but largely uncomplicated: grow pot, sell pot, avoid cops. When and if cannabis becomes legal, it becomes part of the mix between corporate juggernaut and the leviathan, something inconceivably more complex.

To paraphrase a band synonymous with the cannabis counterculture of old—*welcome, cannabis.*

Welcome to the machine.

CHAPTER ONE

Supply and Demand

For as long as cannabis has been illegal, people have tried to legalize it.

It's a matter of personal freedom, some said, the personal freedom to partake of a historically beloved plant no more damaging to a person than alcohol—considerably less so, in fact. Others said it was a matter of social justice, that making it illegal in the first place simply created more crime than necessary and more oppression of the already oppressed lower classes, who take to the black market to get the economic success denied to them in the regulated world. Even if the United States stripped the social justice and human rights questions away, they said, it would still make more sense for cannabis to be legal considering the billions of dollars in law enforcement costs U.S. states and the federal government shell out every year at the expense of the American taxpayer who, likely as not, has smoked cannabis sometime in the past year.

Even without the humanitarianism, the governmental fiscal common sense, or the classic liberal notion of personal choice, cannabis's illegality is a medical contradiction, others say. It is inconsistent and suspicious, they claim, for one of the world's most medically advanced nations to demonize a substance that lessens the lethal nausea of chemotherapy, or that helps those with multiple sclerosis find solace from their muscle spasms, or that could provide one more option for the thousands of post-traumatically stressed soldiers to ease their Iraqi-born emotional scars.

In the mid-2010s, they say, the nation's ongoing and crippling opioid addiction epidemic—caused not by street-bought baggies of smack but by a flood of U.S. Food and Drug Administration (FDA)–approved narcotic pills—would benefit from a more natural detox alternative or even an alternative to opiate-based medications in the first place.

None of those arguments is out of commission in 2017, and none without merit. They do, however, draw attention away from an argument that draws less on philanthropy or civic virtue—for all the human rights rhetoric, cannabis is worth lots and lots and lots of euros; pounds sterling; South African rand; Uruguayan and Mexican pesos; and Australian, Canadian, and U.S. dollars.

For exactly as long as it has been illegal, people have made money from cannabis, too, billions of dollars across the globe that stayed untouched and untallied by economists and public officials. Until recently, that money stayed locked in the underground black economy of human trafficking, monetized sex, smuggled small arms, and untaxed and untested teenths of illegal drugs.

Colorado and Washington made history in 2012 with a pair of ballot initiatives that legalized recreational cannabis. Only five years later, a political blink of the eye, and six more U.S. states joined them, including California, home to one-fifth of the world's most powerful nation's population.

Together, this makes 29 states and one federal district that have legalized either medical or recreational cannabis, along with 16 states that have legalized cannabidiol, one of the cannabis plant's nonpsychoactive compounds that is used for medical treatments of epilepsy and other neurological disorders.

The two U.S. states were not trailblazers in legalization entirely. Many other nations and other states had allowed cannabis sales. Colorado and Washington took the conversation somewhere new, however; cannabis, under their laws, is simply another consumer product, albeit one with medical applications and a way of thinning jail ranks.

The Consumerism of Cannabis

In five years—three if you count forward from the date cannabis was on shelves available for retail sale—cannabis has morphed into a chemical consumer product every bit as popular as alcohol. In fact, no single illicit drug in the world is as popular, and arguably none as versatile. You can smoke cannabis, spread cannabis butter onto whole wheat bagels, make cannabis into tinctures to spread on skin, extract from cannabis its vital components and bake them into a pie, or dissolve them in oil that can be smoked in concentrated form from a superheated titanium nail or in steady controlled doses from a designer vape pen. Customers can attach loyalty to favorite retail chains or to branded products created by Willie Nelson or Snoop Dogg or Bob Marley's family.

From the supply side of venture capitalists, advertising and public relations firms, farmers, retailers, and all their associated ancillary businesses, all that branding and product development is a gold mine. Wall Street economists or pot-funded data analytics firms churn out revenue projections for the U.S. cannabis industry every month. The numbers vary as revenues and business structure grows, but they are always large.

If every state were to legalize recreational marijuana, the cannabis industry would be worth at least $14.8 billion and up to $113 billion,[1] according to financial market analysis by the Anderson Economics Group, which provides public policy analysis for private, public, and government sectors. Cowen and Company, an investment banking group, confirmed that the domestic cannabis industry could be worth as much as $50 billion by 2026,[2] and that without even legalizing commercial cannabis across the board. Estimates keep climbing as more states legalize cannabis. In partnership with ArcView Group, New Frontier Data pegged the American pot trade at $21 billion in the next five years.[3]

As of publication, the numbers in the United States haven't risen so high, but the world is keeping close watch. The media is drenched daily with new tax income figures, new sales figures, and new news of mergers and acquisitions that still peg the U.S. cannabis industry alone as a multibillion dollar enterprise. As of September 2016, the cannabis industry's overall domestic value is $7.2 billion, according to Bloomberg News.[4] Colorado and Washington take a majority share as of 2017, but California alone is projected to make untold billions from the sheer size of its population, almost certainly to replace Colorado as the cannabis trade mecca. Some industry leaders predict Los Angeles alone will overshadow the entire Colorado market once the system is up and running.[5]

Everyone with an appetite for risk is getting in on the cash influx.

States welcome the millions in tax revenue; the large-scale and small-player investment communities want to establish themselves on the ground floor of an entirely new economy; and entrepreneurs of all stripes are cropping up across the nation as suppliers, manufacturers, retailers, and assorted support industries. The U.S. federal government is so far the only party involved that makes no money from the growing industry, making most of its cannabis revenue from the Drug Enforcement Agency's (DEA) raids of black market producers and distributors.

Consumer Demand

Broadly, cannabis has two commercial brackets: personal pleasure and medicinal use. Domestically, many legalization campaigns and many consumers argue the U.S. government's classification of cannabis as a nonmedical substance is bogus and have decided to move forward without the federal government's say-so. Three-fifths of U.S. states have decided by ballot or bill that cannabis has medical value and should be publicly available either by prescription or the consumer marketplace. This puts the majority of Americans against their government, which itself is changing more slowly than the rest of the Western world. The U.S. government's position on cannabis's medicinal qualities makes it very nearly the last holdout in the G7 power structure.

Nations in Europe, South America, North America, Africa, and Oceania started legalizing medical cannabis decades ago and have recently sped up the process.

The DEA's scientific literature focuses more on finding the bad cannabis parts than finding the benefits, but studies continue to show cannabis has a wide range of medical applications. Opiates are still the world's unmatched gold standard for pain relief, but some medical evidence points to cannabis as an effective pain reliever and nausea treatment. Pharmaceutical companies already have cannabis-based drugs in development under the exact U.S. federal government that still declares cannabis illegal.

According to the World Health Organization:

> Several studies have demonstrated the therapeutic effects of cannabinoids for nausea and vomiting in the advanced stages of illnesses such as cancer and AIDS . . . Other therapeutic uses of cannabinoids are being demonstrated by controlled studies, including treatment of asthma and glaucoma, as an antidepressant, appetite stimulant, anticonvulsant and anti-spasmodic, research in this area should continue. For example, more basic research on the central and peripheral mechanisms of the effects of cannabinoids on gastrointestinal function may improve the ability to alleviate nausea and emesis.[6]

The National Academies of Science, Engineering, and Medicine collaborated on a report of the available research and made the same conclusion.[7] According to the organization, there is substantial evidence that cannabis is useful for the treatment of chronic pain, as an anti-nausea treatment for chemotherapy patients, and for multiple sclerosis–related muscle spasms. Moderate evidence exists that it is effective as a sleep aid.

With such studies, cannabis law reformers find it hypocritical that the federal government will not take the substance off the Schedule I listing. However, the federal government and several medical associations make it clear that full-scale federal legalization, or even a rescheduling, will not happen until there is a greater body of scientific evidence in the United States exploring the effects of cannabis use.

"A drug must be carefully studied in many people before it can be approved by the FDA," reads a statement from the *Journal of the American Medical Association*. "There have not been enough large studies of marijuana to definitively show that it is a safe and effective drug."[8]

The National Academies of Science, Engineering, and Medicine report agreed:

> Despite the extensive changes in policy at the state level and the rapid rise in the use of cannabis both for medical purposes and for recreational use,

conclusive evidence regarding the short- and long-term health effects (harms and benefits) of cannabis use remains elusive. A lack of scientific research has resulted in a lack of information on the health implications of cannabis use, which is a significant public health concern for vulnerable populations such as pregnant women and adolescents.[9]

Cannabis reformers disagree that the federal government does have not enough evidence to reclassify or legalize cannabis. The National Organization for the Reform of Marijuana Laws, or NORML, points to over 22,000 studies and reviews about cannabis's medical effects,[10] enough to make it one of the most heavily investigated substances in science, NORML says.

But the research goes nowhere with the federal government.

Despite international research, the only American entity approved to research medical cannabis is the federal government itself through cannabis grown at the University of Mississippi.[11] For all the research that the United States does, by admittance it focuses mostly on finding reasons to keep it illegal rather than mining for its potential uses. Michael Boticelli, Trump's Drug Czar as of press time, said the U.S. government has not tried to focus on anything but cannabis's negative impacts.[12]

Often as not, of course, healthy people use cannabis because they want to get high—the kind of consumer demand that Colorado and Washington opened, the kind that continues to drive legalization campaigns, and the kind that grows the cannabis market in ways the medical market cannot. Recreational use, or adult use, is the secondary market for cannabis, though some industry leaders estimate the global demand for recreational pot may be twice the global medical demand.

Nonmedical cannabis uses go back in history as far as medical uses. Cannabis gives mild euphoria, relaxation, and perceptual alterations, including time distortion, and the intensification of experiences like eating, watching films, listening to music, and engaging in sex, according to researchers.[13]

Researchers recognize the nonmedical, pleasure-boosting cannabis uses, but do not know how to control them and therefore do not put much effort into studying them. The human body does not respond to cannabinoids in the same predictable manner as with other substances. Depressants depress and stimulants stimulate, but the effects of cannabinoids are more varied and depend in no small part on the user's mood and psychological makeup.

In a study on the cannabis market, RAND Corporation noted the difficulty:

We believe that such benefits are real and that they should matter, but they are far more difficult to quantify than other benefits, and they have received far less research attention than the harms of marijuana use.[14]

Why Is Cannabis Illegal?

Despite the now all-too-apparent market demand, cannabis has an intense amount of U.S. and international rancor directed against it. The U.S. government's decision makers keep it on the strictest listing, despite both a long-standing movement to legalize and even internal disputes at the Drug Enforcement Agency.

America's legal history with cannabis only heated up after World War I. The United States has kept cannabis out of trade for 80 years. The federal government made cannabis effectively illegal with the Tax Act of 1937, but it was not until after the dope decade that it was a controlled substance worth potential prison time. At that time, the U.S. government did not single out cannabis for no reason. International laws govern the drug trade, not U.S. laws. Despite the furor against the DEA, it is only responding to international treaty.

The Single Convention on Narcotic Drugs of 1961 is the United Nations' governing law on drugs, among others, focusing in large part on the big three: cannabis, coca, and opium poppies. The treaty places cannabis as a Schedule IV drug, the highest level of control alongside synthetic opioids, but it has recognized and encouraged medical use of controlled substances, including cannabis, in recent years. The worldwide swing toward medical cannabis makes cannabis line up with the other globally illegal drugs. Opium farms and coca farms are, in fact, legal so long as the supply chains are carefully controlled to funnel the products into pharmaceuticals.

It would appear most countries don't want to break with the UN treaty altogether. Internationally, most treaty-bound nations are not going the Colorado route of recreational pot—they are sticking with the international convention and medical usage.

The U.S. government passed the Controlled Substances Act in 1970 to comply with the UN's Single Convention, like most other UN nations did. Just like the Single Convention, the U.S. law put cannabis in the most restrictive category. The Controlled Substances Act rates drugs on five different schedules. Schedule I, where cannabis is listed, is the Controlled Substances Act's Do Not Invite list. Those items listed as Schedule I are designated to have both a high potential for abuse and have no recognized medical use, according to the act. Considering former president Richard Nixon's hatred for the 1960s counterculture movement, Schedule I contents seem almost punitive in hindsight. Apart from heroin, the schedule reads like a list of Hunter S. Thompson's favorite drugs—psychedelics like LSD and mescaline, other era treats like Quaaludes, and newer synthetics like MDMA.

Cannabis legalization advocates say cannabis's Schedule I placement was wrong in the first place, grows more antiquated by the month, and ignores the impacts of lesser schedules. Aside from the medical arguments, many long argued the lower-scheduled drugs feed more into social harms like violence, overdose, and health problems. Schedule II drugs, which have a "high potential for abuse" but also an accepted medical purpose, include cocaine, methamphetamine, OxyContin, and angel dust.

Groups have regularly challenged the listing in the last few decades, but with no luck. Only two years after the CSA's birth, the National Organization for the Reform of Cannabis Laws petitioned the DEA to knock cannabis down to a Schedule II substance. Congressmen have had the same feelings and tried to challenge the CSA nearly as long as NORML. Rep. Stuart McKinney, R-Conn., in 1982 submitted a bill to declassify cannabis as a Schedule I drug, but it died in committee. Rep. Barney Frank, D-Mass.—one of the industry's biggest supporters and favorite contribution recipients—has introduced several pieces of legislation to the same effect, each of which has failed. Citizen petitions sprung up as well in 1995, 2002, 2009, and 2011, each of which failed.

Even the DEA itself has gone back and forth on cannabis. Assistant Secretary of Health Roger O. Egeberg had insisted before the CSA was passed that "cannabis be retained within Schedule I at least until the completion of certain studies now underway to resolve the issue."[15]

Subsequent studies have either not been performed or not been heeded, sometimes from within the federal government itself. In 1986, Administrative Law Judge Francis Young gave an order to take cannabis off the Schedule I listing, but was overturned by DEA administrator John Lawn.[16]

Consumer Safety

In the nearly 50 years since the CSA passed, state laws have chipped away at cannabis while the federal government held fast to its ruling. Now, with most of the country's population having some kind of access to cannabis, the feds seem to be losing ground. The federal government and the opposition to cannabis legalization say the conversation is simply moving too fast for the public's safety.

Internationally, cannabis is indeed a safer substance than either tobacco or alcohol in terms of deaths, neither of which are scheduled as controlled substances. Though it is the most heavily consumed illicit drug, cannabis has not been responsible for a single reported overdose death, according to the World Health Organization's report.[17] Unlike opium or coca leaves, so far nobody has been able to make anything that can stop a human heart with cannabinoids. The National Cancer Society concluded that cannabis overdose simply does not happen.[18] So far, few studies have linked tetrahydrocannabinol (THC) and death. German researchers have found instances where cannabis could have been the cause of fatal heart irregularities,[19] but little in the scientific literature exists to link cannabis or THC with direct health hazards aside from the dangers of smoking.

Regardless of reformer objections, the federal government does not appear to have any will to budge. The Drug Enforcement Agency has refused for 50 years to reschedule cannabis. This has less to do with cannabinoid chemicals themselves than how a person gets to them, according to statements.

The DEA's position statement, released in January 2011, does not take issue with cannabinoids per se.[20] Rather, it takes issue with "smoked marijuana," saying smoked cannabis is clearly and definitively harmful, while acknowledging the cannabinoid-based medicines of several multinational pharmaceutical companies.

This opposition has crystallized in the mid-2010s under one overarching concern—the U.S. government says it does not want what happened with tobacco to happen with cannabis, namely that corporate profit motive will fuel a preventable public health crisis.

The American medical community is somewhat divided, with many physicians and patients advocating for medical cannabis use and others clamoring for more studies. Cultural criticisms that Big Pharma wants to monopolize cannabis have some merit considering a wealth of connections between the two, as we'll see in later chapters. Leaders in the U.S. medical community want the laws to revolve around cannabinoid *medicines*, not necessarily the unrestricted personal choice to consume cannabis at will—clearly the route the American public is choosing more and more. The American Medical Association said "that marijuana's status as a federal Schedule I controlled substance be reviewed with the goal of facilitating the conduct of clinical research and development of cannabinoid-based medicines."[21]

Despite cannabis and cannabinoids being federally illegal, the U.S. Food and Drug Administration has in fact legalized cannabis facsimiles. The FDA approved dronabinol and nabilone as nausea and pain medicine—both are simply synthetic THC. See Chapter 9 for an even more in-depth look at the connections between cannabis and the pharmaceutical industry.

Consumers

In the United States and other nations, market statistics can break out recreational vs. medicinal cannabis demand. The Marijuana Policy Project, which funded the legalization campaigns in states like Colorado, estimates there are 2.3 million medical cannabis patients throughout the states where marijuana is legal[22]—roughly 1 percent of those states' combined population as of early 2017. In the United States, consumption rates differ according to the source, though they generally agree with the United Nations statistics.

Legalization patterns in the United States relate to a national trend. Cannabis use is becoming more normal. Nationwide, more people are smoking, or at least, more people are willing to admit to it, than they were before adult use legalization took place in 2012.

In August 2016, Gallup polls[23] said 13 percent of U.S. adults used marijuana in the last year—double the rate from only three years before.

Consumer demographics are scant. The industry had no quantification until the last five years, when the legal market exploded. Still, there are some nuggets of guidance for who smokes cannabis and who doesn't.

The Gallup poll didn't find a big link between cannabis use and education levels or income, even though the study's poorest bracket reported the highest use levels. It did find decisive links in three areas: age, sex, and church attendance. Younger, less religious, and male are the market characteristics more than others.

The poll gives evidence that the older people get, the less they consume. Nineteen percent of respondents ages 18 to 29 reported cannabis use, more than twice as much as the next oldest group. That percentage dwindles to 3 percent by age 65 and up.

Y chromosomes are linked to higher use rates. Twice as many men (14 percent) reported using cannabis than women, according to the Gallup poll. This follows international research that points to men as heavier consumers of several drugs and several state studies on consumer trends. According to the 2016 World Drug Report, men are three times more likely to use cannabis, cocaine, or amphetamines than women, who are more likely to use opiates and tranquilizers.

Religion is another key consumer factor. According to Gallup, churchgoers are even less likely to use cannabis than geriatrics. People who seldom or never attend church had a 14 percent use rate. Weekly churchgoers had only a 2 percent use rate—even less than the 65 and up age category.

Geography also plays a part in who uses cannabis and who doesn't. The laid-back Western United States overwhelmingly leads adult use legalization efforts. As of the 2016 election, six of eight states with legal recreational pot are Western states: Alaska, California, Colorado, Oregon, Nevada, and Washington. Either Western folks are more comfortable talking about their pot use or they use more—14 percent reported that they smoked marijuana, up from 9 percent in the East and Midwest and 6 percent in the South.

Statistics will develop with time. By the UN's logic, use rates could be clearer in the future as legalization normalizes pot use more.

States' willingness to legalize cannabis could be a reason for the uptick in the percentage of Americans who say they smoke, regardless of whether it is legal in their state. Gallup finds Western Americans are far more likely to say they smoke cannabis than Americans in other U.S. regions.

More Users of All Kinds—Except Kids

Cannabis use is undeniably going up, but not in the way some fear. The cannabis consumer base is getting deeper, not wider.

Legalization picked up international steam in 2010, trailing behind it much hand-wringing from worried parents and politicians about increased drug use rates. So far fears have little ground to stand on. From a commercial viewpoint, cannabis business is doing a bad job attracting new customers. Worldwide, use hasn't gone up in recent years.

> Despite major changes in some regions, global cannabis consumption has remained somewhat stable in recent years. In 2014, some 3.8 per cent of the global population had used cannabis in the past year, a proportion that has remained stable since 1998. Given the global population growth, this has gone in parallel with an increase in the total number of cannabis users since 1998. The Americas, followed by Africa, remain the main production and consumption regions for cannabis herb, with about three quarters of all cannabis herb seizures worldwide taking place in the Americas in 2014, the largest amounts in North America, while Africa accounted for 14 per cent of all cannabis herb seizures and Europe for 5 per cent.[24]

Instead of new customers, legalization patterns tell us the cannabis market is much like the alcohol market—advertising courts regular users instead of trying to create new ones from nonsmokers.

The most comprehensive studies say the cannabis market only intensifies use. The UN tells us that the number of daily cannabis consumers has risen, but not the total number of cannabis consumers. The RAND Corporation estimates that 80 percent of cannabis consumed is consumed by daily or heavy users. Likely, the people who smoked black market weed simply bought more when it started becoming legal.

> Although it is still too early to evaluate the impact of new cannabis policies, the evidence collected to date in the United States points to an increase in cannabis use in states where referendums have led to the legalization of recreational marijuana use . . . In the United States, the number of daily (or near-daily) cannabis users, measured by the number using cannabis on 20 or more days in the past month and the number using cannabis on 300 or more days in the past year, rose significantly after 2006, by 58 and 74 per cent, respectively. However, this increase in daily (or near-daily) cannabis use has not translated into an increased number of people seeking treatment, even when those in treatment referred by the criminal justice system are excluded.[25]

Legalization opponents often lobby legislators to hold back on cannabis for the youth. The data is divided the idea cannabis legalization will intensify youth consumption. Advertising up until now has stayed far away from children due to strict regulations, again mirroring the kinds of restriction placed on the alcohol and tobacco industries.

The lack of targeted youth ad campaigns and the strict state regulations seem to be working. In Colorado, youth marijuana use rates dropped from 2009 to 2015, according to the Colorado Healthy Kids Survey.[26] A 2016 report from Washington found a more neutral theme; despite legalization, teen use rates have stayed steady since legalization.[27]

Teens are only one of several groups that have a hard time buying cannabis, but unlike the others, the teens' blackout is purposeful. Buying cannabis makes a consumer a federal criminal at all times. Unlike prescription drugs, alcohol, or tobacco, federal laws either restrict or cause problems for consumers of even legal medical or adult use cannabis. Naturally, this causes some contentions where otherwise viable consumers either can't consume or can't do so without implicating themselves as felons.

International Trend

In the United States, Colorado's successes and the resulting legalizations of several other states somewhat overshadow a global market view, but the media is catching on. Worldwide, cannabis is a massive well of untapped consumerism.

Illegal drugs are one of the world's biggest businesses, and in terms of market size, cannabis tops harder drugs by far. In the United States cannabis is the world's most heavily consumed and most heavily produced illicit drug.

Every year the United Nations Drug and Crime Office compiles the World Drug Report,[28] aimed at giving international policymakers all the latest news. In 2016, cannabis again topped the charts for most consumed drug. As many as 183 million people globally consumed cannabis in 2015. This is most of the roughly 250 million adults globally who took an illicit drug in 2014—about 1 in 20 adults worldwide. Unfortunately, UN numbers don't break down international demand any finer than that. Gathering reliable data on the use of an illegal substance is tricky.

Globally, estimates vary for how much money the international medical cannabis trade is worth. Brendan Kennedy, CEO of international cannabis private equity firm Privateer Holdings, said it could climb as high as $100 billion in retail value annually in the next 5 to 10 years, according to company financial projections.[29] In other words, the legal international market could equal half the current demand. According to Kennedy, the current global total retail demand for cannabis in the black, gray, and illegal markets is roughly $200 billion—around what Exxon Mobile's total revenue was in 2016.[30]

Part of cannabis's widespread use is its biology, which makes it available to any nation that might have a mind to join the frenzy. It can grow in most global populated areas, unlike poppies and coca leaves, which need more specific climates. The versatility pays off.

According to the UN:

> The most widely cultivated drug crop continues to be cannabis, which was reported by 129 countries over the period 2009–2014, far more than the 49 countries that reported opium poppy cultivation (mostly located in Asia and the Americas) and the 7 countries that reported coca cultivation (located in the Americas). Leaving aside the disparity in their respective numbers of cultivating countries, opium poppy cultivation has been decreasing in the past year while coca cultivation has been rising.[31]

Indeed, cannabis is not just the world's most grown drug but the world's most transported. Nearly the entire world has law enforcement reporting cannabis as the biggest portion of seizures:

> Cannabis also continues to be the most trafficked drug worldwide, while there has been a large increase in seizures of synthetic drugs. Although there were 234 substances under international control in 2014 (244 in January 2016), the bulk of trafficking (based on reported drug seizures, which reflect both law enforcement activity and drug flows) was concentrated on a far smaller number of substances. Cannabis in its various forms was intercepted in 95 per cent of reporting countries in 2014 and accounted for over half of the 2.2 million drug seizure cases reported to the United Nations Office on Drugs and Crime (UNODC) that year, followed by ATS, opioids and coca-related substances.[32]

The Big Players

The business world is scrambling to get in on the blossoming cannabis demand.

Companies around the world, but especially in Canada, are capturing the market. As of early 2017, the international cannabis trade is already booming and growing. Companies are already shuffling cannabis around the globe for medical purposes and studies, with major markets and producers in the developed world in the Americas and Europe.

Canada is the first G7 nation to have a national medical cannabis system and is now the leading exporter of medical cannabis. Over the past year, medical cannabis facilities like Canopy Growth, Peace Naturals, Tilray, and Tweed in Canada have exported to Europe, Australia, and South America.

European countries are not far behind. Germany, whose parliament passed medical marijuana legislation in January 2017, is the second, making it Canada's largest export destination and the largest medical market outside the United States. Nations that accept medical marijuana imports include the

Czech Republic, New Zealand, Brazil, and Chile. Bedrocan in the Netherlands has shipped to Canada, Australia, and European Union nations.

Israel—one of the United States' leading pharmaceutical suppliers—is also a world leader in medical cannabis research. Conservative rabbis used to forbid cannabis for its psychological impacts, but more recently rabbis said cannabis is kosher for any Jew if used medically, not recreationally.[33] Israel decriminalized cannabis possession in 2017, expanding medical access and allowing medical cannabis exports with an eye toward the United States, though U.S. states still cannot receive cannabis imports.

International exports are not for recreation, but for medical distribution and clinical research, overseen by the importing nation's health agencies. The International Narcotics Control Board requires detailed reports on the number and quantity and purposes of exports and imports.

Black Market Impacts

As the new market develops, the old market is beginning to dry up. Nothing kills the black market like a full-fledged industry, but only to a point. Because the country is legalizing on a state-by-state basis, the black market can sometimes take advantage of the legal market. Further, the state laws tend to block former black marketers from entering the legal industry.

Before legalization measures, cannabis was, by definition, an almost entirely criminal market. Despite being quasi-legal in some states, beginning with California in 1996, the regulated market did not reach full vigor on these programs alone.

One of cannabis reform's goals and biggest talking points is how legalization will shift the industry from the black market to the regulated market. In theory, this will sweep up the violent crime associated with the drug trade the same way repealing Prohibition did with alcohol in 1933.

To some degree, this worked, in no small part because of market demand. In legalized states, consumers have more access to specialized strains as opposed to the brick-packed Mexican "ditch weed" that largely makes up cartel shipments. Even as early as 2015, Mexican drug cartels started pushing harder drugs across the border[34] as demand for low-quality Mexican weed gave way to high-octane American strains. Within a short amount of time, Colorado noticed a dent in the black market. According to Marijuana Policy Group, only 6 percent of the state's market is supplied by black market product.[35]

State lawmakers, it seems, ignored lessons in black market demolition[36] learned when Prohibition ended. Lawmakers in the 1930s followed a basic structure: incentivize former black marketers to come back into the regulated world by ignoring their former status, keep taxes low to keep the new businesses financially healthy, and punish rule breakers severely. As we will see, the cannabis world hasn't evolved the same way.

The black market is still healthy, though diminished. In gold-standard Colorado, the legal cannabis industry was even shown to have fed the black market in at least one instance. A retail store employee at Denver's Buddy Boy—which is owned by a former National Cannabis Industry Association director—was accused of trying to sell a backpack of legal cannabis to an undercover police officer. The incident prompted further development of state tracking systems designed to keep legal cannabis in the legal market.

Law enforcement in cannabis-legal states still seizes illegally produced or illegally imported cannabis and still makes cannabis-based arrests. According to municipal data, though, those arrest rates have dropped, along with their associated court appearances. Arrests in all states and in Washington, D.C., dropped dramatically between 2012 and 2014. In Colorado, total marijuana arrests dropped by 46 percent over that time. Court filings dropped 81 percent. The total number of low-level marijuana court filings in Washington fell by 98 percent from 2011 to 2013. Marijuana arrests in Oregon declined by 50 percent from 2011 to 2014. There were 4,223 arrests for all marijuana offenses in 2011, which dropped to 2,109 in 2014.[37]

Whether the decreases are due to decreased police activity or to decreased black market activity, though, is still up to interpretation. Alaska's arrests dropped[38] from 669 in 2013 to 290 in 2015—even though sales had not even begun until the end of 2016. In Washington, D.C., marijuana arrests decreased 85 percent from 2014 to 2015, though Washington, D.C., only decriminalized possession instead of establishing a regulated industry like the other states.

Blowback

While former black marketers linger in the U.S. prison system, the massive demand for cannabis in the United States is making thousands of others very rich. Over the last five years, cannabis legalization has unlocked deep reservoirs of capital, employment, and entrepreneurship that went unseen in the underground.

Long-time medical users, aficionados, compassionate access advocates, black market growers and sellers, and closeted recreational fans clamored and will continue to clamor to get into the legal market. When it began in Colorado, the industry didn't need the kind of capital and expertise normalized commerce has. Clearly, it had plenty of demand to get through whatever challenges the shortages of experience and revenue would present.

As time passed, however, the cannabis industry is growing more stratified to reflect similar industries in agriculture, alcohol, tobacco, or pharmaceuticals.

At the top of the pyramid are those from the well-capitalized and well-established business and political worlds who are trying to fold their knowledge and lessons and experience into the new industry. Lower on the free market totem pole are the former black market actors, bootstrapped mom-and-pop shops, and independent contractors. The market's complexity is daunting for each.

CHAPTER TWO

Federal Laws vs. State vs. Local Control

Cannabis operates on a state-by-state basis, at odds with federal legislation. When legalized, localities only intensify the complexities.

Use and supply are plentiful, but access is another story.

Business is never easy, but the cannabis industry has a distinct set of hurdles so vast and varied this book can only address the biggest themes. Consumers consume and producers produce only in the states where cannabis is not illegal, instead of nationally as most industries do. The single most defining characteristic of the industry is this disparity between the Controlled Substances Act and whatever state laws are in place—a division we will call the federal/state gap.

For the cannabis industry, the federal/state gap distorts every single possible facet of ordinary business. Taxes are different, licensing processes are different, the regulations on businesses are different, community reactions are different, and consumer habits are different from state to state and from nation to nation. A map of cannabis laws looks like a piece of mottled fruit rather than a single, smooth shade of green.

On the surface, this is not extraordinary. Cannabis is only the most popular and most visible example of a larger theme of forbidding nonviolent, noncoercive products, habits, or practices. The U.S. federal government forbids several industries that flourish in rebellious states. Usually, these industries fall in the same category as cannabis—vices.

Vice is, of course, a broad category. Morals dictate vice laws, most often, but social and health arguments creep in almost intended as proof of the morals' morality. Drugs, prostitution, gambling, alcohol, or tobacco use all have health and social impacts, too, argue those who use the government to outlaw them. It was the social arguments of the temperance movement that outlawed alcohol in the United States in 1920, cracking off the gangster era of the 1920s.

Still, outlaw vice as it will, national governments have never had luck stamping out the consumer's appetite for vice. If the market does not legally supply it, the market will illegally supply it—most typically through criminals and the poor, the kind of people already familiar with imprisonment and violent death. Al Capone will supply smuggled rum. Human traffickers will supply prostitutes. Loan sharks will supply sports betting. Mexican cartels or Taliban insurgents will supply drugs.

Governments know this, to some degree, and turn a blind eye where some vices are concerned. Just like cannabis, which is globally very popular, vices are popular, and where there is demand there is industry. Gambling is federally illegal, yet it nets states like Nevada and Connecticut, or Indian reservations, billions of annual dollars.[1] Prostitution is not federally illegal—one of the few items the federal government does not claim authority over. It is therefore a state-by-state industry—certain districts in Nevada allow legal prostitution in the United States.

Alcohol is federally legal, but still has an enormous amount of complexity among states, counties, cities, and towns. Like cannabis in the 2000s, when Prohibition ended, states and localities were allowed to reintroduce the alcohol industry as they saw fit, including banning it altogether. There are still dry counties and dry cities in the United States.

For cannabis, the root of all industrial evil comes from this kind of patchwork vice law management.

Cole Memo

Businesses live in fear of the federal government at every moment, and more so since the 2016 election and Attorney General Jeff Sessions' 2018 repeal of a key policy, the Cole Memo. That fear affects every facet of business. Banks do not involve themselves with the cannabis industry because of that fear. State governments slap heavy restrictions on the business because of that fear that in turn make the cannabis industry—as profitable as it can be—a distorted mess.

This fear comes from a lack of clarity. Before Sessions, the federal government's communications about cannabis were carefully crafted to allow states some leniency to make their own laws but also offered zero concrete protection.

Former president Barack Obama was not well loved by the cannabis industry during his first term,[2] but in his second term fared better. The most important pieces of federal cannabis communications came from Obama's administration. Their content varies, but the most important one that governs the cannabis industry's pace is cloudy.

Obama's early communications led pot reformers to believe he would leave them alone. U.S. Attorney General Eric Holder issued a memo in October 2009 telling federal prosecutors they "should not focus federal resources in your states on individuals whose actions are in clear and unambiguous compliance with existing state laws providing for the medical use of marijuana."[3]

This meant little in practice. Obama's first term overseeing the executive branch's Drug Enforcement Agency yielded an *increase* in cannabis seizures, and Obama ended up ranked as an unfriendly president.[4] When Colorado and Washington legalized the same month as his second election, the tune changed. In August 2013, just before legal sales started in Colorado and Washington, U.S. Deputy Attorney General James Cole issued a memo[5] to all U.S. states attorneys that built on Holder's memo. Industry and state governments refer to this guidance as the "Cole Memo" and discuss it the same way clergy talk about the 10 Commandments.

Indeed, the Cole Memo issued a kind of Eight Cannabis Commandments for whichever states decide to legalize. The memo implied the federal government will leave states alone as long as regulators do whatever possible to keep the product away from minors, keep it away from gangs and cartels, prevent leakage into other states, prevent cannabis from being a front for other illegal operations, prevent violence and keep it away from guns, prevent drugged driving and other public health consequences, prevent growing on public lands and whatever environmental dangers, and prevent possession or use on federal property.

One or several of Cole's commandments is behind every industry controversy, every piece of slow-moving legislation, and every industry hurdle. State legislatures, regulatory boards, industry attorneys, and business owners did not make a single decision without considering how it fulfills or does not fulfill the Cole Memo.

What read like an instruction manual, though, was little more than a blind eye agreement. The feds reserve the right to do what they will, including prosecute. The final portion of the memo creates a cloud of doubt especially for the financial industry (see Chapter 5).

"Neither the guidance herein nor any state or local law provides a legal defense to a violation of federal law, including any civil or criminal violation of the (Controlled Substances Act), the money laundering and unlicensed money transmitter statutes, or of the BSA, including the obligation of financial institutions to conduct customer due diligence."[6]

The 2016 election has added panic where once there was only uncertainty. President Donald Trump said little about cannabis leading up to his election, but what he did say has been mixed. On the campaign trail, he said he does support medical cannabis and does support states' right to change laws on their own.[7] In 2017, though, he wrote he would reserve the right to prosecute medical cannabis states.[8] His administration, however, has proven itself vocally anti-cannabis. Trump's former press secretary, Sean Spicer, said in early 2017 that states with legal cannabis should expect more enforcement of federal laws.[9]

Trump also appointed long-time drug warrior Jeff Sessions as U.S. attorney general, who in his position has grown to Cannabis Public Enemy Number One. Although he and the DEA both have acknowledged that cannabis is low on the federal priority list, the attorney general has made it clear he will not follow the zeitgeist.

He has sent letters to governors questioning whether their cannabis programs are legal, drawing from the reports of anti-cannabis lobbying groups (see Chapter 3). He has said "good people don't smoke marijuana,"[10] claimed cannabis is only "slightly less awful" than heroin,[11] relaunched drug war rhetoric in saying the country must create culture that is "hostile to drug use,"[12] and is directing state prosecutors to harsher drug sentences than under the Obama administration amid a national opioid abuse epidemic. And finally, in January 2018, he rescinded the industry-bolstering Cole Memo.

Media, the governors and congressional delegations, state attorneys general, and industry leaders cry foul on Sessions, saying he claims falsehoods to defend his anti-cannabis stance and that he defies states' rights and voter will, but as of mid-January 2018, Sessions has created fear but no new prosecutions. If the Cole Memo offered no concrete protections, Sessions' repeal offers no concrete threats, either. The Congressional delegations and U.S. attorneys of states where marijuana is legal insist prosecution decisions are still up to states' U.S. attorneys. Still, the U.S. attorney general caused unease across the cannabis industry, about which the president has stayed entirely silent.

Consumer Problems

Even if there were no fear or attorney general loathing, the federal government's Controlled Substances Act would still make the drug hard to consume. To begin with, the industry's customer base is still largely unshaped after a century of cannabis stigma—there is nowhere to smoke, and if there were, consumers could get fired, ridiculed, fined, or imprisoned for their use. Breaking old habits is hard. On top of the hurdles of employment, gun ownership, or veteran status, the effects of the reefer madness era linger in the form of stigma.

Aside from its health impacts, alcohol has a venerable history and is mostly tolerated in U.S. society, if not exactly condoned by every social group. Cannabis is another story, the product of decades of social programming that painted users as stoners or worse. The tide is changing quickly, though. Over 52 percent of American adults have smoked cannabis in the last year as of a 2017 poll from the Marist College Institute of Public Opinion.[13] This makes cannabis still less common than alcohol—70 percent of American adults say they have had an alcoholic drink in the past year.[14]

Some of the most far-reaching impacts to the cannabis industry concern the consumers. The impacts of cannabis's stigma on consumer base are eroding somewhat, but the actual illegality has concrete effects tied directly to law. Whether for medical use or for recreational use, the federal/state gap makes cannabis a niche drug that cannot reach the maximum consumer base even in the states where it is legal.

The federal/state gap could potentially produce millions of felony liars simply over gun laws, or conversely turn millions of Americans to unwilling abstinence. There are an estimated 300 million guns in the United States,[15] and among the third of American households that own one, there is bound to be cannabis use crossover. This market segment is strictly off limits to the cannabis industry, though. An American cannabis user cannot buy a firearm from a federally licensed gun dealer without being a federal criminal.

The Bureau of Alcohol, Tobacco, Firearms and Explosives (ATF) made it clear in a 2011 letter to firearms dealers[16] that state laws offer no protection for cannabis users who want to buy a gun:

> Any person who uses or is addicted to marijuana, regardless of whether his or her State has passed legislation authorizing marijuana use for medicinal purposes, is an unlawful user of or addicted to a controlled substance, and is prohibited by Federal law from possessing firearms or ammunition.

Federal gun purchase forms ask whether the buyer uses cannabis, which will get their application denied. The only way to smoke cannabis and buy a gun would be to lie on the form—a felony punishable by up to five years in prison.

The ATF makes no exceptions for gun buyers who might also have a state-issued medical card. In 2016, the Ninth U.S. Circuit Court of Appeals issued a decision on a Nevada case that cardholders are still unlawful drug users.[17]

The federal/state gap also stops federal employees—including U.S. veterans—from consuming cannabis. A 2011 Veterans Health Administration directive stops Veterans Administration (VA) doctors from even talking about medical marijuana with their patients.[18] Veterans organizations have asked for years to allow the option, citing therapeutic benefits to post-traumatic stress disorder sufferers. The directive was set to expire on January 31, 2016, then a proposal to reverse it was shot down in the House Rules Committee in July 2017.[19]

Federal employees themselves—all 2 million of them,[20] not counting the millions more nonsalaried employees—are forbidden from touching cannabis. The U.S. Office of Personnel Management sent an uncompromising letter to federal employees in 2015[21] that reads much like the other federal directives: "Federal law on marijuana remains unchanged."

Jobs that deal heavily with safety are among the hardest to make consistent with federal law, stigma, or the lack of information available on how cannabis consumption affects performance behind the wheel or in other places. Commercial truck drivers, train engineers, pilots, and other Department of Transportation–licensed positions are strictly drug free.[22] This is not only an issue of soldiers and bureaucrats.

Because the drug is federally illegal, many private companies screen employees for its use alongside cocaine, amphetamines, opiates, and other illegal drugs. Even if a state legalizes cannabis, employers within that state can still maintain their drug testing policies. Cannabis lasts longer than most other drugs in a person's bloodstream as well, meaning employees cannot safely rely on sneaking past their company policies at a weekend party.

Even while use rates nose closer to alcohol, however, cannabis is still abnormal in how and where and when a person can have it. Adult use states have been too terrified of the federal government to allow cannabis users a venue outside their homes like a bar or an Amsterdam- or Spanish-style café. It has not been for lack of trying, lack of customers, or even for lack of state government support.

Alaska, Colorado, Washington, and Oregon each had a rash of these clubs immediately following their ballots. Most often, the clubs are on the wrong side of public consumption laws, or the legislature does not have a license type to allow them anyway. Federal laws do not help either—indoor clean air acts states have set up over the last several decades to comply with federal standards outlaw tobacco smoking in public places like restaurants and bars. States with clean air acts still do not know exactly how to treat cannabis under these laws.

In some cases, lawmakers expressed interest in legalizing clubs or cafes, partly because they recognize an inconsistency with alcohol and partly because the absence of clubs and cafes leads to problems. Without them, cannabis tourists who flock into legal states have nowhere to smoke—hotels, motels, restaurants, rental cars, and public spaces are all off limits. Instead, consumers simply break the rules.

Though these states know they have a problem to fix, the federal/state gap has a chilling effect. Regulators in Alaska and Colorado have both talked about legalizing clubs and cafes, but laws change slowly. Alaska regulators have postponed several times in two years and as of publication time have yet to allow any kind of public consumption.[23]

Only Colorado has taken the lead in moving forward with a venue option. Even though Colorado lawmakers stopped plans to legalize clubs and cafes outright in April 2017—they said explicitly they did not want to bring the federal government down on Coloradoans heads[24]—Denver will have some kind of bar or café operating in 2018. Voters passed a city ballot that allows the Denver authorities to license on-site consumption.[25]

Workforce Problems

The federal/state gap complicates the industry's workforce, as well. For being one of the highest-velocity job creators in the modern United States, lawmakers and regulators are in no hurry to open cannabis employment to the same levels as other industries. By the end of 2015, Colorado issued nearly 27,000 occupational licenses. These numbers only include businesses that deal directly with the product, not support industry. According to estimates from Marijuana Business Daily, the number of employees in the industry nationwide is between 100,000 and 150,000,[26] and those before California has launched.

Because cannabis is so new and so legally tricky, job creation statistics aren't normally included in the usual state studies. Most businesses can hire whoever they want—decisions about who can and cannot work in a bookstore, bar, or ballet studio are made generally by the bookstore, bar, or ballet studio owners and managers.

State governments have a tighter leash around cannabis employment. Cannabis license employees often complain the permitting requirements are "unreasonably impracticable"—employees are held to the same kind of strict standards that apply to the actual business license holders. States with legal adult use marijuana have different occupational licensing practices. Colorado requires an occupational license for industry workers. Any conviction for a controlled substance–related felony over the last 10 years or any felony over the last 5 years will immediately disqualify an applicant.

Others are more lenient. The Oregon Liquor Control Commission may refuse a permit over a felony involving controlled substances or cannabis, violence, theft, fraud, or forgery in the last three years, but does not deny an applicant with a misdemeanor. The Washington Liquor and Cannabis Board does not require occupational licensing at all.

These laws differ from even strict alcohol laws, which usually require workers to apply for licensing but have fewer criminal restrictions.

No Unity in Regulation among States

Just like with customers, the federal/state gap turns the actual practice of cannabis business into a warped version of normal national industry. Each state sets up its own regulations, and none of them are anything less than strict. Fear of the federal government makes state lawmakers very cautious when it comes to cannabis—the rest of this book will examine the impacts of these rules in detail.

A clutch of industry boards serves as the root of the cannabis industry's rules. Typically, a state's governor puts bureaucrats and business owners at the helm of these boards to come up with regulations, hand out business licenses, and in general steer the industry in a way that complies with the now-defunct Cole Memo. Washington's Liquor and Cannabis Board, Oregon's Liquor and Cannabis Control Commission, and Alaska's Marijuana Control Board all fit this model, while Colorado's Department of Revenue has a Marijuana Enforcement Division to perform most tasks. On occasion, the state's legislature will step in when the issue at hand demands an actual change to state law, like taxes or adding new license types.

Because cannabis is new, highly regulated, and highly lucrative, the boards themselves have pressure from all sides. Industry interests seek looser regulations that will let them do more business, or in some cases tighter restrictions where it means blocking competitors. Government representatives usually want tighter restrictions—most of the time, specifically because they do not want to give the federal government any reason to come knocking. These boards and their regulations are the gatekeepers of the industry.

People rarely get to simply sell product and make money in the United States. Most states require extensive professional licensing. A person looking to open a business must first pass education requirements, business planning requirements, and background checks and pay the necessary fees for everything from a liquor store to a barber shop to a nail salon. In each state, applicants get approved on a case-by case basis by the regulators. Depending on the state, the board can approve the licenses in public meetings or privately.

On the one hand, this does keep the industry from disreputable people, and therefore that much further away from a Washington, D.C., magnifying glass. Most states have waves of former black marketers and quasi-black marketers who try to grow pot, sell pot, deliver pot, or open pot social clubs without getting the state and local authorities to approve a license for them. In general, the owners of the pre-license businesses end up on a state prosecutor's to-do list, though there are a few notable exceptions mostly relating to cannabis social clubs.

On the other hand, the cannabis versions of these licenses are high barriers to entry. Many pin the licensing process as the reason minorities—hardest hit by the War on Drugs—are conspicuously absent from a cannabis industry dominated by well-educated and often wealthy whites.[27]

To get approved for these licenses, hopeful cannabis business owners submit detailed information for the governing authorities to comb through for regulatory compliance, criminal background, and financing. When necessary, they bring their many problems directly to the regulatory board for a fix in a never-ending cycle of revisions.

This makes the industry incredibly complex, which in turn makes it incredibly risky and expensive. Media often points to the small businesses that pop up in the early, heady days of the Green Rush, but more and more the larger and more well-capitalized companies are getting ahead as the licensing process and regulatory compliance expense block those without backers and experience.

Licensing is so complex and laborious that many cannabis businesses devote themselves to it. Many of the most successful businesses hire cannabis business attorneys to prepare their license applications, which can be intensely complex in places with dual licensing requirements like Denver or Anchorage. Others, from individuals to companies like AmeriCann, sell themselves as license-getting wizards who will help aspiring shop owners cut through the red tape for a healthy fee.

Local Controls

The federal/state gap can sometimes be only the beginning. Most states with legal pot let local governments create their own regulations, including an option to opt out of state law and keep cannabis illegal within local borders. So far only Washington does not allow local opt-out options, though several towns in Washington do so anyway. This creates layers and layers of complexity and cost. For example, a retail shop owner in Denver does not just deal with the federal/state gap. The owner must go through two separate licensing ordeals—one from the Colorado Marijuana Enforcement Division and one from the City of Denver—pay taxes to two different entities, and adjust the business to two sets of zoning standards—all the while complying with whatever they must do to stay out of the federal spotlight.

Other towns may simply ban cannabis, in many cases after businesses have already started their plans to operate there. Colorado Springs, the state's second-largest city, does not allow commercial cannabis, though it does allow medical cannabis. In California, over 160 local governments, including Anaheim, banned cannabis,[28] and 89 local governments have banned it in Oregon.[29] Massachusetts, Maine, and Nevada's cities are in the process of carving up the state similarly. Occasionally, some of the state's most potentially profitable regions will ban cannabis. Alaska's city of Wasilla, the urban center of the famously pot-fertile Matanuska and Susitna valleys, banned cannabis along with similar farmer havens elsewhere in the state—including the home borough of the Alaska Marijuana Control Board's chairman, who even gathered signatures for the ban.[30]

This has varied effects. It can give some companies a leg up in the statewide business, whereas other move under burdensome rules, or it can kill businesses altogether. In some instances, local governments are hungry for commerce. A rural American city bleeding young people to tech-centric cities welcomes the industry with eager arms as often as it passes cannabis bans.

Colorado media hoisted Pueblo County as a success story that had equivalents throughout the weedy American West.[31] High unemployment rates from manufacturing, mining, or farming job loss were reversed as new people migrated in to work in pot and customers drove in bringing tax dollars with them. Arizona-based American Green, an investment firm, bought Nipton, California outright in the summer of 2017, with plans to make Nipton to cannabis as Las Vegas is to gambling—an entirely cannabis-centric tourist spot.

Indian Reservations

Although states have their own problems, American Indians have a mixed relationship with cannabis, flavored by an already-tense relationship with the U.S. government. Some tribes court it, some oppose it. When tribes enter a compact with a state government or pass their own laws, the federal government has unpredictable reactions to it.

In theory, the feds view cannabis on tribal lands the same as cannabis in Colorado or Washington. The U.S. Department of Justice (DOJ) sent a memo to all U.S. tribes in 2014 after several asked what to do following the 2012 ballots.[32] The DOJ told them what it told U.S. state attorneys in the Cole Memo: nothing keeps a state or tribal government from legalizing, but nothing keeps the federal government from crashing the party if they do not regulate it to the Cole Memo's guidelines.

> Nothing in the Cole Memorandum alters the authority or jurisdiction of the United States to enforce federal law in Indian Country. Each United States attorney must assess all of the threats present in his or her district, including those in Indian Country, and focus enforcement efforts based on that district-specific assessment. The eight priorities in the Cole Memorandum will guide United States attorneys' marijuana enforcement efforts in Indian Country, including in the event that sovereign Indian Nations seek to legalize the cultivation or use of marijuana in Indian Country.

Commercial cannabis is a western U.S. phenomenon, putting pot alongside most of the country's reservations.[33] Every recreational state also has tribal land, as does almost every medical state.[34] In theory, cannabis could generate the kinds of tribal revenue casinos have in the past. Despite the numbers, however, tribes seem reluctant. Of 562 federally recognized Indian Nations—nearly half of which are in pot-legal Alaska—only a scant handful have asked to grow cannabis, and some American Indian or Alaska Native organizations vocally opposed legalizing ballots or tried to install cannabis bans. Tribal governments are often leerier of cannabis than state governments, considering the well-documented substance abuse and drug trade impacts on American Indian communities. Alaska tribes opposed legalization and lobbied hard for rules that would let rural districts opt out of sales.

The federal government has not taken kindly to tribal cannabis, and in fact seems to make tribes subservient to the state laws in which the reservations are found. South Dakota's Sioux Nation started growing cannabis, then destroyed the crop after the federal government threatened to raid,[35] wrecking plans for an entire cannabis-based tribal resort. Before California's ballot passed in 2016, the federal government raided Pit River tribal grows in northern California.[36] Cannabis pillar *High Times* wanted to hold its annual Cannabis Cup on Moapa tribal land outside Las Vegas. The DOJ sent two letters warning the tribe to dial back.[37] This event took place before Nevada's 2016 ballot took effect. In Wisconsin, feds told the Menominee Indian Tribe to stop growing industrial hemp, which is legal under federal law but not under Wisconsin law.

In states with recreational pot laws, though, the feds have stayed away as tribes join the states in raking in tax revenue. Two Washington tribes, the Suquamish and the Squaxin, are in the cannabis game, along with Oregon's Warm Springs Tribe. The Navajo Nation, which has a reservation the size of an Eastern state that spreads across New Mexico and Arizona, is considering a cannabis and hemp legalization measure as of press time,[38] only two years after vocally opposing it.[39]

Diversion

In whatever case, bans do little to keep cannabis away from outsiders looking to buy. There are differing accounts for how much the legal markets feed into the black markets of neighboring states. Law enforcement calls this "diversion," and it is strictly illegal—but then again, so is cannabis.

Some measurements point to a rise in black market activity fed from legal states. Without citing any statistics, the states of Oklahoma and Nebraska filed with the U.S. Supreme Court to sue the state of Colorado in 2014, hoping to reverse the ballot initiative that legalized cannabis. The proposed lawsuit claimed Colorado pot would overflow into their states and fuel the black market there. The U.S. Supreme Court dismissed the case, but Nebraska and Oklahoma's accusations do have some basis in fact. Law enforcement has experienced several instances of cannabis grown both illegally and legally smuggled to neighboring states in the Midwest.[40] This contradicts another trend, however, as mail deliveries of drugs dropped after 2014.[41]

Consumers find ways around their own states' cannabis laws, anyway. Just like Amsterdam, long a haven for drug-seeking tourists, Colorado and Washington became destination points for cannabis users. State tourism organizations have not pumped their states' legal pot as a selling point—doing so would cross state lines and veer into federal law territory. As in all things cannabis, data is scarce this early in the game, but cannabis tourism does contribute at least some to the economies of cannabis-friendly states. Companies like Kush Tourism in Washington or 420 Tours in Colorado pick tourists up from the airport for a blunt-laced tour to grow facilities, retail shops, and other cannabis business attractions.

Where tourism is a factor, though, it is not as much as some advocates have touted. Regulators, bureaucrats, and business owners from Alaska, Colorado, Oregon, and Washington often advocate loudly that cannabis tourism will be sizable. So far, it has been very visible and very good for certain businesses, but overall not a big part of the total demand. An early Colorado report suggested that over half of the year's tourists came at least in part because of interest in cannabis. Later, the study admitted its findings were wrong—only 23 percent of visitors' travel plans were influenced by legal pot.[42] Though mountain ski resort areas see 90 percent of their cannabis sales go to tourists, tourism only makes up 7 percent of the total cannabis retail demand in the state.[43]

Colorado is the friendliest state to pot tourism, as well, not only centrally located in the Intermountain West but with more toleration for clubs and hotels that advertise themselves as cannabis friendly. In Washington, regulations make the state less so.[44]

Just as out-of-state tourists have access to legal pot, local restrictions simply lead to a kind of residential pot tourism, as residents travel outside city limits to purchase their pot and bring it back. Even at the producer level, local laws often fall short of total bans. The headquarters for several cannabis businesses, including one of the state's largest retail chains, Native Roots, are in Colorado Springs.

Simply arguing about the Cole Memo and the other laws is a privilege, though. For that, a cadre of cannabis advocate groups fronts the money, time, and rhetoric to change the laws. Afterwards, the resulting regulatory landscape is treacherous and peppered with attorneys to guide the fledgling industry through the muck.

CHAPTER THREE

Lobbyists and Lawyers

Apart from voting in the ballot box and buying in the retail shop, the average American has little to do with the gears and levers behind cannabis.

The voters didn't create the ideological arguments behind the ballot, staff the think tanks and nonprofits behind the arguments, spend the decades convincing state and federal legislators, or fund the ballot's signature-gathering process. Nor did they shape the industry through an endless process of writing, reviewing, and rewriting rules; fighting with feds; and in general overcoming the twin velocities of the federal/state gap and the free market.

Lawyers, lobbyists, and policy advocates did and do these tasks, without which cannabis would still be nationally and internationally off limits and commercially dead. These professionals play into a long-established pattern of U.S. politics and industry.

In these early days of the cannabis industry, there is a green version of the kind of Beltway geometry that links advocates, funders, industry leaders, and politicians. In this case, special interest groups funded by assorted billionaires, industry leaders, and voter donors pass legalization measures. The associated attorneys then help the states craft the resulting business regulations and represent the businesses that follow them.

This is not only an embedded feature of U.S. commerce, but a pronounced feature of the cannabis industry. Any American business deals in laws and regulations along with buying for a dime and selling for a dollar. Cannabis does so much more because of the federal/state gap. This lends a unique flavor to the cannabis industry—whether advocates, lobbyists, prosecutors, regulators, business advisors, or criminal defense specialists—everything cannabis related starts moving with, moves through, moves around, is moved by, and stops with lawyers.

Lobbying and Advocacy

There is money behind the Green Rush.

The public supports legalizations through the ballot box, but those ballots take well-established and savvy organizations to spearhead. Whether it comes from business-minded people or from those motivated by social justice, though, it is large donors who made and still make legalization possible.

Cannabis legalization has its roots in academic arguments as much as in common public outcry. Private money flows into academic institutions, which feed policy and eventually change law. Industry, which will profit from the academic and the political arguments, helps and intensifies the effort.

Laws make much of the cannabis lobby's money difficult to track, both in the pro- and anti-legalization camps. Many organizations involved are public nonprofits. Nonprofits have unique donor and expenditure reporting requirements with the Internal Revenue Service (IRS) and are notoriously incestuous, circuitous, and opaque.

This distorts the view of cannabis legalization financials. From the money that can be traced, however, a picture emerges of a strange world of strange bedfellows. Democratically aligned groups are taking conservative business-boosting stances to advance their cause, whereas the stereotypically business-minded Republicans oppose legalization with liberal anti-corporate and public health concern rhetoric. It involves a proxy war between two of the world's wealthiest men who fight each other on a worldwide political stage centered around the state of Israel, competing pharmaceutical interests, and the shuffling of federal taxpayer money to anti-legalization advocates.

Politically, it fosters bizarre partnerships.

Naturally, the cannabis lobby has developed deep relationships with liberal leaders. The four largest lobbying groups contribute almost entirely to the same Democratic elected officials and committees and funded in large part by notable Democratic Party supporters. As the industry has grown, however, lobbyists court Republicans more and more as business interests coincide with social justice. Despite libertarians' rabid support for legalization, few lobbying dollars are thrown toward that party, though there have been a great many libertarian donors to legalization efforts.

Other industry interests come into play, notably alcohol and tobacco. In Chapter 9, these connections will be explored further, including two of cannabis's most prominent advocates courting the existing industry interests for funding and even the eventual hope of a collaboration between pot, booze, and smokes.

Broadly speaking, the most grassroots part of the cannabis debate is the actual votes on the state ballot initiatives. Anything further on the political front is connected to big, or at least not-so-small, money.

Main Street and K Street

Whether by design or coincidence, liberal causes and apolitical business mix in cannabis, which by now is its own special interest. The four main national lobbying organizations are closely related. They receive their funding from many of the same donors. One organization's leadership often bleeds into the leadership of another, and many cannabis lobbyists worked for rival cannabis lobbying groups before launching their own. Each group donates, funds, and supports the legalization campaigns and policy efforts of the others. Industry leaders sit in leadership or advisory roles for one or several groups or make large contributions to them.

This is standard in U.S. business. Few commercial concerns go without hired guns to prop favorable policies, block rivals, and make political inroads with friendly officials. Few social justice movements go without them, either.

Crossover between cash and the cause make cannabis. Intentional or not, social justice reform ends up fueling industry, and the industry advocates and lobbyists have roots in social justice. The leadership and donors of both the industry and social justice groups are a web of the industry's most influential people, whose products and services the social justice advocates endorse.

Opposing groups, of course, display the same patterns: large funders, deep political connections, and social arguments—in their case, the public health.

The cannabis lobby is the newest addition to the lobbying one-two punch combo of philanthropy and commerce. Only the youngest of the four big cannabis advocacy groups focuses exclusively on business, but the others still open huge business opportunities for their financial backers by pushing legalization agendas. The leaders of each of the four main cannabis advocacies have recognized that profit drives the conversation more and more.

Simple numbers show that cannabis legalization is dialing back on its original humanitarian goals now that money is in the mix. Of the eight states that legalized recreational cannabis, none have addressed cannabis-related incarceration except California.

Industry lobbyists aren't unaware of this, and the cannabis industry's development even causes some to quit their long-time advocacy jobs because they fear the corrupting influence of profit motive. Former Marijuana Policy Project lobbyist Don Riffle left his work with the organization. "Drug policy is all about reducing demand, and a company that has a profit motive is only going to increase demand," Riffle said. "Having a big commercial marijuana industry runs counter to public health goals."[1]

Other longtime advocates spurn the industry associations of newer groups. NORML founder Keith Stroup sent a fundraising email to NORML supporters, reminding them that the country's most well-established cannabis lobbying group relies on grassroots support, not industry backing.

> The marijuana legalization movement is only incidentally about marijuana; it is really about personal freedom. We are entering a new phase in which some of the most powerful interests will be profit driven.
>
> In the 47 years since we founded NORML, I have been proud of the fact that we are the consumer's champion rather than an industry group. From fighting for an end to marijuana related arrests, searches, and other intrusions of privacy—to working to ensure that people have access to high quality marijuana that is safe, convenient and affordable—our strength has and always will be people powered (NORML mass email to subscribers).

As we'll see, it is indeed a handful of industry interests and deep-pocketed liberal cause supporters who fund the bulk of the cannabis lobby and its successful legalization efforts.

Whatever the feelings from former or current cannabis advocates, and whether they are profit or people driven, the reality is hard to avoid. If we measure altruism by how many states have legalized cannabis, altruism gained real-world steam after it became profitable.

DEA, George Soros, and the Green Lobby Money Men

A few groups dominate the cannabis industry and cannabis legalization efforts: the National Organization for the Reform of Marijuana Laws, the Marijuana Policy Project, Drug Policy Alliance, and the National Cannabis Industry Association. Each has varying degrees of connection to industry as much as ideology.

The U.S. Drug Enforcement Administration fears the cannabis lobby, or rather, fears the money behind it paints too pretty a picture of legalization and medical use. The DEA points to how cannabis legalization efforts began and how they have developed in the last half decade, noting that what started as medical cannabis and cannabis decriminalization campaigns have morphed into adult use campaigns—an intensification it says exposes money as the true aim of legalization.[1]

> A few wealthy businessmen—not broad grassroots support—started and sustain the "medical" marijuana and drug legalization movements in the United States. Without their money and influence, the drug legalization movement would shrivel. According to National Families in Action, four individuals—George Soros, Peter Lewis, George Zimmer, and John

Sperling—contributed $1,510,000 to the effort to pass a "medical" marijuana law in California in 1996, a sum representing nearly 60 percent of the total contributions.

In addition to the continuing support from these businessmen, other contributors have supported the Drug Policy Alliance and the Marijuana Policy Project and their initiatives, including David Bronner, Rick Steves, Sean Parker, Dustin Moskovitz, Richard Lee, Bob Wilson, Jacob Goldfield, and Irwin Mark Jacobs.[2]

Money isn't the only way to measure support for the cause. Several public polls show a majority of Americans support legalization, and the ballots in each state should be proof enough.[3]

However, the DEA's point about cannabis legalization money is valid and doesn't contradict cannabis advocates' aims. The public does support some lobbying organizations with membership fees, but the cannabis lobby also has a deep, narrow pool of liberal and cannabis industry leaders as its biggest contributors.

The DEA's pro-cannabis business list is a helpful guide to some of drug reform's biggest funders. Hedge fund manager George Soros, Progressive Insurance founder Peter Lewis, former Men's Wearhouse CEO George Zimmer, and University of Phoenix founder John Sperling were indeed some of the biggest funders for early Californian cannabis measures and subsequent measures.

The DEA's list is out of date, however. Men's Wearhouse founder George Zimmer does contribute to legalization efforts, but since 2010 he's stayed quiet on the issue. John Sperling passed away in 2014 while Colorado and Washington were still building their recreational industries.

Soros and Lewis, however, are still very much a part of cannabis efforts, cofunding many causes peripheral or directly involved with cannabis along with multimillion dollar contributions to liberal organizations like America Coming Together and MoveOn.org.

Both are heavy funders of the American Civil Liberties Union (ACLU), a wellspring of cannabis legalization arguments and prominent business attorneys. Marijuana Policy Project and Drug Policy Alliance make yearly contributions to the ACLU, whose leadership crosses over into both organizations and which itself backs legalization efforts.

Both funnel wealth into cannabis research. Lewis also funds the Multidisciplinary Association for Psychedelic Studies for medical cannabis and other psychoactive drugs listed on the DEA's Controlled Substances Act. Soros's hedge fund also has many potential cannabis profiteers who have spent decades studying it as a market potential, which is explored in Chapter 9.

Apart from large funders, the cannabis lobby simply harnesses the donations of smaller businessmen set to profit from the drug's legality.

The Four Horsemen of Cannabis

NORML

Cannabis lobbying has been a Beltway mainstay since long before the recreational industry roared to life, thanks mostly to the National Organization for the Reform of Marijuana Laws, or NORML.

NORML has spearheaded cannabis efforts since 1970, lobbying in both state and federal buildings as a public nonprofit and one of cannabis's ideological proving grounds. It promotes responsible nonmedical use and led successful campaigns and ballot initiatives to decriminalize small amounts of cannabis in several states and to deprioritize cannabis law enforcement in others.

NORML's power lies in its broad chapter network and education campaigns, rather than from spending or from sponsoring the ballot initiatives younger and richer groups use. Internationally, NORML has chapters in Australia, Canada, France, Ireland, Jamaica, Spain, Norway, New Zealand, South Africa, and the United Kingdom.[4] In the United States, NORML chapters exist in every state but the Dakotas, Kansas, Maine, Mississippi, Utah, and Vermont. Many states have several chapters and subchapters diced up by cities and counties—Texas alone has 14 NORML chapters.[5]

NORML is less of a mover than a motivator of legalization campaigns. Maine and Vermont, neither of which have NORML chapters, legalized cannabis, and states like Texas or Missouri each have multiple NORML chapters but some of the nation's stricter cannabis laws.

In terms of political financing, NORML has never been either well capitalized or a big donor compared to other cannabis advocacies. Until 2001, NORML had no political action committee, or PAC, to make political contributions. Since then, the NORML PAC made only light contributions, not even donating enough at the federal level for the organization to need to report anything. Between 2001 and 2016, NORML donated only $80,000 directly to elected officials who supported cannabis legalization both in state and federal office.[6]

At the federal level, NORML has a history of donating almost entirely to the House of Representatives, having in 20 years made only two Senate contributions in 2014 to New Jersey and Maine Democrat Senators Cory Booker and Shenna Bellows.[7]

By far, NORML's favorite politician is former Massachusetts Congressman Barney Frank, one of drug reform's historically key Capitol Hill allies and one of the favorite fund recipients from other cannabis lobbying groups. NORML supported him with $10,000 of campaign contributions, more than double the amount any other federal or state elected official ever received from the group.[8]

More than direct donations, NORML influences through endorsements, an extensive network of information campaigns to educate readers about laws, along with recommended attorneys for cannabis-related crimes. Though Stroup prides his organization on staying away from industry funding, NORML does have industry connections.

Advocates use commercial apps to advance their case. NORML endorses the MyCanary app, which has impairment tests that can tell when a cannabis user needs to get off the road. Venture capitalist and Weedmaps founder Justin Hartfield (Chapter 8) sits on NORML's board of directors.

Drug Policy Alliance

If NORML is the oldest advocacy group, Drug Policy Alliance, or DPA, is the biggest and broadest: a collaboration of some of the deepest pockets and most well-established social justice connections. DPA formed in 2001 when the Lindesmith Center and Drug Policy merged, keeping Princeton University professor Ethan Nadelmann as executive director. An early founder, Kevin Zeese, once directed NORML.

For DPA, cannabis law reform is part of a bigger goal to end the global War on Drugs entirely. Efforts center mostly around a health-based approach to drugs instead of a punitive approach—rehabilitation and jail time reduction programs, reduced drug sentences and treatment plans, decriminalization, and education programs not just for cannabis but for all illicit drugs.

DPA set the scene for the last five years of explosive growth. Nadelmann said the turning point for cannabis legalization was in 1996, when he cobbled together the funding of Soros, Lewis, and Zimmer into the medical cannabis measure in California—the nation's first—and another medical measure in Arizona. Since then, he and DPA have chipped steadily away at medical ballots and recreational ballots in concert with Marijuana Policy Project and with New Approach PAC, a political action group funded by the family of Peter Lewis and run by attorney Graham Boyd.

DPA, along with Marijuana Policy Project, is the most impactful group. It has financially and operationally supported most of the successful legalization campaigns in U.S. states, as well as many unsuccessful ones. It gave $1.7 million to Washington State's successful 2012 ballot initiative, $100,000 to Alaska's successful 2014 ballot initiative, nearly $1 million to various California ballot initiatives, was the single largest donor for the Oregon campaign, and funded the Washington, D.C., measure. DPA was also the single largest driving force in Uruguay's legalization measure. California's 2016 ballot, unlike each of the prior states, was written by DPA.

Drug Policy Alliance has spent millions lobbying elected officials. Since 2001, DPA has spent $4.5 million on lobbying and supporting bills like the Synthetic Drug Control Act of 2015, the Comprehensive Addiction and

Recovery Act of 2016, and the CARERS Act of 2015. Over time, lobbying spending has increased, rising from $493,000 in 2001 to over $700,000 in recent years, according to tax filings.[9] Between 2002 and 2016, it gave $340,000 to federal candidates, parties, and committees, almost all of which went to Democrats and Democratic committees. Since 2002, DPA has made only one contribution to Republicans.[10]

Like NORML, DPA's funding relies heavily on gifts. Between 2011 and 2016, DPA has received over $52 million in gifts, grants, contributions, and membership fees.[11] On average, DPA brings in $11.4 million in annual revenue, several times that of the other three.[12]

Somewhat in line with DEA's accusations, DPA's financial support is deep, not wide. It does receive moneys from citizen donations and fees, but more comes from large donors, though Nadelmann insists little comes from the cannabis industry.

For the tax year ending May 31, 2016, Drug Policy Alliance brought in $10.4 million in total revenue. Of that total, $6.8 million, or 65 percent, came from 11 individual donors, with the largest being $1.5 million.[13] George Soros, DPA's biggest funder, spends between $4 million and $5 million a year in contributions.[14]

DPA has close relationships with other Soros projects. Soros has donated millions to the ACLU, whose Drug Policy Director Alison Holcomb was one of Washington State's initiative fund raisers and who consulted with the Uruguayan government prior to that country's cannabis legalization[15]—another Soros connection discussed in Chapter 9. Former ACLU director Ira Glasser is DPA's board chairman and was paid as a DPA consultant in 2003.

It also has an administrative services agreement with the Open Society Foundation (OSF), which granted $50 million to DPA during the recreational cannabis banner year of 2012.[16] Open Society Foundation is one of the world's most well-financed grant-making organizations, founded by Soros in 1993 to help transition Eastern European countries away from communism. OSF supports many social justice causes, including support for developing democracies; government accountability; education; public health issues; and human rights issues surrounding minorities, women, and the LGBTQ community.

Soros is one of the Democratic Party's biggest financial backers. DPA's money flows to Democratic Party candidates and causes along with cannabis ballot measures, too.

Whereas NORML is a heavily volunteer-based organization, DPA pays its people well, and the numbers have gone up as cannabis efforts increased. Salaries are by far DPA's biggest expense. In 2016, the group paid $7 million in salaries and payroll taxes, about half of its total expenses.[17] Founder and executive director Nadelmann is the highest-paid employee, making over $300,000 in 2016,[18] roughly twice the amount he made in the group's first years of operation.

DPA, of course, has industry funders, including some of the same business-men who bankroll the other three, including John Gilmore, Philip Harvey, and Rene Ruiz.

Marijuana Policy Project

If DPA is more broadly focused than NORML, the Marijuana Policy Proj-ect (MPP) could be seen as a more forceful NORML spinoff, with the same connections to industry and to George Soros. Founder Rob Kampia, a former libertarian political candidate, worked for NORML until he and NORML man-agement had a disagreement on methodology. Kampia and MPP cofounder Chuck Thomas wanted to focus more on direct lobbying.[19]

So far, they've accomplished this goal. Apart from spending nearly $1 million in direct lobbying costs since 2002, MPP donated twice as much as NORML per candidate and to far more candidates.[20] MPP's greatest successes, though, do not come from federal lobbying but from its trademark state bal-lot initiatives, most of which are funded or supported heavily by DPA.

MPP's Campaigns to Regulate Marijuana Like Alcohol are behind adult use of cannabis in Colorado, Alaska, Nevada, Massachusetts, Maine, and Califor-nia, as well as the successful Arizona Medical Marijuana Policy Project cam-paign in Arizona in 2010, among earlier decriminalization efforts.

MPP is more well funded than NORML, with most of its cash coming through grants and contributions. From 2000 to 2015, MPP's revenue aver-aged $1.7 million per year, according to tax filings. Wealthy funders play a large role in MPP's financing, as they do in DPA's. Like the Drug Policy Alli-ance, MPP got its first round of funding from George Soros. Peter Lewis gave the group $3 million in 2007. Like DPA, MPP's contributions swell in heavy cannabis legalization years. In both 2004 and 2012, MPP clocked revenues of $3.3 and $3.5 million, respectively.

MPP's largest individual donors are businesspeople, some with histories of advocacy and some with established industry connections.[21] Peter Thiel's Clarium Capital, billionaire Jeff Yass of the Susquehanna Foundation, Joseph Benjamin Pritzker and Jacqueline Pritzker ($50,000), Robert Field and wife Karen of the Manor Group and of Common Sense Drug Policy ($45,000), Elec-tronic Frontier Foundation founder John Gilmore ($50,000), Phil Harvey of DKT International, J. Edwin Holiday of Campbell and Company, Woody Kaplan of the Kaplan Group, Jonathan Lewis and Associates founder Jona-than Lewis ($25,000), and Steve Persky of Dalton Investments, among others, are the largest and most frequent donors, among them some of the more well-financed cannabis firms. Many of the cannabis industry's leaders are natu-rally donors to MPP campaigns, including Justin Hartfield of Weedmaps and Patrick Macmanamon of Cannasure.

Since launching its political action committee in 2004, MPP has contributed over half a million dollars to federal election campaigns. Like NORML, MPP's donations concentrate on Democrats, but recently have veered hard toward courting Republicans. In every election cycle since 2004, contributions have been at least 60 percent Democrat and typically around 90 percent. In 2016, though, donations to federal candidates were 65 percent Republican.

This switch can mostly be chalked up to Kentucky Republican Senator Rand Paul, a cannabis legalization supporter to whom MPP gave $13,000 in 2016 and just under $15,000 since its inception. This makes Paul one of MPP's most heavily supported candidates, alongside Congressman Sam Farr (D-CA) ($13,000), Sen. Mark Udall (D-CO) ($11,000), Rep. George Miller (D-CA) ($13,000), Rep. Maurice Hinchey (D-NY) ($13,000), Rep. Steve Cohen (D-TN) ($13,500), and Rep. Barney Frank (D-MA) ($8,250)—each of whom has equivalent war chests from DPA contributions.

The contributions are politically pointed to the states with powerful Democratic leadership and large populations. Though Paul and his Texas Senator father Ron Paul are some of MPP's most supported candidates, MPP funnels most of its money to California and New York Democrats. Between 2004 and 2016, MPP contributed $92,450 to California federal elected officials, 90 percent of which went to Democrats. Aside from California, only New York candidates have attracted more than $20,000 of contributions from MPP—100 percent of which went to the state's Democrats.

MPP also donates to liberal and Democratic committees, including the Vermont State Democratic Committee; the Committee for a Progressive Congress; PAC to the Future; United for a Strong America; Blue Dog PAC; Democratic Congressional Campaign Committee; DNC Services Corp; 21st Century Democrats; Democratic Freshman PAC; the Democratic parties of Arizona, New Mexico, Louisiana, Colorado, and Indiana; and the Democrats Win Seats PAC—many of which are favorites for DPA and the National Cannabis Industry Association.

It has also started shuffling money around to Republican campaigns, including the Republican Main Street Partnership and the National Republican Congressional Committee. Between 2004 and 2016, MPP has contributed only $16,000 to libertarian candidates—about 4 percent of the total $380,000 went to federal candidates. Aside from that, MPP gave $5,000 to former Libertarian Party presidential candidate and former New Mexico governor Gary Johnson, now a cannabis businessman himself.

Many of MPP's former staff and board members left to found businesses. Neal Levine served as MPP's department head, spearheading several of MPP's medical or recreational ballots. He now works for LivWell Enlightened Health, one of Colorado's largest retail cannabis chains. Mason Tvert, MPP's former communications director, now works for cannabis business law firm Vicente

Sederberg. MPP naturally donates to other cannabis lobbyists, notably to the National Cannabis Industry Association.

National Cannabis Industry Association

MPP's founder and former NORML employee Kampia was also one of the founding members of the National Cannabis Industry Association (NCIA), the youngest and fastest growing of the big four cannabis lobbying groups, which describes itself as the "only industry-led organization engaging in industry efforts to expand and further legitimize the legal cannabis market in the U.S."[22]

NORML, DPA, and MPP have well-established criminal reform goals, despite the growing industry focus and backing. NCIA, however, is straightforward about its Beltway commercial lobby role:

> To promote the growth of a responsible and legitimate cannabis industry and work for a favorable social, economic, and legal environment for that industry in the United States.
>
> The National Cannabis Industry Association was founded on the principle of power in numbers. The thousands of American businesses involved in the state-legal cannabis industries represent a tremendous economic force in this country. As the industry's national trade association, NCIA works every day to ensure our growing business sector is represented in a professional and coordinated way on the national stage.[23]

As the mission statement might suggest, NCIA's offerings for members are geared to enhance business opportunities rather than correct the negative impacts of the drug war.

NCIA runs on the fees from now over 1,300 member businesses, which range from $1,000 a year to $5,000 to be a "sustaining member." The membership fees bring the industry's forefront together to collaborate on best practices and regulation ideas. In exchange, members have access to the many networking and trade shows NCIA presents—complete with speakers from cannabis-focused law firms and business leaders—discounts with other members, prominent brand placements on the NCIA's webpage for the higher-paying members, and discount market data from BDS Analytics, one of the country's foremost industry data firms, among other industry partnerships.

NCIA's revenue, though still heavily dependent on grants, also comes from membership dues and shows the industry's rapid growth. In the last half decade, the organization's bankroll has swelled 10 times. In 2011, NCIA brought in $160,720 in revenue. By 2015, annual revenue had grown to $1.5 million.

The National Cannabis Industry Association's lobbying also went up with time, starting low with $20,000 and working up to $430,000 by the 2016 cycle. In total, the group has spent over $1 million in lobbying.[24] NCIA uses two established Beltway lobbying firms, Heather Podesta & Partners and Jochum and Shore & Trossevin, as well as its main lobbyist, Michael Correia.

Contributions to politicians have grown rapidly along with the cannabis industry. Contributions between 2013 and 2014 only clocked just over $30,000, then spiked to $104,066 the following cycle.

Unlike the other three cannabis advocates, NCIA spreads its money more evenly to parties. NCIA's political action committee has given over $100,000 to mainly Democratic candidates and committees during the 2014 and 2016 campaigns. During the 2014 and 2016 election cycles, NCIA contributed $67,400 to Democratic candidates and $16,350 to Republicans—clearly not a majority, but still far more raised for Republicans than any of the other three groups.

Like NORML and MPP, NCIA's state chapters are active and played key roles in drafting the regulations that followed MPP's initiatives. In New Jersey, the New Jersey Cannabis Industry Association has pumped money into state policy makers, hiring firm CLB Partners to help craft legislation.[25]

NCIA's leadership is stacked with some of the most influential names in cannabis, and although some of them have advocacy histories, each of them now leads a business concern. Many also have leadership roles with either the national or the state affiliates and chapters of NORML, DPA, and MPP. Most, if not all, took roles in drafting the local or state regulations the rest of the cannabis industry must follow in Colorado, Washington, California, and Oregon. Through the rest of this book, many of these names will reappear as leaders in their respective industry spheres.

The founders alone are among the industry's heaviest power hitters, with many ties to the other lobbying organizations. NCIA's executive director, Aaron Smith, was the California state policy director for MPP. Capital-raising firm ArcView Group CEO Troy Dayton is also the founding board member of the NCIA and a board member of the Marijuana Policy Project. ArcView founder Steve DeAngelo is president of ArcView Group, founder of one of the largest cannabis producers, Harborside Farms; cofounder of one of the largest testing facilities, Steep Hill Labs; and an NCIA founding board member. Vincent Keber is a founder of NCIA, director and CEO of Colorado's megaproducer Dixie Elixirs & Edibles, and director of MassRoots, one of the cannabis industry's most powerful information sources.

Board member Kris Krane formerly worked for NORML and now runs the cannabis business consulting firm 4Front Ventures. Board member Jessica Billingsley founded MJ Freeway—one of the foremost companies that sells tracking software state regulations require. Board member Shannon Fender works for Native Roots, one of Colorado's new breed of Starbucks-like cannabis retail chains. WeedMaps, another of the largest cannabis apps, has many of the same lobbying connections.[26]

This list is not exhaustive. Current and past board members represent some of the top law firms, top business consultants, top retailers, top extraction experts, etc., in the country.

Opposition

The same kind of ideological connections and wealthy funders exist against the cannabis industry as in favor of it, but so far are losing the battle. Apart from the actual arguments and public opinion, legalization advocates outspend anti-legalization efforts substantially.

Much like the connections and ideological spinoffs in the pro-cannabis lobby, the anti-cannabis lobby's most powerful voices have a few genesis points in common—supporters of conservative causes, candidates, and thought leaders and the industries that profit from the drug war, including federal anti-drug money.

Opposing groups typically argue against the cannabis industry over some kind of safety concern—public health, driver safety, or criminality top the list—but like the cannabis lobby, money isn't far off. There are naturally competing industry lobbying interests try to halt, slow, or latch onto the cannabis industry. Some of these anti-legalization commercial interests—pharmaceuticals, alcohol, and tobacco—will be addressed in Chapter 9.

Arguably the most vocal and politically relevant anti-cannabis voice is Smart Approaches to Marijuana, or SAM, which has spent millions in opposition to cannabis legalization ballots. SAM is the child of two high-profile voices in both the public health and drug policy worlds and one of the more prominent neoconservative commentators in the country. Former Rhode Island Democrat Rep. Patrick Kennedy founded SAM, along with a former advisor to President Barack Obama's Drug Czar, Kevin Sabet, and David Frum, a prominent neoconservative journalist and author who founded news site The Daily Beast and now works as a senior editor at *The Atlantic*.

Sheldon Adelson

Much of the money used in anti-legalization efforts comes from Sheldon Adelson, the anti-pot billionaire equivalent of George Soros. Adelson has lobbed tens of millions of dollars against medical and recreational cannabis legalization measures. He was the single largest contributor to the opposition of the 2014 medical legalization campaign in Florida, donating $2.7 million to the Drug Free Florida campaign and another $1.5 million to the No On 2 campaign. During the following 2016 Florida medical initiative, he gave another $1.5 million to opposition. In 2016, he donated millions against the recreational ballots in Nevada, Massachusetts, and Arizona.

Adelson is chairman and CEO of the Las Vegas Sands Corporation, which includes the Venetian and Sands casinos, among others. His reasons are ostensibly motivated by public health concerns, but he does have an interest in rehab facilities and in Israeli drug research. Israel, as one of the leading pharmaceutical research nation's in the world, has criticized the United States' recreational program as untested and unmedical, a view Project SAM shares.

Both he and his wife, Miriam, have extensive histories with drug addiction issues and stakes in recovery centers, she as an Israeli-born researcher and he as a philanthropist. Two of Adelson's sons suffered addiction issues, one of which was fatal. He established several drug treatment centers as a result, including the Miriam and Sheldon G. Adelson Clinic for Drug Abuse—one in Tel Aviv, Israel, and one in Las Vegas.

In recent years, he's branched into media. The media to which he is attached has different takes on cannabis legalization, depending on their country. He owns the *Las Vegas Review Journal*, which he bought for $140 million and which promptly withdrew its endorsement of Nevada pot legalization after his purchase. He is also closely tied to Israeli daily newspaper *Israel Hayom*, whose editors, Elia Berger and Steve Ganot, took a very supportive view of cannabis legalization in a 2014 debate with one of their contributors.[27]

Adelson has the same history of supporting conservative causes and candidates as Soros does supporting liberals, spending hundreds of millions of dollars on election contributions. He is close friends with Israeli Prime Minister Benjamin Netanyahu—who is known for his hatred of Soros—and has been known to pow-wow with Netanyahu on policy. Like Soros's connections to the Clintons, Adelson is deeply linked to the administration of former President George W. Bush. Prominent Republicans with vocal anti-cannabis views rank among his largest contribution recipients, including former Speaker of the House Newt Gingrich and California Republican Sen. Carly Fiorina. In the two most recent election cycles, he was among the top individual contributors in the country. In the 2016 election cycle alone, he contributed nearly $83 million to House and Senate candidates, 100 percent of which went to Republicans, including $25 million to President Donald Trump's campaign.[28]

Some of Adelson's projects aim specifically to combat Soros's Democratic focuses. For example, Adelson founded and funded Freedom's Watch, a short-lived conservative lobbying organization that supported drug war policies and the invasion and war in Iraq until disbanding in 2008. In practice, it functioned as a counterweight to Soros's MoveOn.org. It featured heavy collaboration with the Republican Jewish Coalition, of which Adelson is a major funder, and conservative voices from the American Enterprise Institute for Public Policy Research, a conservative think tank. However, these are not Project SAM's only ties to any of these groups.

David Frum

David Frum, a Canadian American journalist and commentator, has the same connections to conservative candidates and causes and Adelson-backed organizations. Known for his support of conservative Israeli policies, Frum is on the board of directors of the Adelson-funded Republican Jewish Coalition. He is a senior editor at *The Atlantic,* which has published such pieces as "The Failed Promise of Legal Pot" regarding the persistence of racially disparate drug-related arrests. He is also a regular contributor to CNN.

Frum volunteered for former President Ronald Reagan's campaign in 1980, and he served as a speech writer for former President George W. Bush from 2001–2002. He also served as an American Enterprise Institute fellow and as vice chairman of the R Street Institute, which is one of several conservative think tanks associated with the State Policy Network.

Patrick Kennedy

Breaking the trend of conservative voices on SAM, former Rhode Island Congressman Patrick Kennedy is the sole Democratic anti-cannabis voice. He and Adelson have similarities—a wealth of personal drug use baggage and personal involvement with rehabilitation facilities, with pharmaceutical connections to boot.

Kennedy has been an outspoken critic of cannabis legalization since 2011, ostensibly over his own past with addiction. Kennedy is himself a recovering alcoholic, former cocaine user, and admitted oxycodone addict.

He has also been aggressive in promoting measures that deal with mental health, both in policy and through his book *A Common Struggle: A Personal Journey Through the Past and Future of Mental Illness and Addiction.* Among other projects, he founded several rehabilitation facilities, like Adelson has.

His voting record is in concert with SAM's arguments, which support medical cannabis studies but not recreational legalization. Kennedy supported several medical cannabis–focused bills in the 2000s, including the Rohrabacher-Hinchey amendment. Like the Rohrabacher-Farr amendment in the 2010s, this bill denied the federal government any funding to prosecute cannabis in states where it is medically legal.

Like the pro-cannabis lobby, whatever anti-addiction and pro-health arguments Kennedy uses also have dollars attached at some point. Some of Kennedy's efforts have connections to the larger pharmaceutical industry that lobbies against cannabis legalization, in part over the opioid crisis (see Chapter 9). Casino interests and health professionals were among his biggest contributing industries over the course of his career.[29]

Kennedy served as a spokesperson alongside conservative icon Newt Gingrich for Advocates for Opioid Recovery, which the *Boston Globe* uncovered is backed by Apple Tree Partners, a private equity firm that owns Braeburn Pharmaceuticals, a psychiatric, neuropathic, and addiction recovery drug manufacturer. The same company backed another addiction nonprofit of Kennedy's, CleanSlate Addiction Forum.[30] Among Braeburn's products is Probuphine, its branded version of buprenorphine. Buprenorphine's medical purpose is to lessen an opioid addict's cravings during withdrawal.

Kenney's legislative fights involved the drug when Congress was churning through the Comprehensive Addiction and Recovery Act, a $181 million spending bill that broadly addresses the national opioid epidemic. Among other items, Kennedy argued[31] in favor of an expensive bill feature that expanded the criteria for federally funded health workers to prescribe the buprenorphine and expanded federal funding for such medication.

This is only one example of anti-cannabis play from interests connected to pharmaceuticals and the opioid crisis. Chapter 9 will discuss more, including those with interests in the cannabis lobby world itself.

Project SAM

Kennedy's Project SAM itself does not have any backing from pharmaceutical companies, but does count among its supporters and leaders some with connections to the pharmaceutical industry, along with pediatrics and mental health professionals, and others with personal wars with drug addiction or drug-related traumas.

SAM's cofounder, Kevin Sabet, lost a friend to a drug-related accident in high school[32] and has since devoted his career to combatting drug use. He worked as a drug policy advisor for the federal government from Bill Clinton through Barack Obama, whose toleration of states' cannabis legalization spurred him to start SAM. He currently works as the director and assistant professor of psychiatry for the University of Florida's Drug Policy Institute, which claims cannabis research has been bought by George Soros though Open Society Foundation grants.[33]

The group's board and staff are mostly pediatrics and psychiatry professors from four universities: Johns Hopkins Medical School, University of Colorado at Denver, the University of Kansas, and Harvard Medical School. Others are pharmacology researchers and addiction recovery advocates, including the president of the American Society of Addiction Medicine, or social activists and judges opposed to drugs in the African American community.

The group drops the public service announcement (PSA) tone of the 1980s, calling the War on Drugs "ineffective and counterproductive." Project SAM says no government should legalize cannabis, but says it agrees with decriminalizing small possessions; expunging low-level cannabis criminal records; and other missions related to the social justice crusades of the ACLU, DPA, and NORML. Instead, it echoes the DEA.

Sabet says Wall Street advertising is as ruthless as a Mexican cartel and denies there are any reasons for cannabis legalization beyond profit motive. He says "Big Marijuana" is simply Big Tobacco 2.0 in waiting and uses the same marketing and lobbying tactics tobacco once did and that cannabis legalization's breakneck pace from state ballot initiatives will have unintended consequences without the proper time to study health outcomes:

> Legalization is about one thing: making a small number of business people rich. If it were about ending the War on Drugs, recent law changes would be limited to decriminalization. Rather, a host of business interests are getting involved with the legal marijuana trade in Colorado and elsewhere. They have set up private equity firms and fundraising organizations to attract investors and promote items such as marijuana food items, oils, and other products.[34]

To illustrate this, SAM argues against points it claims medical cannabis advocates use to disguise or mislead the public about public health dangers, addiction, connections between cannabis and mental health and suicide, lung cancer, and traffic fatalities. Virtually all cannabis advocates say SAM and Sabet skew the data, make straw claims, and unfairly catastrophize the cannabis industry.

SAM has weathered accusations of unethical financing, which doesn't amount to nearly as much as the pro-cannabis groups. Among the smaller individual donors, whose names SAM is not required to disclose, the contributors to SAM's campaigns include pharmaceuticals, alcohol interests, Sheldon Adelson, law enforcement groups, and federal drug trafficking watchdogs.

In 2017, the California Fair Political Practices Commission tried to slap SAM with a $6,000 fine for failing to include in its campaign committee name the name of its major California campaign donor, Pennsylvania millionaire Julie Schauer; failure to disclose other Schauer donations in a timely fashion; and failure to file its top 10 donors.[35] Schauer gave SAM $1.4 million for the campaign and tens of thousands of dollars apiece to similar campaigns in Nevada and Massachusetts.

SAM's campaign against the 2016 Arizona recreational ballot received $500,000 from Insys Therapeutics, a pharmaceutical company currently developing synthetic cannabinoids. More on Insys and pharmaceuticals companies will be discussed in Chapter 9.

SAM also receives funding and assistance from partly federally funded groups. Californians for Drug-Free Youth, or CADFY, partly funded and works with SAM.[36] CADFY receives federal High Intensity Drug Trafficking Area (HITDA) funding reserved for organizations and law enforcement targeting drugs. SAM promotes and distributes the studies and research of HITDA organizations, including a controversial report from Colorado's

Rocky Mountain HITDA that met heavy media and industry criticism for misrepresenting data to paint a negative picture of cannabis in Colorado.[37]

Law Enforcement Groups

Apart from SAM and the federal government itself, nobody lobbies harder against pot than law enforcement, though some states like Oregon earmark a percentage of cannabis taxes specifically for police. Legal or not, cannabis is worth money to somebody. Drug criminalization brings millions of dollars into police departments from drug-focused U.S. Department of Justice grants and the seizure of drug suspects' homes, vehicles, and personal property, a practice called civil asset forfeiture that netted the nation $1 billion from 2002–2012.[38]

During California's 2016 ballot campaign, half of the oppositional Coalition for Responsible Drug Policy's funding came from police, prison guards, and associated unions.[39] Similar organizations opposed medical legalization in Minnesota and opposed recreational cannabis in Washington and Colorado.

Private prison organizations like Correction Corporation of America and GEO, which collectively spend millions on lobbying, receive less money and need fewer employees the fewer prisoners they have. These groups have extensive histories of lobbying against measures that would reduce incarceration rates.

Lawyers

Once the lobbying groups pass their initiatives, lawyers take over the day-to-day realities of navigating regulations. Nearly all the large cannabis business, and a big bulk of the small ones, contract with specialized cannabis business attorneys to walk them through the now-legal mire of the cannabis industry.

As most industry leaders point out, the cannabis industry is not just risky, but complex for a garden-variety businessman. One prominent cannabis business attorney describes the Controlled Substances Act as the Lawyer's Full Employment Act because of sheer volume of restrictions, the federal/state gap, and the countless snags from cannabis business bans and moratoriums.[40] In short, the legal complexity of the cannabis industry almost forces entrepreneurs to work with attorneys.

As we'll see in later chapters, the regulatory structures for cannabis businesses create high barriers to entry both fiscally and operationally. Cannabis businesses cannot open bank accounts; secure loans; rent question-free retail or cultivation space; advertise through traditional channels; sell their products in grocery stores or online; write off employee expenses on their tax forms; pay taxes through traditional channels; work across state lines; hire at will; or operate without heavy licensure, endless collaboration with local authorities, background checking, and spot checks for regulatory compliance.

For a garden-variety, mom-and-pop retail shop or small farmer, having a lawyer isn't at the top of the business priority list. But because virtually any issue in a cannabis business needs deep regulatory and legal knowledge to navigate, it borders on a necessity.

The industry's youth plays into the necessity. Many cannabis entrepreneurs have little business or legal experience (outside criminal courts), and those who do are all too familiar with the legal complications of garden-variety commerce, let alone cannabis commerce.

Cannabis plays a part in easing the legal market, which as late as 2010 was saturated with law school graduates looking for work. Now, cannabis business law is the latest legal rage and a lucrative source of legal work.

The partners from several law firms remembered that in the early days of cannabis legalization, they had to convince their mentors they weren't committing career suicide—now an almost laughable stance considering the short track to wealth, prestige, and media stardom cannabis lawyering presents. As experts in the hyperdrive conversation, cannabis lawyers are not only industry fixtures but some of the most heavily consulted media sources (see Chapter 8), as well as the moving hands behind the endless regulatory tweaks at state and local levels.

Some cannabis attorneys are stars in their respective world. Prominent lawyers lecture at countless industry seminars. The media mines them constantly for quotes and context and crowns them Super Lawyers, Lawyers of the Year, Most Powerful People. The prestige comes with money. Because big firms and many established attorneys stay away, and because cannabis is so legally irregular, cannabis lawyers have a leg up on the competition simply by accepting the risk of entering the space.

In interviews, lawyers openly acknowledge the career boost cannabis has given them. Arizona's Ryan Hurley, who leads Rose Law Group's cannabis office, said he doubts he could have gained the same kind of status had he entered the already-saturated banking law.[41] At least two attorneys who specialize in cannabis businesses, Nicole Howell Neubert and Jana Weltzin, left their plans of working in Indian law to represent pot clients after finding Indian law practice less than friendly to young attorneys.

Ethics and Malpractice

The federal/state gap can propel the indispensable lawyers into lucrative practices, but lawyers aren't immune from the same traps, hurdles, and patterns seen in other industry segments. As with the businesses themselves, attorneys had to fight for the ability to take on cannabis clients in the face of federal law.

Critically, the federal/state gap opens a nest of ethical considerations. Simply taking on cannabis clients is an ethical gray area that can put smart and forward-thinking attorneys at personal risk of damaging their own reputations, or even exposing themselves to federal criminal liability. This has not yet happened, but the possibility remains because of the federal/state gap.

State bars and state bar associations have changed their advice to attorneys over the last decade, but just like a cannabis farmer, attorneys have no concrete protections from federal law. At the national level, this is still the case, even though national firms are loudly and proudly representing cannabis businesses.

At first, the message to attorneys was clear: don't do it at all. It would be irresponsible, many bars said, for a lawyer to have anything to do with an enterprise that is still illegal at the federal level. The American Bar Association (ABA) said lawyers should not assist cannabis clients. According to its Model Rules of Professional Conduct, Model Rule 1.2(d), they can't directly assist with anything illegal:

> A lawyer shall not counsel a client to engage, or assist a client, in conduct that the lawyer knows is criminal or fraudulent, but a lawyer may discuss the legal consequences of any proposed course of conduct with a client and may counsel or assist a client to make a good faith effort to determine the validity, scope, meaning or application of the law.[42]

When medical programs started coming online, state bars started loosening up. By the 2010s, bar associations bucked hard against the ABA's guidance. In 2011, the State Bar of Arizona Ethics Committee not only allowed for cannabis law practices, but lionized the attorneys that would go against federal law and refused to follow the ABA model rule:

> The maintenance of an independent legal profession, and of its right to advocate for the interest of clients is a bulwark of our system of government. History is replete with examples of lawyers who, through vigorous advocacy and at great personal and professional cost to themselves, obtained the vindication of constitutional or other rights long denied or withheld and which otherwise could not have been secured.[43]

Others followed. The state bar associations of recreational states were standoffish at first, but the adult-use craze blew the legal industry's doors open. When Colorado legalized in 2012, the state's bar association opined that lawyers could advise a cannabis business, but not help it do business.[44] Shortly after, Colorado lawyers looking for entry points into the cannabis business lobbied for a different opinion and eventually got one in 2014:

> A lawyer may counsel a client regarding the validity, scope, and meaning of Colorado constitution article XVII, secs. 14 & 16, and may assist a client

in conduct that the lawyer reasonably believes is permitted by those constitutional provisions and the statutes, regulations, orders, and other state or local provisions implementing them. In these circumstances, the lawyer shall also advise the client regarding related federal law and policy.[45]

Florida, Massachusetts, Minnesota, Nevada, New York, and Washington bar associations and legislatures passed similar opinions and policies—in those states, cannabis lawyers have some state protection to ply their trade in cannabis.[46] Whatever issues remain, ethically speaking, are in the past as far as legal practice is concerned.

To link attorneys with each other, three San Francisco business attorneys founded the National Cannabis Bar Association (NCBA) in 2015 to "educate and connect with other cannabis industry lawyers for the purpose of providing excellent, ethical, and advanced legal assistance to this growing industry." More member attorneys are either from Colorado or California, but span all over the country.

Ethics of the Green Rush

Ethics, however, are a moving target. The law may protect lawyers in some states, but there are fewer laws protecting cannabis businesses from attorneys. Just as there can be dishonest cannabis businesses, some attorneys complain that a few bad lawyers are giving cannabis lawyers in general a bad name, though the Cannabis Bar Association denies there are any shadier deals than in other industries.[47] The opportunities for dodgy deals come from regulations, not despite them.

Lawyers verge on a requirement for cannabis businesses due to the density of regulations. The complexity and federal illegality often scare away experienced businesspeople, leaving behind unsophisticated entrepreneurs who may not know the basics of securing counsel. Further, because of the banking and general financing hurdles, many have no startup cash and have no choice but to enter certain kinds of financial structures with their attorneys.

The way a lawyer charges a client can bring up ethical breaches if done incorrectly. Traditionally, lawyers charge hourly fees for service, but lawyers can take a piece of investment in their client's business or a percentage of the profits instead.

This isn't necessarily a bad thing, according to American Bar Association guidance and guidance from other legal committees, but they strongly recommend against it.[48] The practice of lawyers doing business with clients has been increasing in the last few decades, according to an ABA report, and is reputedly one of the more common features of attorney–client relationships in the cannabis industry. One of the cannabis legal industry's flagship firms,

Vicente Sederberg, works in collaboration with a business advising company, VS Strategies.

Zoning regulations alone can make the situation even more ethically risky. In many localities, zoning laws force cannabis businesses to clump nearby each other. A cannabis attorney with stake in a business could potentially represent several competing businesses in the same area.

Legal Education

The Ivory Tower of law has noted the successes of cannabis lawyers and is adjusting to prepare its followers. Broadly speaking, cannabis attorneys come from three pools: former criminal attorneys turned business attorneys, former business and regulatory attorneys using their expertise for commercial cannabis benefit, and young attorneys who enter the legal world with cannabis representation in mind from the get-go.

With examples from Harvard to the University of Denver, professors and deans see the money in cannabis too. Law schools have been offering cannabis-related courses for decades as a criminal law study. In the last decade, though, many started offering coursework for two basic purposes: how to write state regulations and or how to manage and bill the companies that must follow the regulations they write.

The trend naturally began in the first two states to legalize recreational cannabis. The University of Washington launched the Cannabis Law and Policy Project, which tries to tie together the mishmash of law studies to make sound policy recommendations. The University of Denver Sturm College of Law offers classes like Representing the Marijuana Client and now has a designated professor of marijuana law and policy, Sam Kamin, who is affiliated with both the ACLU and with Denver's top cannabis law firm, Vicente Sederberg.

The trend quickly spread to other states. Ohio State University teaches Marijuana Law, Policy and Reform. Hofstra University offers Business and Legal Issues Related to Marijuana. Vanderbilt University Law School offers marijuana-related business and law classes. Lewis and Clark Law School offers Cannabis Law and Policy.

Lawyers even dispense advice to each other. Washington cannabis law firm Gleam Law, CannaLaw Blog, the CLPP blog, and dozens of others swap ideas and best practices. Legal consortia exist for the express purpose of linking lawyers with other lawyers for classes for best practices.

Practice Areas

The sheer density of problems caused by federal, state, and local laws means countless billable hours for an energetic lawyer, but also means the practices must be specially tailored. In practice, cannabis business lawyers must either be excellent generalists or be highly skilled specialists with connections to a firm full of other specialists. Cannabis business lawyers need to know at least the rudiments of intellectual property (IP) law, zoning, criminal, regulatory compliance, estate, day-to-day legal, corporate formation, etc., just to navigate a single retail store's development.

Most of the prominent cannabis firms either grow from a single general practice to teams of specialists or move into cannabis from an already established firm with many lawyers of differing expertise.

Like the cannabis lobby, cannabis law has shifted as more and more business opportunities opened. Before the cannabis rush of the early 2000s, cannabis attorneys were focused on the social justice arguments used by the ACLU and NORML: reduction of incarceration rates, personal freedom, racial disparities in law enforcement, etc. Early criminal defense attorneys like Bruce Margolis, director of the Los Angeles NORML branch, made a name for themselves defending high-profile cannabis crimes. As the industry developed, both business and criminal attorneys moved into the territory where once defense attorneys were the norm.

Many cannabis business attorneys simply fold their operations over from the criminal world—both in defense and in prosecution. Cannabis attorneys like Lauren Davis and others began their careers as prosecutors before they represented now-legal pot businesses. John Vardman, now with cannabis financing company Hypur, formerly worked for the U.S. Department of Justice. Shellie Hayes, a retired Illinois judge, is both a founding member of the National Cannabis Bar Association and co-owner of Sweet Leaf Kitchens, an edibles company.

The business focus hasn't taken attorneys away from criminal matters entirely. Because the cannabis industry is still toddling out of the black market, criminal and business matters often blend. When legalization passes, businesses sometimes jump the gun and start operating before regulations are ready. Even when they stay within the state laws, they may still run into snags with federal laws.

Indeed, this is the rule in states where recreational pot is legal. Alaska, Colorado, and Washington each had one or several instances where state or feds prosecuted early business owners, both licensed and unlicensed. It is often the cannabis business attorneys who take the criminal defense case. Cannabis business lawyers Jana Weltzin, Henry Wykowski, and Christian Sederberg, among others, have all represented clients in high-profile criminal cases that fit this description.

The Firms

Like the businesses they represent, lawyers are starting to carve out their niche. The cannabis industry already has a loose framework of dominant firms shaping the regulations and therefore the industry.

Just as with the other business sectors we'll examine, the federal/state gap has kept much of the established legal industry out. This guarantees market share for those lawyers willing to accept cannabis's risk and stigma. The long-standing and powerful clients of top-tier law firms might not want their firm representing businesses that are, in the strictest federal definition, drug dealers and money launderers. Many cannabis attorneys say the legal establishment sees cannabis practice as a joke and will until Washington, D.C., changes federal law.

Big-ticket international firms like Holland and Knight or Latham & Watkins have either not entered the sphere or not given comment to the book's author about their level of involvement. In the meantime, some of the founders of internationally operating cannabis companies like Canada's Canopy Growth have backgrounds in international law, and most others retain private counsel with those who do.

Still, high-profile firms are trickling into cannabis law. Perkins Couie contracted with a cryptocurrency startup called POSaBIT (see Chapter 5), which is entirely cannabis-centric, to see whether the former Microsoft-based company is breaking any rules.[49] Further, cannabis firms can sap talent—Vicente Sederberg is home to a former Latham and Watkins attorney who left the multibillion-dollar New York firm for Denver's ever-greener pastures.

In the mid-2010s, the most prominent cannabis firms were first mover types in boutiques and solo practitioners. Colorado's Vicente Sederberg and Hoban Law Group, California's Frontera Law Group, Washington's Harris Bricken, and Florida's Greenbridge Corporate Counsel, to name a few, were among the most visible pioneers in establishing cannabis business law as a legitimate practice in and of itself.

Despite the reluctance of the power broker firms, larger regional, state, and national firms are getting into the business too. National law firms like Dymeka, Thompson Coburn, Much Shelist, Fox Rothschild, and Rose Law Group have all entered the new industry from other highly regulated areas like gambling, zoning, or corporate law. Other attorneys are launching their own firms. Chicago's Rollman & Dahlin, California's Clark Neubert, and Alaska's JDW, LLC (whose founder, Jana Weltzin, formerly worked at Rose Law Group), were each founded expressly focused on cannabis business law and consulting.

The firms are the guiding hands behind the business framework, working in concert with the ballot makers. Most attorneys have direct connections to the cannabis lobbying world, and many directly contributed to the industry regulations in the states where they operate.

International and across State Lines

In a way, cannabis lawyers are bypassing the federal/state gap and setting up a national legal system outside the boundaries of the federal government.

The industry is already developing a rubric for a national regulatory scheme and even an international commercial model. The appetite for paying clientele, connections with lobbying groups, and constantly changing regulations mean lawyers and the legal lessons make footholds throughout the world.

Like most of the ancillary businesses we'll examine in Chapter 8, cannabis attorneys have a leg up on actual cannabis producers. Cannabis itself cannot cross borders thanks to federal law. Cannabis-centric attorneys are unlike the businesses they represent in that they spread across several states and sometimes even across international borders.

Most, if not all, of the most prominent cannabis firms associated with the National Cannabis Bar Association operate across state lines. Vicente Sederberg has offices not just in Colorado, but Washington, D.C., Massachusetts, and Nevada. Hoban Law Group has attorneys and offices in half of the U.S. states where cannabis is legal, including some of the attorneys most responsible for their respective states' regulations. Harris Bricken's Canna Law Group has clients in California, Florida, Oregon, and Washington.

Some of these attorneys are already working in established markets across international borders as well. Aird & Berlis Cannabis Group has brokered deals with both Canadian and Uruguayan cannabis companies. Florida-based law firm Greenspoon Marder has offices in Florida, Tennessee, Colorado, New York, Oregon, California, and Nevada, as well as across international lines in Israel.[50]

Ties to Pro-Legalization Groups

Cannabis business attorneys in general—especially those affiliated with the National Cannabis Bar Association—are largely the tactical arms of the driving lobbying forces behind the cannabis industry's legalization and growth. Most are connected to one or more of the four main national cannabis advocacy groups or their state chapters.

Along with some of the more well-known brands and ancillary businesses, NCIA has some of the most recognized industry attorneys as current and former board members. Christian Sederberg was the first director of the National Cannabis Industry Association. Hilary Bricken served on the board of directors as well. As its general counsel, NCIA uses Henry Wykowski, a California tax trial attorney specializing in cannabis matters.

There are the same connections between the NCBA and the ACLU—the driving ideological force behind legalization—and NORML. Shabnam Malek, president and executive director of the NCBA, works for the ACLU. Sam Kamin, a professor of cannabis law at the University of Denver Sturm College of Law, worked on an ACLU panel. Jason Brandeis, an NCBA member Anchorage attorney and assistant professor at the University of Alaska Anchorage, advises municipal governments on cannabis regulation. Prior, he worked for the Alaska ACLU.

Vicente Sederberg is a haven for ACLU-connected attorneys. Vicente Sederberg's Chloe Grossman interned for the ACLU and currently is a research director for NCIA. Allen Hopper, a counsel attorney for Vicente Sederberg, also worked a high-level position at the ACLU. Joshua Kappel, one of Vicente Sederberg's partners, interned for ACLU.

NCBA's connections to NORML run as deeply as its ACLU connections. California's Omar Figueroa is a member of NORML's legal committee. Nicole Howell Neubert, another California business attorney, has a seat on the California NORML board along with attorney Robert Raich. Mathew Abel, a Michigan defense attorney turned business attorney and one of NCBA's founders, is both the executive director of Michigan NORML and on the Michigan ACLU's legal committee. Leland Berger, the primary author of Oregon's cannabis measure, is both a founding member of NCBA and a member of the NCIA and the NORML Legal Committee.

Nearly all of these people were instrumental in not just the passage of the cannabis measures, but in their implementation. Many were already thoroughly embedded in the legal and political community as well, as members of state bar associations, legislative and quasi-legislative committees, regulatory boards, and nonprofits, along with the multibillion-dollar industry whose interests they oversee.

Attorneys have their work cut out for them. Once they get to the starting line, nothing is easy.

CHAPTER FOUR

Going to Market: Cultivation, Testing, Manufacturing, Production, and Retail

Entrepreneurs lock up investment, launch their outfits, and try to beat their competitors on the open market, but what should be garden-variety economics hits a wall with local, state, and federal regulations.

When lobbyists are done changing laws, the lawyers take over for a good reason. Functionally, the Controlled Substances Act makes business as usual harder than usual. Starting a cannabis business looks a lot like starting any other business in the United States, just more complex, laborious, time intensive, capital intensive, and susceptible to potential federal prison sentences than other businesses. Growing, selling, and testing cannabis for the consumer are hassles unlike what most industries endure to get their products to the market. Half the trouble comes from the federal/state gap and half from the states' self-imposed limitations in the form of business licensing.

The only thing separating legal pot from drug war pot is a state-issued license, the magic portal through which a black marketer can dance to become a media-anointed entrepreneur in exchange for licensing fees, taxes, and agreeing to play by certain rules, called regulations.

The growing, selling, and testing of cannabis are the market's gatekeepers and state governments' insurance policy against the feds. The federal government's Cole Memo made it clear that states' rights only exist for the states that make sure the black market isn't involved. To make sure the new industry doesn't invoke an army of DEA agents and IRS auditors, state licensing programs make sure no buds get packed in pipes, no oils get vaped, no brownies get eaten without a chain of licensed farmers, retailers, and testers keeping the cannabis supply in traceably legal sources only. On purpose or by accident, the regulations also tend to make the cannabis industry very hard on Mom and Pop. Combined with the larger problems of the federal/state gap, licensure and regulations have a way of choking out smaller players who can't keep up with the expense of regulation, leading, as in other businesses, to more and more big businesses buying out, vertically integrating, and franchising to give cannabis its own class of top dogs. Across the nation, the top dogs' rules get spread out.

From state to state, regulations get more consistent with each other as advocacy organizations and the National Cannabis Bar Association's attorneys continue to shape the industry. When consumers want something to change, the cannabis industry changes it to suit, rather than waiting on federal guidelines. Of course, every state has its own take still, and the regulations are far from uniform. As with all things cannabis, the conversation around licensing involves so many other problems and questions that a single chapter—or a volume of books—cannot give more than a broad overview about basic structure and basic problems. Chapter 6 will give a more detailed look at how the different regulation systems of medical and recreational states have different impacts—and what this means for the bottom lines of both the industry and of the state treasury that makes money from it.

First on the list of any businessperson's plan is having an idea, crafting a business plan, and securing funding from bank-backed business loans, private lenders, debt financing, etc. Cannabis businesses, however, do not have widespread access to most of the components of the U.S. financial system due to the federal/state gap. The book will discuss this issue at length in the following chapter.

Requirements for Licensure

The federal/state gap has a chain reaction–like impact on virtually every facet of U.S. business. An entrepreneur has a hard time even getting a business license in the cannabis world. To start, no business can exist without a building. As part of the licensing approval process, applicants usually must show they have a planned location—in some cases, they must even show proof they've started renting it when they apply. Though common sense enough a rule, the requirement bites businesses especially in recreational markets. It has two common side effects, neither well loved. Landlords routinely overcharge for building space if they lease to cannabis businesses at all, which can hold up the licensing process. The building requirements also force pot businesses to cluster, which often riles neighbors who didn't want legal cannabis in the first place. Real estate for the cannabis industry is scarcer than the Western United States' many pot shops would make a person think. Despite the money involved, the stigma of cannabis hasn't dissolved enough for real estate options to match those of regular business. Real estate owners aren't always eager to rent to cannabis businesses, whether from risk or from personal feelings about the drug's legality.

And the law itself doesn't help. Regulations require cannabis business to be set back from schools, churches, child care centers, playgrounds, etc., most often by 1,000 feet between properties required by the federal Drug Free Zone standard. In heavily commercial areas, this can be challenging—some small towns can even zone the cannabis industry almost entirely out of existence. Eagle River, Alaska, officially allows commercial cannabis, but the city's legislature purposely expanded the restricted areas so much that there are no buildings available for rent.[1]

These zoning regulations affect some businesses worse than others. Most states force cultivation spaces into agricultural or industrial zones where they theorize the smell of an industrial grow won't bother residents. This has several impacts. First and foremost, the scarcity means paying high rates. In Washington, Colorado, and Alaska, real estate brokers and media reported industrial warehouse space in cannabis-zoned areas being leased up to four times the average rate.[2] Real estate owners raised prices on cannabis businesses in Washington when it rolled out its recreational cannabis industry. In Washington in 2013, Seattle area landlords charged cannabis real estate deals of 150 percent to 200 percent premiums. Similar situations rose in Oregon.[3] In Denver, prices spiked to highs not seen since 2004.[4] In 2015, industrial lease rates climbed to $7.05 per square foot. Like Seattle, cannabis tenants paid two or three times the average lease rate.[5]

Limited space and washy landlords not only push cannabis businesses' rental overhead up, but sometimes backfire against regulations. Some regulations aim to keep cannabis businesses out of the public eye—instead, in large cities like Denver, Seattle, and Anchorage, zoning creates clusters of cannabis businesses that have aroused the ire of nearby schools, business associations, and residents. Further, building scarcity and regulations can hurt the business owner. Owners must have proof of a building lease, in many cases, before they present their license for approval. In places where the licensing process takes a long time, owners can be paying the inflated lease rates without having started their business—for months or even years in the most extreme cases.

Though real estate can be tricky for shop owners, landlords have found a gold mine. The premium on cannabis-ready real estate makes it one of the most attractive and low-risk ways for noncannabis business investors to get into the industry. Steve Berg, a co-founder of Arcview Group (see Chapter 8), said cannabis real estate speculation is some of the most prominent and prolific investment in the entire industry.[6] Real estate ownership requires no cannabis knowledge. Further, the licensing requirements and the general hot market of cannabis businesses typically mean high profits—and if they don't, the owner of the building still owns the building to rent to the next business.

Like with high cannabis business concentrations, the real estate situation can sometimes thwart the intent of regulations. In several states, investors can use real estate to bypass residency restrictions, which forbid nonresidents from taking a piece of a cannabis business license. Instead of blocking outside investors, these regulations simply open opportunities for real estate speculation.

Licenses

For the money crop—recreational cannabis—licensing regimens look similar in each state. Oddly, medical cannabis programs can have less strict licensing regulations than medical states. Chapter 6 will dive into a state-by-state analysis.

Most states approach legal cannabis regulations like alcohol, in part because of the Marijuana Policy Project's (MPP's) "Regulate Marijuana Like Alcohol" campaigns. This is for two reasons. First, the oldest legalization argument says cannabis is no more dangerous than alcohol, is in fact considerably less so, and should be treated at least as normal as spirits. Philosophy aside, though, regulators treat it like alcohol anyway for convenience's sake.

Like alcohol, cannabis has tight, stiff regulations. Part of this is ostensibly for public health—regulators don't want cannabis marketed at kids, don't want to allow dangerous overuse, don't want to see public intoxication, and in general don't want to see cannabis get looser rules than the next closest thing, alcohol. Like alcohol, regulations can vary widely from city to county to state. Like cannabis in the early 2010s, alcohol prohibition ended by letting local governments opt out of alcohol if they wanted to—even the Jack Daniel's distillery is located in a dry Tennessee county, an irony several cannabis businesses are catching up to.

Regulators usually chop the cannabis industry into a handful of licenses that match a particular business type. Depending on the state, these licenses can include retail, cultivation, testing, transportation, production, manufacturing, or medical care givers. In recreational states, the most common setup is a cultivation license, a retail license, a production license, and either a laboratory testing license or simply a requirement for testing. Depending on the state, some licenses are blended with another, and some cities will have entirely different licensing schemes.

Each license type carries its own unique difficulties. The federal/state gap, along with state and local regulations, distort each business type, or at the very least, prevent it from looking like any other regulated product that falls along the same lines in the noncannabis world. Still, the high consumer demand for cannabis keeps the industry growing.

The Green Rush met initial waves of fear that the industry would be irresponsible and sloppy. Contrary to these fears, each segment of the industry has rapidly evolved to look mostly like any other consumer-based product, albeit in a limited fashion due to the federal/state gap. This means a certain amount of consolidation among license types, along with a clear trend for the most well-capitalized and well-run companies to control larger and larger shares of the market, many of whom have extensive connections with moving hands discussed in Chapter 3.

Regulations squeeze businesses, but business is still business.

Cannabis Agriculture

Before it became vape oils, wax and shatter, brownies, or infused drinks, cannabis was a simple agricultural product. To grow it in a recreational state, farmers must get a cultivation license, arguably the most popular license type in the business.

The cannabis trade begins with farms, but regulations and the federal/state gap keep cannabis from the most important feature of American farming—scale. Cannabis farmers simply aren't part of the larger agricultural machine. By keeping cannabis on the Controlled Substances Act (CSA), the federal government ensures cannabis farming is dramatically out of step with the rest of U.S. agriculture and out of step with a global cannabis agriculture system in hyperdrive, both in terms of economies of scale and in environmental practices.

Whatever the hurdles, cannabis growing is still a hot prospect. For whatever reason, cannabis-growing licenses are often the most popular in states where cannabis becomes recreationally legal. Home growing cannabis for personal use or for the black market has been a mainstay for everyone from college juniors to backwoods survivalists since the CSA listing went into effect in 1970, and many are eager to make a legal buck from their knowledge. By the end of 2014, Washington had granted just under 100 retail licenses but granted 320 cultivation licenses.[7] Alaska's early licensing days saw nearly three times more cultivation license applications than any other license type.[8]

Beyond growing for sale, cannabis lovers can grow their own. Most recreational states let residents grow 6 cannabis plants per person and up to 12 per household. Like home-brewing laws, citizens are fine to grow and consume their own—without undergoing any safety or impurity testing required of commercial grows—as long as they aren't selling it.

The popularity has limits, though. Most states force cannabis grows into either agricultural or industrial zoned areas. Depending on the state, regulators can put a cap on how much growers can grow, or limit which retail stores they can sell to, or whether they can sell to nonmedical consumers—more on this in Chapter 6.

Can't Get State or Federal Help

Domestic cannabis has a long way to go before it becomes a large-scale crop by Bread Basket standards. Apart from the regulatory hurdles, the smaller-scale cannabis farmers cannot take advantage of the resources offered to other farmers. The federal government lends a federal-sized helping hand to the nation's farmers in some ways. The U.S. Department of Agriculture has a treasure trove of businesses resources for small and midsize farmers.[9] A noncannabis farmer can get a federal subsidy for crop insurance, which paid 60 percent of such premium costs in 2014.[10] Cannabis farmers have no guaranteed level of revenue, like many other crops. For roughly 20 crops, a federal agricultural risk coverage subsidy can pay farmers if their annual pay falls below that guaranteed level.

There are literally hundreds of federal programs for farmers that cannabis growers will not be able to touch. Farms can access loan programs for specific needs like storage, or microloan programs. Organic farmers can apply for cost-share support or tax breaks. U.S. farmers have access to risk management help, market directories, help with crafting land and water management plans, and endless educational programs and grants for everything from rural development to needy youth. The federal government plays such a hand in state politics that even state agricultural programs are off limits for cannabis farmers.

Some states have federally funded farming programs meant to help farmers market their product. Alaska's Department of Natural Resources allows products made in the state to use the highly visible Alaska Grown logo. To make the cut, however, products must meet U.S. federal standards. The Alaska Marijuana Industry Association protests the exclusion, but the state has remained adamant that allowing farmers to access a federally funded program will mean exposure to federal laws.

Out of Step with Environmental Regulations

The industry's youth and the federal/state gap have led to a shortage of agricultural and environmental information as well. In some cases, the federal/state gap directly conflicts with federal policies like the Clean Water Act, the Endangered Species Act, environmental concerns like carbon emissions, and a host of other factors.

Although many U.S. states are legalizing recreational and medical marijuana possession and use, it remains illegal at the federal level, putting the industry in a semi-legal gray area in these states. This status separates marijuana from fully legal agricultural commodities and greatly complicates regulation of the industry. Without adopting a position on liberalization of marijuana use and possession policies, we argue here that (a) the environmental harm caused by marijuana cultivation in both the semi-legal and black-market context is significant and merits a direct policy response, (b) current approaches to and funding for governing the environmental effects are inadequate, and (c) neglecting discussion of the environmental impacts of cultivation when shaping future marijuana-use and -possession policies represents a missed opportunity to reduce, regulate, and mitigate environmental harm.[11]

Some of these problems come from black market grows, not legal ones, which in turn shot federal goals in the foot. By simply having made cannabis illegal in the first place, the federal government in fact forced domestic cannabis growers off the grid, where federal priorities and regulations are even less likely to be followed.

Illicit cannabis grows in northern and central California have been linked to large-scale poisoning deaths of local mammals. Mice and rats love to eat cannabis stalks. The rodenticide used to keep them away was found in 80 percent of sampled fishers, a weasel-like animal currently a candidate for listing under the federal Endangered Species Act.[12]

In Humboldt County, the so-called Emerald Triangle that is northern California's cannabis basket, other federally protected animals may be threatened. The region's river systems are home to steelhead trout and Chinook salmon, which are threatened and endangered under federal law.[13] Further, indoor cannabis grows are notoriously less green than one might think. As early as 2012, researcher Evan Mill estimated illegal cannabis grows contribute as much carbon emissions as 3 million cars.[14]

Whether or not states can find ways to fix those problems—and regulators are trying—is beside the point. Agribusinesses in the United States are simply too bound in federal red tape, as a rule of the general reach of federal government, for cannabis to look anything like a modern crop until federally legal—even when keeping farms out of the U.S. agriculture system backfires against federal goals.

Testing Labs

After being farmed, the next licensed stop a gram of cannabis takes is to the testing lab, which itself adds a big bulk to retail cannabis's price. In most recreational states, regulations require cultivators to send their product to a lab before it hits retail shelves. The lab will test the cannabis for a range of possible chemicals: the tetrahydrocannabinol (THC) and cannabidiol (CBD) concentrations in each batch, the terpene profile that gives a batch its unique flavor and smell, and any traces of pesticides or contaminants that might have made their way into the plant through the soil or through growing techniques.

Labs are a complex and tricky industry segment, and add yet another layer of complication and overhead to cannabis businesses. Cultivators and retailers abound, but the licensed testing facilities most states require are few. They make less profit and have a unique set of challenges, both from the federal/state gap and from states themselves.

Like growers and retailers and cannabakers, the Colorado-style open market led to the boom in labs, such as it is. The movement towards rigorous testing standards like those seen in the agricultural industry did not start with medical cannabis, but with recreational cannabis. Many medical states do not require testing at all, like Arizona, Maine, Michigan, Montana, New Jersey, and Rhode Island. Others like Vermont only specify that the state *may* require testing.

Since the Colorado dam broke, the adult use world looks far different. Except for Maine, every recreationally legal state requires extensive testing, though it took a few years for the testing to get as extensive as it is.

Apart from a state safety requirement, labs are the root of branding. Growers and manufacturers send samples into a lab, and the lab provides them the THC concentrations and terpene profiles they can use as marketing points like a beer's alcohol content and hops profile.

Unlike cannabis growing or sale, testing is not a popular license type. In the first four states to legalize adult use cannabis, there are roughly 50 cannabis testing licenses, by far the least numerous license type.[15] Colorado alone has just over a dozen labs.[16] It isn't hard to see why. Labs are costlier and harder to run than the relatively simple grows or retail shops.

The federal/state gap starts the avalanche of problems the testing sector faces. Most consumable or medical products in the United States require testing for contaminants, pesticides, and any other potential health impacts. These testing programs have their root in the Food and Drug Administration (FDA), however, and the FDA will give no guidance until cannabis is federally legal.

Despite some of these expertise-focused laws, the federal government's safety mechanisms do not filter down to testing facilities. The Food and Drug Administration has taken a hands-off stance with regard to cannabis. As mentioned, until cannabis is legal at the federal level, the FDA will not step in to devise a framework for testing as it does for virtually every other commercial consumable product.

Not only are they murkier in the operational sense, but testing labs also are less a part of the commercial machine as is cultivation or retail. In most recreational states, cannabis testing labs must apply for their own licenses— labs that already test agricultural or food products cannot simply pivot to accept cannabis. Labs do not have the same opportunity for vertical integration that retailers have, either. Often, states forbid any kind of co-ownership of lab licenses with retail, cultivation, or manufacturing to prevent conflict of interest and favoritism.

Testing labs themselves are not among the most profitable of industry segments, mostly due to the high costs of entry and operation. Due to regulations and the nature of lab work, overhead is simply too high. Testing labs demand at least half a million dollars of capital for even basic, refurbished testing equipment. To run a state-of-the-art lab, industry leaders say that the bill runs as high as $5 million for startup costs.[17]

State laws inflate payroll costs, as well. Most states that require testing also require labs be run by highly experienced professionals with advanced degrees in biology, chemistry, or another lab-based hard science. States with limited capital and smaller academic populations have a harder time finding staff. In sparsely populated, rural states like Alaska, there are only three licensed labs.[18]

Brief History

Like the regulations in the other licenses, testing labs' regulations let the market solve problems the federal government gives no help for. Two issues control the history of testing facilities: pesticides and industry standards. Testing labs show a contradiction between cannabis legalization advocacy and the cannabis industry. First, early mover states with medical cannabis programs did not require testing—this became the norm only after recreational states popularized it. Second, there seem to be few proven incidents that back the need for safety testing beyond the pesticide issue. Cannabis legalization supporters typically argue cannabis is safer than many pharmaceuticals, and indeed the World Health Organization seems to back them—black market cannabis has never been responsible for a single death worldwide. There have been no reports of consumers getting sick from commercial cannabis in states where it has been legalized—including in the several states that recalled large batches of cannabis shown to have been grown with risky pesticides. Some states acknowledge that labs aren't doing much in the way of safety—Colorado's advertising regulations forbid retailers from telling customers their product is safe just because a lab has tested it.

In the recreational U.S. market, though, testing labs and states try to find the right balance between more tests, more accreditation, and higher standards to protect consumers from whatever harmful substances might be in their pot. Where there is more money, there is more testing, and the more money has piled up, the more rigorous the testing has gotten.

Colorado first required lab tests on solvents, pollutants, and potency, but not on pesticides. Eventually, mass amounts of cannabis grown with unapproved chemicals were recalled.[19] Even when Colorado started requiring pesticide testing, it had to set its own standards—the U.S. Environmental Protection Agency (EPA) oversees national pesticide regulations, so naturally as a federal entity, it has none for cannabis. The Colorado Department of Agriculture issued a list of approved pesticides, but left it to local governments to

enforce. Since then the state has continued to ratchet up its testing requirements. Similar scenarios played out in Washington and Oregon. By turns, each
ramped up its testing requirements.

By the time the third round of recreational states came online in 2016, state
governments came out of the gate with stricter regulations. Nevada requires
the same kind of pesticide reporting the EPA would require for similar crops.[20]
California, which began cannabis legalization in 1996 without any testing
requirements at all, now requires testing for over 60 individual pesticides.[21]

For many industry leaders, California is taking the matter too far. Leaders
at the Association of Commercial Cannabis Laboratories (ACCL), a confed-
eration of roughly half the country's labs, say the regulations are overkill. They
agree there should be regulations. Cannabis farmers are not allowed to use
the federally approved *organic* stamp, so growers have no incentive to avoid
pesticides other than brand recognition. ACCL says those growers need
accountability, but that the tightening regulations are fear based, not science
based. It rarely finds any more than 20 of California's pesticides in a sample,
and rarely finds heavy metals.[22] Besides being unnecessary, the regulations are
expensive. ACCL estimates California's regulations will cost a producer roughly
$1,000 per pound of product—which the consumer will then pick up.

Standards

While states tighten regulations on what to test for, labs are lobbying states
to add more restrictions on lab procedures themselves in the absence of any
guidance from the federal government. The relaxed initial rules in the first
mover states did have a positive impact in that they allowed the industry to
steamroll ahead at a quick pace, but some feared the pace was too quick and
the rules too loose. Dozens of labs sprouted that gave varying results and had
varying levels of expertise. In some cases, consumers were lied to about the
product.

Here, both the cannabis industry's youth and the federal/state gap play a
part in consumer trickery. The most educated cannabis consumers know the
differences in THC, CBD, and terpene profile the way educated beer consumers might know what hops, malt, and alcohol by volume (ABV) are. Cannabis's chemical properties are far more advanced, though, and unscrupulous
labs can take advantage of the burgeoning market's lack of education and the
lax regulations.

This can play out in several ways, either from the cultivator side or from
testing labs themselves. Cultivators can send only their best buds to testing
labs to get the most favorable reading. Because THC content is a major selling
point, testing labs themselves might overstate the concentration in each product. This happened in Colorado in 2014, when one lab's THC content results
turned out to be dramatically overstated,[23] and more recently in 2017, when

one of Washington's leading labs produced inconsistent and inflated samples.[24] To cure both this issue and the ongoing lack of data, labs continue to call for higher standards.

However, leaders in the testing lab space—some of whom helped create state regulations—continue to decry the lack of central guidelines from the federal government. ACCL, which employs a full-time lobbyist, has gotten at least part of its wish list. Massachusetts, Nevada, New Hampshire, and California require accreditation from the International Organization for Standardization by the American Association for Laboratory Accreditation. New Hampshire requires accrediting by the American Association for Laboratory Accreditation or under the Clinical Laboratory Improvement Act (CLIA), the same body that oversees blood banks and tissue sampling facilities. States in which recreational cannabis is legal have no standard set of best practices for labs to follow. Typically, federal agencies mandate and control testing for consumable products—but not for cannabis.

Because there is no list of best practices, and because the wind is blowing towards stiffer regulations, more and more labs are adopting the Steep Hill Labs franchise—otherwise, they would have to start from scratch. Some labs are hesitant to share trade secrets and best practices with competitors, and others simply don't have them collated.

Sacramento-based Steep Hill was one of the first commercial cannabis labs and started in 2008. In Washington, the company served on a contracting team to help the then-Washington State Liquor Board craft its regulations.[25] This company is, of course, not without its connections. Co-founder Steve DeAngelo is also the president of ArcView, founding member of the National Cannabis Industry Association (NCIA), and co-founder of Harborside, one of the largest retail brands.

Retail

The regulations governing retail shops don't help price points, either, though retail shops are arguably the least legally problematic businesses to run in the cannabis universe. Shops that sell directly to consumers need a retail license to do so—and in medical states, a dispensary license. Colorado alone has nearly 500 retail licenses,[26] and hundreds more dot the rest of the Western United States as business develops further.

Retail businesses are the most consumer facing of all the plant-touching industry types. The federal/state gap, in turn, keeps them from most ways retailers reach their customers in the digital age. First on the list of any cannabis retail store's complaint is cash. The fact that banks will not take cannabis money affects consumer habits. Instead of paying with credit or debit cards directly at the point of sale, cannabis retailers must take cash. This means installing ATM machines in the store or finding workarounds. It also means cannabis retail shops store lots of cash, which becomes a security concern and a tax concern. These issues will be discussed the following chapter in greater detail.

Along with the payment type, retail cannabis stores simply don't have the ability to function according to best practices for young consumers in 2017. For now, cannabis retailers must have physical store locations, which is rather un-Millennial of their very Millennial product. Brick-and-mortar retail isn't at its healthiest in 2017, as chains like Macy's, Sears, and JCPenney downsize rapidly along with smaller chains in the face of retail e-commerce sites like Amazon or the panoply of box delivery services for special interests.

Cannabis isn't the same—most brick-and-mortar downsizing is, in general, one-stop shopping retail, not with niche items—but the point stands that cannabis retailers, who already have no ability to go truly national, aren't allowed to engage in the most cost-effective modern retail methodology, which blends digital, delivery, and physical shopping.

Delivery services attached to retail stores, for the most part, aren't available to cannabis retailers, even though the target demographic for cannabis buyers is the same demographic that prefers digital shopping and delivery for certain products. Retailers don't have a legal option for delivery in most cases. The U.S. Postal Service refuses to ship cannabis, as does United Parcel Service and FedEx—though doing so and simply not informing them is still a popular way to move cannabis. Delivery is almost entirely relegated to local delivery services, which often are a ball of legal trouble unto themselves.

Retailers and producers alike have problems even reaching their customer base. Logos and brands are, of course, common and necessary for every licensed product, store, and grower, but showing off the brands and logos is another story. Advertising rules vary by state, but traditional advertising channels almost entirely touch the federal government in some way. Advertisements in newspapers and magazines are growing, but only in regionally circulated print, not with larger publications that move through the mail—the U.S. Postal Service does not allow cannabis advertising to be distributed through the mail.[27] The Federal Communications Commission certainly won't allow ads on television or over federally regulated airwaves.[28] Even on a state-by-state level, advertising isn't much easier where it doesn't concern the federal government.

As usual, the recreational states tend to have stricter rules than the medical states do. Some medical states outlaw any advertising at all, whereas others like New Mexico simply have no regulations at all regarding advertising. In adult use states, the advertising regulations are more uniform on the side of strictness. Most recreational states only allow minimal signs attached to the building itself, never in the form of leaflets or billboards or any other movable signage. Typically, cannabis consumers can't window shop, either—regulations in most states forbid windows.

Usually, retailers take to social media to shore up their customers, but this isn't always possible for cannabis businesses. Large-scale advertising on social media is not an option, because Facebook does not welcome cannabis store advertising on its pages, nor does Twitter or Instagram. Regulatory boards have had to come down on their state's cannabis businesses for advertising over these social media channels, though it remains one of the most popular ways for cannabis retailers to reach their market base. Over time, however, regulations have gotten looser to match alcohol. In Colorado, advertisements can be in statewide radio, TV, print, or Internet channels if less than 30 percent of the expected viewership is under 21 years of age.

The laws and regulations just distort the market, not end it. The endless advertising difficulties open big opportunities for advertising with apps (see Chapter 8). Weedmaps, one of the premier cannabis apps, even has a billboard advertising, not for any stores, but simply promoting pro-legalization propaganda in Michigan. Regardless, federal laws keep cannabis retail advertising at only a shade of its mainstream industrial equivalent. Still, business acts as business will, and cannabis retail is growing to look as structured as anything else within the confines of the state, complete with branding, vertically integrated supply, and chains. Retail shops in recreational states are starting to see McDonald's- and Starbuck's-like chains and franchises. Colorado's Native Roots alone has 20 locations. Competitor LivWell Enlightened Health—a branded partner of Snoop Dogg's—has 15. The Green Solution has 12.

Also like Starbuck's or McDonald's, these chains rarely exist solely as retail outlets and have no plans to stay within their state boundaries. Each owns cultivation licenses that produce proprietary strains, extracted products, and branded packaging. Each has expressed plans to operate across state lines in Oregon, Washington, or California, as well. Here, the trend towards big business strategies gets more evident. These successful companies are not the venue of bootstrapped family savings, but of the meatier parts of the cannabis capital machine that span across international boundaries. The Green Solution's main investor is iAnthus Capital Holdings, a Canadian financing company focused on cannabis that has investments in Massachusetts, New Mexico, and Vermont as well as Colorado. Native Roots' first funding came from a millionaire real estate developer.

The aggressive expansion has drawbacks. It is the larger retailers that bring in some of the first large-scale legal troubles. The Green Solution was embroiled in a lawsuit with the IRS over tax deductions, a matter Chapter 7 will explore in more detail.[29] LivWell was the first company to be sued by consumers for alleged irresponsible use of pesticides, though the Denver courts dismissed the case.[30]

Some states fold retail licenses together with production or manufacturing licenses, which make the cookies, brownies, concentrate oils, wax and shatter, candies, gummies, and all other products that are not simply the plant cannabis. Edible cannabis products in particular are a major sticking point for states with legalized recreational cannabis. Even those who supported legalization typically have concerns about the effect edibles have on both children and adults—the products are harder to distinguish and the effects are less predictable than that of smoked cannabis. The goal is to keep edibles and other cannabis derivatives away from children and away from consumers who might confuse a cannabis cookie for a Milano. To this effect, the advertising around edibles is usually quite strict. Some states forbid any brightly colored packaging to keep children away, which in turn keeps an entire line of products away from common advertising.

Price Points

The industry's development, crawling from inflated black market prices, is already hurting itself. Aside from cannabis, a fruit, vegetable, or herb rarely passes a retail price of three or four dollars per pound, even for pricy organic products. A pound of cannabis, though, would cost several thousand dollars on the retail market if any individual could buy that much at once. On a per gram basis, even legal cannabis is more expensive than delicacy white truffles or the world's most expensive spice, saffron—though it is not quite as dear as beluga caviar.

The open market in recreational states has knocked holes in cannabis' black market price, but federal and state regulations keep farmers and retailers from the mass production and best practices of any other crop. As the growers and retailers and product manufacturers continue to consolidate and mass production and distribution are more and more possible, economists predict the price per gram could drop lower than a dollar—as cheap as virtually every similar plant grown on an industrial scale.

This is already happening in a limited way. When retail sales first came online, many medical cannabis proponents feared the recreational market would gouge consumers on prices. This has not happened. In most states, recreational prices start high and steadily drop. For example, when sales first started in Alaska, patrons paid $420 per ounce or $22 per gram—a cute price, but also roughly $100 dollars more than what the Alaska black market charged. When Colorado opened legal adult use sales in 2014, Denver metro area prices averaged $323 per ounce according to a survey performed by Colorado Pot Guide. Outside the Denver area, the price rose to $367 per ounce. By October 2016, that price was cut roughly in half.[31] Cannabis-legal states have in total seen wholesale cannabis prices plummet by more than 50 percent.[32]

License Consolidation and Licensing Agreements

The costs associated with securing and maintaining licenses and keeping up with regulations—all while unable to access startup funding from banks—has led to a steady death in the early days where mom-and-pop shops scrambled into the industry. The industry has gotten more consolidated as it developed. In Colorado, 20 percent of cannabis business licenses are owned by only 10 people,[33] most of whom secured their franchises by buying out smaller companies. As the book progresses, this trend will continue to be seen not only in direct cannabis business licenses, but with ancillary cannabis businesses as well.

Part of the trend towards larger businesses comes from regulations. More specifically, it comes from the inability of smaller business owners to keep up not only with the intense regulations, but also how often they change. The rules are in a constant state of flux, so much so that businesses are constantly complaining of being behind the eight ball. Even the basics of licenses themselves change according to market demands and public scrutiny—size of signage, the markings on edibles, tax rates, inspection requirements, canopy growth space, etc., all must be worked out over time in an endless collaboration between industry, industry attorneys, legislators, and regulators.

Most industry figures accept that it is simply an effect of being in an early industry and anticipate the rules will become more concrete as time goes. States follow each other's lead and have ended up, in a matter of years, with some of the same regulations. Residency requirements were among the first to change. When Colorado and Washington legalized recreational cannabis, regulations would not let anyone except a resident of those states invest in a cannabis license, ostensibly to keep criminals and black market money out of the new industry. Oregon and Alaska followed suit two years later.

It didn't take long, though, for regulators to recognize that the residency restrictions mostly just squeezed the licensees, who now had no access to available outside financing. Instead of keeping criminals out, it guaranteed a head start for the licensees in each state who had access to deep resident pockets. Furthermore, regulators and attorneys saw that nonresidents simply found loopholes, like real estate or license management agreements. Colorado, Washington, and Oregon have since rescinded their residency restrictions, saying they shot themselves in the foot.

Home grows developed in the opposite way, starting far more lenient than they finished. At first, the home-grow allowance in Colorado was fairly loose and even allowed residents to band together to form cannabis co-ops—the psychoactive version of a community garden. These didn't turn out as law abiding as voters might have liked. In 2014 and 2015, local police and the DEA noted huge black market–bound nonlicensed grows in individual homes.[34] Eventually, Colorado changed the rules to only allow 12 plants per household, which other states adopted in their own regulations afterwards.

Regulators also didn't anticipate the swell of pot clubs that followed each recreational ballot. In Colorado, Washington, Oregon, and Alaska, venues styling themselves as "social clubs" started offering cannabis users a place to smoke, vape, or ingest cannabis they bring from home but do not buy at the establishment itself. Invariably, this issue relates to public use. None of the recreational states allow cannabis users to smoke in public, relegating consumers to only their private homes. To make use consistent with alcohol, social clubs popped up in Alaska, Oregon, Washington, and Colorado that argued they charge a membership fee or cover charge and are therefore not a public place. Each battled back and forth with law enforcement, regulatory boards, and elected officials, and most petered out after admitting defeat. The social club closures, however, might have been premature. Colorado ended up carving rules for social use, becoming the first state nationwide to make allowances for the pot equivalent of a bar.

But even if a business wades through the muck of regulations, finding a way to process the profits is a challenge.

CHAPTER FIVE

Banking and Financial Implications

When your money is green, banks will take it. If your money is cannabis green, however, banks mostly won't have anything to do with it. Most industry leaders agree commercial cannabis's biggest, worst problem is lack of access to the U.S. finance industry. Major financial institutions, particularly those banks and credit unions that receive insurance from the Federal Deposit Insurance Corporation or the National Credit Union Administration, will not take cannabis-related monies. As of December 2015, 60 percent of cannabis-related companies have no access to the backbone of commerce in the United States: a relationship with a bank, according to an industry survey by Cannabis Business Daily.[1] The balance tips in favor of ancillary businesses. For businesses that involve the plant itself—grow operations, retail outfits, or manufacturing facilities—that number rises to 70 percent.[2]

The banking industry's reluctance is not groundless. Because of the federal/state gap, the federal government can and has prosecuted financial institutions involved with cannabis for a host of financial crimes, including money laundering.

The federal government sends somewhat mixed signals regarding cannabis, which have only intensified under the Trump administration. Guidelines state that if banks follow certain procedures, they will not be prosecuted. Without solid legal protection, though, banks only have a half-hearted yellow light to accept any of the industry's deposits, dole out loans, and in some circumstances even keep legitimate business owners' personal accounts open. Risk-averse banks—including the biggest banks in the country—prefer not to be involved.

Like most other areas of the cannabis industry, though, the lure of the cannabis cash piles is too much to resist entirely. Even in the most risk-averse and most likely to be prosecuted business, the market draws businesses in like a flame.

Smaller credit unions and banks are more willing to accept the risk and, as such, make up a majority of the growing number of institutions willing to accept cannabis deposits. These banks are often state-chartered institutions with slim national profiles, often only operating in one state or sometimes only in local communities. Between 300 and 400 banks across the nation now take cannabis accounts.[3] In the meantime, other types of financial organizations and state treasuries have recognized a potential cash cow and have adjusted accordingly. Silicon Valley investors, for example, are buying into cannabis because they recognize the growth potential for the industry, similar to how technology took off in 1997.

In this manner, the federal government is causing several problems. The public doesn't get access to the industry through initial public offerings (IPOs), it pumps no money back into the financial industry and into consumers' pockets, it keeps consumers from spending their money as they're used to in the modern digital economy, and it deepens a growing cannabis industrial complex where the finances are self-contained.

Without a federal fix to banking prohibitions, the cannabis industry will never reach its full potential of maximum efficiency of production and distribution. Without banks, cannabis entrepreneurs have only debt financing or direct investor lending to rely on for their businesses. Twenty-first-century consumer channels—online and mobile shopping, credit card purchases, etc.—are out of reach. Any kind of true interstate commerce is off limits. Furthermore, it only locks most cannabis capital into the hands of the many cannabis capital firms springing up to fill the void. Little can be done to goad federally insured banks and credit unions into accepting cannabis deposits until Congress changes the Controlled Substances Act designation or codifies some kind of exemption for banks in marijuana-legal states.

The Cole Memo

Although they often do not actively prosecute, the federal government does not give any exemption from criminal prosecution to banks when cases are pursued. Banks followed the Cole Memo till Sessions rescinded it, meaning they see only the risk of federal prosecution rather than the promise of new cash flow.

According to the federal courts weighing in on the issue, they are right to be cautious. The federal government's letter of guidance amounts to little more than a flimsy hint that it will turn a blind eye. In Colorado, banks were the first to touch on the issue. However, they have wobbled back and forth between accepting cannabis money and denying it. A well-publicized battle between the state-chartered Fourth Corner Credit Union and the state of Colorado eventually decided that the cannabis industry couldn't store cash in banks, setting precedent for the other 24 states where cannabis is legal in some form. The credit union had filed a suit with the federal government to force the Kansas City branch of the U.S. Federal Reserve Bank to give the credit union a master account. Fourth Corner set itself up expressly to serve cannabis businesses. According to the judge, the federal government simply cannot ignore marijuana's place on the Schedule I list. Cole's guidelines, he said, do not equal approval of the business model.

> U.S. District Judge R. Brooke Jackson said in a nine-page opinion that he was compelled to reject The Fourth Corner Credit Union's suit because cannabis remains illegal under federal law.[4]
>
> The U.S. Department of Justice has issued guidelines on how banks can work with legal cannabis businesses, making it clear that prosecutors would not pursue investigations unless certain conditions were not met. But Jackson said he could not take that tack.
>
> "These guidance documents simply suggest that prosecutors and bank regulators might 'look the other way' if financial institutions don't mind violating the law," Jackson wrote. "A federal court cannot look the other way."[5]

Even if banks decide to take the risk and accept marijuana-related deposits, the Financial Crimes Enforcement Network, or FinCEN, makes the operation difficult enough to make banks think twice. FinCEN requires a daunting amount of effort for banks that want into the industry.[6] Not only are cannabis accounts dangerous within a risk-averse industry, but FinCEN makes them too expensive and time consuming to administer anyway. For each transaction related to a cannabis business account—deposit, withdrawal, transfer, etc.— the bank or credit union must file three separate suspicious activity reports. Any missteps or misreports could result in a stiff fine or an audit, which could lose the bank its Federal Deposit Insurance Corporation insurance.

Besides access to banks themselves, the federal Schedule I classification for cannabis extends to other financial businesses.

Credit Crunch

Until banks have a clear direction, cannabis merchants themselves face a limited range of payment options. Visa, MasterCard, and most major credit card companies have punted the issue to banks, relying on the financial institutions themselves to decide whether to offer merchant services for cannabis businesses. In some cases, this amounts to a *de facto* ban on all electronic payments, and in others the lines are less clear.

When states started legalizing medicinal cannabis beginning with California in 1996, credit card companies processed payments from cannabis retailers.

After federal drug enforcement officers raided several medical cannabis companies in California and Colorado in 2012, they tightened their rules. Most cannabis retailers still make a point to install ATMs in their lobbies to ease cash transactions.

In 2012, after Colorado legalized recreational cannabis and the Cole Memo had been issued, the credit card companies' stand on cannabis changed. Rather than denying access outright, the companies kicked the issue back to banks for them to decide. A company representative's statement to the *Wall Street Journal* resembles Cole's vague guidance:

> In offering our payment service, Visa adheres to the rule of law and seeks to prevent our network from being used for unlawful purposes. In this instance, the federal government considers the sale of cannabis illegal but has announced that it will not challenge state laws that legalize and regulate cannabis sales . . . Given the federal government's position and recognizing this is an evolving legal matter with different standards applicable in different states, our local merchant acquirers (banks) are best suited to make any determination about potential illegality.[7]

Simply put, banks assume the liability for any illegal transactions. MasterCard issued a similar statement to the same effect, and American Express closed the accounts of several business vendors connected with marijuana.

In some cases, credit card companies processed cannabis business payments unaware. That is because every credit card transaction carries a code for food, gas, liquor, or whatever category the purchase falls under. The cannabis code is not welcome over credit card transaction wires, called "the rails," so some businesses simply changed the transaction code. Some retail shops in Denver, for example, intentionally miscoded transactions as "herbal tea" or "food" to cloak the purchase.

In response to these contract violations, credit card companies threatened to drop the bank as a customer. The banks ended their relationships with the cannabis businesses following an investigative exposé of 27 Denver area retailers who willingly accepted credit card payments under these disguised codes.[8]

Workarounds and State-Sanctioned Gray Markets

States and industry find ways to make banking work, but the solutions are by necessity complex, somewhat shadowy, and leave out the national financial institutions largely necessary for a full-scale commercial enterprise. As of March 2016, over 300 banks nationwide accept deposits from cannabis businesses.[9] These banks are largely small community banks and credit unions rather than national, federally insured institutions. Local credit unions like Seattle's Salal Credit Union, Spokane's Numerica Credit Union, and Oregon's

Maps Credit Union are among the larger of the Pacific Northwest's cannabis banking services. Some rely more on word of mouth rather than direct advertising to attract clientele, whereas others are starting to proudly announce that they take cannabis money.

In states with booming recreational markets, the state government itself becomes complicit in what would be considered money laundering or accepting legal payment as defined by federal law[10] and tries to draw non–federally insured banks into the industry. With millions of tax dollars at stake in tax revenue, the state needs banking almost as badly as the pot growers.

In Washington State, officials say the cannabis stigma is largely mythical. The reality is more nuanced. Roughly 90 percent of all marijuana-related taxes and fees from the billion-dollar industry[11] pour into the state treasury electronically, not with cash. Washington has at least three credit unions and two banks that accept money from cannabis operations. In July 2016, one even made a loan to a business, which was a national first.

Federal laws and the banking industry's refusal to break them present problems for state treasuries. Most states hold bank accounts for the state treasury and receive tax payments either from direct electronic payments or from electronic bank transfers.

Banks and credit unions at first refused to handle Washington's cannabis-related treasury. A cannabis business law firm and the state of Washington told the bank it would violate contract if it did not, and eventually the bank caved to the state's ultimatum. Still, cannabis businesses can't pay taxes directly to Washington State with credit cards, through which most state treasuries typically accept business licensing fees and tax payments. Washington uses tactics that match those of the Denver cannabis dispensaries that disguised their credit card purchases as "food" or "herbal tea." Both of Washington's tax acceptance schemes allow credit card payments, but under noncannabis transaction codes. The first, called PayQwick, serves as a closed loop system like PayPal. Retailers stock a prepaid card with money, and all transactions take place within that system. The product might be cannabis, but the prepaid card system meets industry standards for credit card companies that depend on a wide range of similar setups. Prepaid cards carry their own transaction code, the same used by PayPal, Target, and any other vendor offering gift cards.

The second electronic system used by cannabis retailers has a customer credit card buy the digital currency Bitcoin and accept Bitcoin payments. Retailers cash their accounts out at the end of the day and deposit the money into their bank. Banks then make electronic transfers directly into the state treasury for taxes and fees.

Still, Washington's position of state acceptance depends on willingness and toleration that aren't in full supply elsewhere, and the transactions used to grease the skids for tax payments are loopholes at best.

At the state level, each of the states where recreational cannabis is legalized makes efforts to encourage their financial institutions to get into the industry. Most states look to Colorado for guidance, but the Rocky Mountain State has few answers. In 2014, the state authorized a cannabis co-op financial structure,[12] but so far none have been formed. Some states have discussed the idea of a state-backed bank, but apart from a non–cannabis-related bank in North Dakota no state has set one up.

Andrew Freedman, Colorado's director of cannabis coordination, has openly acknowledged that until the federal government acts, the states where cannabis is legal will continue to struggle. Some try to encourage the same kind of local bank activity seen in Washington. In March and April of 2016, Oregon Gov. Kate Brown signed a series of laws designed to help the cannabis industry, including a bill encouraging medical market growers to enter the regulated industry, a bill abolishing an Oregon state residency requirement for financial stakeholders of cannabis businesses, and a bill allowing for co-location of medical and recreational cannabis facilities. To encourage state financial institutions, one of the bills exempts banks and credit unions from any criminal liability under Oregon state law if they decide to deal with cannabis businesses.[13] Oregon's intent is to encourage commerce and a regulated market, but analysts say it's a statement of intent more than anything else. Cannabis business law firm Harris Bricken emphasized that the state's financial industries wouldn't change heart substantially without a change in federal law.[14]

Other states in the recreational camp experience no willingness at all from the banking community despite prodding by state officials in the form of informational seminars. The Alaska Bankers Association (ABA) has unequivocally stated that it will not enter into any business arrangements with cannabis businesses until the federal government changes its tune; the current risk of federal prosecution, said ABA president Steven Lundgren, won't equal what bankers anticipate to be a small cannabis market compared to Lower 48 counterparts like Colorado and Oregon.

The state itself has received flak from its own merchant service provider. U.S. Bank cut the Alaska Department of Revenue's credit card service option, leaving license fees to be paid in cash along with taxes. In states like Colorado, this could mean a drive of several hours to the nearest tax collections location with several hundred thousands of dollars in duffel bags. For states with remote communities like Alaska or Montana, a common suggestion is to simply mail cash-stuffed envelopes of tax dollars to a central collector.

Investment

Cannabis business attorneys, including Hilary Bricken, clarify that investment in cannabis companies is technically still illegal, but private investors have grasped the potential of the cannabis industry's growth—tech investors in particular. Publicly traded stocks aside, private venture capital firms have launched to secure funding for cannabis businesses, many of whom directly financed legalization measures and most of whom back the most successful names in the cannabis industry.

Funding has always come from Silicon Valley. Sean Parker, the early Facebook investor, has been a vocal financial supporter of the nascent cannabis industry, and Peter Thiel, founder of PayPal and a Silicon Valley tech icon, is directly responsible for some of the biggest, brightest names in cannabis.

Thiel's $2 billion venture capital firm, Founders Fund, is one of the cannabis industry's genesis points. Founders Fund financed Privateer Holdings, one of the leading international cannabis firms. Privateer Holdings was launched in 2010 by three investment managers specifically to offer development strategies for cannabis companies. The company has solicited up to $82 million in private equity,[15] owns and runs cannabis app and information site Leafly (see Chapter 8), and is a rival of Canadian medical cannabis powerhouses like Canopy Growth through its Canadian subsidiary, Tilray.

Thiel also directly funded Isaac Dietrich, founder of MassRoots, another cannabis information app and rival of Leafly, which will be discussed in Chapter 8. Dietrich, who is himself a former congressional staffer and political strategist, was also a finalist for Peter Thiel's 20 Under 20 Fellowship and was featured in the CNBC documentary *Transforming Tomorrow*. Thiel's other ventures have direct involvement, as well. His Clarium Capital financial group is one of the largest individual donors to the Marijuana Policy Project.

ArcView Group, founded by cannabis high roller Steve DeAngelo, is a collection of 550 accredited angel investors specifically geared towards the cannabis industry. Since inception, the group has raised over $84 million for 130 cannabis companies and over $1.5 million towards direct legalization efforts, and counting.[16]

The inability of the financial sector to get into cannabis has launched dozens of such outfits—Green Growth Investments, Dutchess Capital, Salveo Capital, Poseidon Asset Management, Canopy Growth, Tuatara Capital, Merida Capital Partners, iAnthus, Hypur Ventures, Green Line Investment Group, Viridian Capital & Research, TDM Financial (CFN Media), and half a hundred others. Among them these financial groups control the cannabis industry's most influential and well-capitalized companies and some of the industry's biggest sources of advertising and information, some of which Chapter 8 will discuss.

Despite a growing wealth of opportunities for investors through the venture capital channel, though, cannabis stocks are not high performing. Arcview, Viridian Capital Index, the MJIC Cannabis Index, the Wolf of Weed Street, InvestInCannabis.com, and 420 Investor all provide market research, but the scope of the market makes the analytics unreliable. Even Leslie Bocksor, managing partner of Electrum Partners, a Las Vegas–based cannabis consulting company, acknowledges that few cannabis companies have any reliable data—which, of course, creates an entire market just for cannabis data, discussed in Chapter 8.

Stocks are extremely volatile due to low capitalization and low investor activity. Until then, Eddie Miller, CEO of InvestInCannabis.com, a New York–based cannabis technology investor, advises investors to buy in now and wait until the federal government fully legalizes cannabis.[17] He estimates the return on investment to be 100 times as much after it becomes federally legal.

So far, citizens themselves haven't gotten into the cannabis investing sphere to a large extent. That will certainly change if the federal government makes a move, but until then federal bodies have loosened a few screws. Securities and Exchange Commission rules loosened in 2015 to allow nonaccredited investors to invest in startup companies. Under the crowdfunding rule, known as Regulation 4(a)(6),[18] small, private companies can sell up to $1 million in shares within a 12-month period.

Public Investment

The breadth of education and experience makes the venture capital firms distinct from the self-funded mom-and-pop operators who often spearhead the early days of state legalization programs. There are over 350 publicly traded cannabis companies, and counting. There is a distinction, though, between cannabis companies and companies that deal in cannabis-related matters. The NASDAQ exchange lists several publicly traded cannabis companies, but the companies are mostly involved in industrial production rather than retail or grow operations. Indeed, the publicly traded companies associated with cannabis have more ties to the pharmaceutical industry than cannabis production and distribution. These include GW Pharmaceuticals, a UK–based biotech company with a cannabis-based epilepsy drug; Insys Therapeutics, a Phoenix company developing a cannabis-based drug for the treatment of epilepsy; Cara Therapeutics, a Shelton, Connecticut–based clinical state biopharmaceutical company that develops and commercializes pain relief drugs; and Zynerba Pharmaceuticals, a Devon, Pennsylvania–based company focused on developing and commercializing synthetic cannabinoid therapeutics. In Chapter 9, these companies and their connections to either George Soros or to anti-legalization efforts will be explored further.

Apart from these, smaller companies trade mainly as penny stocks. Investment banking analyst Alan Brochstein and others say the lack of investment banking causes problems especially for these stocks. Opportunistic companies will ride the cannabis hype wave to capitalize on otherwise inexperienced entrepreneurs and investors, and it's hard to get good investors to find the good companies. Many barely even qualify as investment-worthy businesses—they have poor capital structure, little experience, poor public disclosure, and no extensive business track records.

Of the good stocks—Brochstein mentions GW Pharmaceuticals and several other Canadian companies—there are two key traits. First, the companies are ancillary to cannabis, not directly involved. They focus on packaging, hydroponic gear, business and legal consulting, distribution, etc. Second, they have track records both in cannabis and in business, which according to many industry figures, is a very rare combination. Even rarer is the experienced investor willing to give several million dollars to a felon.

Indeed, other cannabis investment bankers and asset managers say risk is the name of the game. Investors and businesses without an appetite for the colossal clutch of legal and business hurdles are told to stay on the sidelines. Those who invest in riskier propositions like oil and gas, subsurface minerals, real estate, life sciences, and resource exploration are among the subtypes mentioned by several of the cannabis industry's wealth managers. .

Stocks and Public Companies

For the most part, the cannabis industry's leading companies are private instead of public, though larger companies like Tilray and MJIC have spoken about being taken public soon. This differs from most other industrialized nations, where industry leaders are publicly traded companies Microsoft, Alibaba, Amazon, Google, etc. For a variety of reasons—political, legal, financial, reputational—cannabis companies either don't have the ability or the desire to go public. Indeed, the publicly traded companies leave a lot to be desired.

FINRA itself, or the Financial Industry Regulatory Authority, isn't friendly to the cannabis industry. It has actively discouraged investors from involving themselves and has kicked companies out of the investing sphere. Cannabis company MassRoots made a hubbub about being the first cannabis stock listed on the NASDAQ—and was promptly denied entry. The NASDAQ denied that the rejection had anything to do with marijuana and that it was simply a poorly performing stock, but has not accepted any other marijuana stocks either.

The federal government's refusal to let cannabis companies operate is in and of itself irresponsible, given its own guidance to states, argues Larry Horowitz. Federal rules simultaneously ask for certain protections and then hamstring themselves from enforcing those protections. For one, the federal government ignores its own infrastructure. Typically, the Internal Revenue Service audits U.S. companies through banking records, which cannabis companies cannot build with any federally chartered or federally insured bank. Even though the Cole Memo wants states to ensure cannabis businesses aren't making any shady financial transactions, it strips state and law enforcement of the most effective tool to do so.

Cryptocurrency

As usual, the federal/state gap doesn't keep business from happening, but instead simply shifts it. To work, the cannabis industry has a quilt of solutions, most of which force them to pay more overhead. Banks are only losing out on a deep well of money that goes in some cases to the netherworld of cryptocurrency or into entire enterprises that exist only to somehow wash cannabis money.

Hypur, founded by a group of former banking experts and officials, circumvents the whole cash transaction by linking the growers and retailers directly with customers through an app and a tracking system.

Black market drugs have always found a home in the deep web through web browsers like Tor, where drugs and guns are sold and mailed under law enforcement's nose. For these transactions, buyers and sellers used Bitcoin, a decentralized cryptocurrency.

These are digital money systems. Potcoin is cryptocurrency explicitly geared to cannabis, where users fill a digital wallet with Potcoins and make purchases from vendors who accept the payment and link it back to their own bank accounts or simply cash it out. Similar products like CanPay also find closed loop systems to bypass the banking conundrum.

Commercial Perks

Without banking access, cannabis operators have none of the necessary business building blocks that are ubiquitous in most other legal commercial endeavors. For example, being able to secure a building loan is more difficult because banks do not issue loans to cannabis business. Owners therefore typically finance through bootstrapping methods, retirement savings, loans from family and friends, or debt financing with private investors. In towns, cities, and counties where local authorities have banned commercial cannabis, several hopeful cannabis business owners have had to eat these losses. Except for Oregon, states where adult use is legal have at times required all cannabis business licensees and financial stakeholders to be residents of the state.

Cannabis grow facilities are typically zoned only in industrial areas where building square footage is plentiful. These are expensive prospects; a mid-sized grow operation of 20,000 square feet can easily cost $3 to 4 million. To secure the building, cannabis businesses often sign building loan agreements with out-of-state investors. These investors, because they own the building and not the business, escape legal scrutiny while charging their tenants rates up to four times the average square foot price for the area. This assumes landlords are willing to rent or lease buildings to cannabis businesses, and if so, those businesses can find insurance companies willing to take them on as customers. Finding a willing landlord within the typically strict zoning requirements for cannabis operations can be difficult.

In the Meantime . . .

State governments will take their taxes and corporations will take their profits—rain, sleet, hail, or snow. More than any other issue, cannabis banking is at the top of the list for politicians and business leaders both. U.S. Congress members from states where cannabis is legal are trying to move federal levers to make banking access a reality for the cannabis industry.

Lawmakers from several of the recreational and medical market states have tried to wrangle protections for pro-cannabis banks, but none have succeeded or even progressed through Congress since being introduced in 2015. All are in subcommittee or committee phases. Sen. Cory Booker, D-N.J., sponsored the Compassionate Access, Research Expansion, and Respect States (CARERS) Act of 2015,[19] alongside an identical House bill sponsored by Tennessee Democrat Rep. Steve Cohen.[20] The bill would amend the Controlled Substances Act to recognize medical uses for marijuana, reclassify it as a Schedule II drug, and explicitly exempt banks from federal prosecution as long as they comply with state laws, whether recreational or medicinal.

Neither the House nor Senate version has moved since the spring of 2015, held in the House Subcommittee on Crime, Terrorism, Homeland Security, and Investigations and the Senate Judiciary Committee. Notably, cannabis has not yet become attached to the larger states' rights battles typically fought by small-government Republicans and Democrats.

Democrats in other states have introduced similar legislation. Oregon Democrat Sen. Jeff Merkley introduced the Cannabis Businesses Access to Banking Act of 2015 in July 2015.[21] The bill would forbid federal authorities from penalizing banks that accept cannabis deposits and forbid the Federal Deposit Insurance Corporation and the National Credit Union Association from denying insurance to banks. The bill was read twice and referred to the Committee on Banking, Housing, and Urban Affairs. An identical House bill was introduced in April 2015 by Colorado Democrat Rep. Ed Perlmutter. Like the CARERS Act, it was immediately kicked to the Subcommittee on Crime, Terrorism, Homeland Security, and Investigations and hasn't seen any action since.

Even legislators who vocally opposed cannabis legalization in their home states have co-sponsored attempts to ensure banking access for cannabis businesses, including Sen. Lisa Murkowski, R-AK.

Tellingly, party lines dissolve when tax dollars start rolling in. The House bill has 16 sponsors, evenly split between Republicans and Democrats. The Senate version has eight sponsors, including two independents and then-Republican presidential candidate Rand Paul of Kentucky. Rep. Dana Rohrabacher, R-Calif., who also would like to remove cannabis as a Schedule I Controlled Substance in the Controlled Substances Act, introduced the Respect State Cannabis Laws Act of 2015. The bill was referred to the House Subcommittee on Crime, Terrorism, Homeland Security, and Investigations on May 15, 2015, and has not moved since.

Industry hopes were crushed in August 2016 when the U.S. Drug Enforcement Agency (DEA) refused a pair of petitions to declassify cannabis as a Schedule I Controlled Substance.[22] Chuck Rosenberg, the DEA's acting administrator, wrote in explanation that the DEA must follow science.[23] Science, in the DEA's view, has still not recognized a legitimate medical use for cannabis, and so it must remain on the Schedule I list where national banks will continue to fear it. On a monthly basis, more and more states and nations will run into the cannabis industry's banking problem.

CHAPTER SIX

State by State, Nation by Nation

The banking system is losing out on a fast-growing economic engine the entire nation and entire world is racing towards. Colorado and Washington got the cannabis fame for their trailblazing into the recreational wilderness, but they were only the latest. Internationally, the pot boom is expanding monthly, though it strays from the Colorado formula.

The classic steered vs. free market debate is already at work in the cannabis industry. Media and politicians overgeneralize when they say "legalize." Deciding how the industry will run is more complex than a simple thumb up or down, and not all legalization schemes are created equal. There are countless ways a state or nation-state can make cannabis not illegal, countless market types to open, and countless regulatory schemes to put in place.

Virtually all cannabis industry is shaped and defined by its restrictions. Fundamentally, state and national governments can either let the market work as independently as possible or take a very active hand in restricting it. States can legalize only medical cannabis, limit the number of licenses in a given area, only allow nonprofits, set prices and control the supply, and take 100 other routes to keep the market under control.

The biggest commercial difference is medical vs. recreational. Most nations start with medical programs, and the U.S. states follow the same pattern. This not only takes some pressure off the black market, but establishes the groundwork for a more well-oiled recreational machine further down the line (though some states and nations deny they have any interest).

In recreationally legal states, medical programs can either be simply disguised recreational programs or be divorced heavily from them. Medical programs generally tightly control their cannabis providers, whereas recreational states have a much looser rein.

Even in two states of a kind, there are big differences. In recreational models like Colorado and Washington, the cannabis industry is not an open market by any sense, but a quasi-free market with infinite variations as to who can enter the industry, what kind of restrictions there are on commercial operations, consumers, and the products available on the market.

Medical programs do not create the same kind of roaring commercialism the recreational cannabis industry produces. More often, medical programs simply produce an array of oligopolies that are then poised to corner the recreational market when that state decides to go all the way with its policy. In terms of money, the recreational industry is king.

The United States is in a legal conundrum, unlike most other Western nations—its Puritanical drug laws war with the Puritan sense of work ethic and profit.

Because of the federal/state gap, the nation's drug laws don't synch cannabis with the American free market machine. Within those states, however, pockets of internationally rebellious policies spring up. The nation has some of the most restrictive federal laws in the developed world, whereas some of its states have the least restrictive cannabis environment in the developed world.

Medical programs have existed in the United States for 20 years, but U.S. states are choosing the souped-up, full-scale commercial legalization model more and more. There are no studies drawing out the causative link between industry growth and legalization success, but the correlation is plain— legalization efforts took on new vigor once Colorado opened it up to consumers and businesses.

State by State

Within the United States, 20 states haven't legalized either medical or adult use cannabis. The RAND Corporation outlines several different models for states flirting with the idea of legalization, whether by ballot initiative or bill. Depending on the model, the future of U.S. cannabis could vary.

> Nevertheless, important consequences flow from selecting who may produce and supply marijuana. So it is very important to systematically consider the potential effects of each strategy. In particular, the marketing and lobbying muscle of a for-profit industry is likely to influence the future trajectory of marijuana policy, whereas other options would allow legislatures and regulatory agencies to act with more regard for the public interest.[1]

The "public interest" concerns health risks, youth risks, crime risks, and a host of other factors—what RAND calls the "net social gain." This concept is hard to quantify—there's no arithmetic formula to add up prison time, court-room clog, medical access, traffic accidents, psychological impacts, cancer risk, violent crime associations, post-traumatic stress disorder treatment, and half a hundred other ways cannabis legalization could either help or harm society. Because cannabis has languished in the black market for so long, data for any of these items will be years in the making, though preliminary reports are starting to address them more and more. To this end, some states choose one of several options or a combination of several.

Partial Decriminalization

Cautious legislators could choose to decriminalize cannabis instead of turning it into an industry. Some U.S. states, and many countries, are mostly interested in keeping low-level drug offenses out of clogged courtrooms with laws that criminalize everything but small amounts of pot. This method may cut down on law enforcement, legal workload, and the life-scarring effects of the U.S. justice system for offenders, but the black market still exists.

Making money from cannabis is more a crime than using it, in these cases. Some of the more conservative states decriminalized possession of small amounts as long as there's no profit motive. In Missouri,[2] Mississippi,[3] and Nebraska,[4] possession of anywhere between 10 grams and 1 ounce (depending on the state) is only a misdemeanor, civil violation, or an infraction, with maximum fines of a few hundred dollars. In each of these states, though, trafficking and cultivation are still felonies that can earn a citizen at least a year of prison time.

In Illinois (which also has a medical program), decriminalization is more ramped up.[5] Sale of up to 10 grams is a misdemeanor, and Illinoisans can grow up to five plants. Ohio has similar rules—less than 200 grams is a misdemeanor and gifts of less than 20 grams is a misdemeanor.[6] North Carolina has a maximum fine of $500 for less than 5 grams of possession, but still classifies sale and cultivation as felonies.[7] Courtroom clog and law enforcement costs have gone down in these states, but only for those low-level offenses. Criminal cannabis seizures are still an everyday reality for law enforcement.

Full Decriminalization

The next step up on the spectrum is to let citizens hold more pot and allow them to grow their own. This has the same benefits of partial decriminalization, but maximized. It keeps more low-level offenders out of the U.S. penal system and allows a much greater range of medical access, albeit in a blind eye way. It also guarantees the market will both grow and remain unregulated, untaxed, and unscrutinized. In these states, there is no cannabis industry to speak of—no new hiring, revenue, or taxes for the state. In a way, this model resembles what the Netherlands has made itself famous for. In that country, law enforcement tolerates cannabis sales but not cannabis cultivation. In certain areas, this leads to problems with organized crime to supply what is a functionally legal market.[8]

Portugal, the liberal gold standard for drug policy, decriminalized small possession of all illegal drugs in 2001 but did not create a market for cannabis the way the United States is doing now with recreational cannabis. Since then, associated low-level arrests and overdoses have dramatically declined, but there is no associated revenue.[9]

The nation's federally controlled capital is the only U.S. space that follows this model for cannabis itself, making it, in fact, friendlier to cannabis than Congress. Any adult over 21 in Washington, D.C., can have up to two ounces of cannabis on his person and grow up to six plants at home. Like with partial decriminalization, this doesn't eliminate the black market per se, and in certain ways guarantees that it will continue to exist. Washingtonians can gift each other cannabis but cannot sell it for profit, though the area has a great many shops that do. Buying and selling simply go unregulated and untaxed.

Full decriminalization does, however, keep industrial nuisances like marketing out of the general public's eyes. This is a concern for those who don't want Americans penalized over pot but don't want to see a cannabis market in general and especially do not want it marketed toward children. Even states that accept cannabis's medical value may be uncomfortable with a full-scale industry that up until the 2010s had been illegal for nearly a century. Other states point out that the decriminalization model's effect on black market pales in comparison to a full commercial model.

Alaska used to have a similar system to Washington, D.C.'s, and some of the country's most unique cannabis laws. Since the 1970s, the *Ravin v. Alaska* decision effectively decriminalized possession and allowed some personal cultivation. Still, when Alaska fully legalized recreational pot in 2014, there is some evidence that the black market shrank. Arrest rates and seizures dropped dramatically,[10] though this could have as much to do with law enforcement deprioritizing cannabis-related arrests.

This decriminalization model is the norm for states that allow cannabidiol (CBD), cannabis's nonpsychoactive compound. Most states, including ultraconservative Utah, allow CBD oil possession for patients with qualifying illnesses, but do not allow its production or sale. Those who want the legal product must obtain it illegally.

Controlled Medical Programs

Medical cannabis programs are the next step up from decriminalization and the first rung on the ladder to establishing a market complete with revenue and taxes. National media attention started with Colorado in 2012, but cannabis has been medically legal in the United States since California legal-ized medical use and cultivation by ballot initiative in 1996.

Consumer access in these states varies, along with how much business can be involved. Some states have medical marijuana laws so stringent that they are virtually ineffective. Louisiana's medical laws only allow for a nonsmoke-able product, with a state-sponsored grower (Louisiana State University) and 10 licensed distributors, none of whom operate yet.[11]

Many of these states didn't legalize medical marijuana per se, but rather shops that can sell it. Hawaii had legal marijuana since 2000, but only allowed medical card holders to grow their own product. Hawaii's 2015 passage of a medical cannabis measure opened the realm to eight initial licensed dispen-saries, none of which may advertise to their clientele through traditional com-mercial means.[12]

Minnesota's medical program is similar, with only eight licensed dispen-saries, each of which is licensed to grow their own medicine.[13] Arkansas licenses 40 distributors and only eight grow facilities, each of which serves a particular section of the state.[14] Illinois' program has 53 licensed distributors, with a cap of 22 cultivation centers, also divided into districts.[15] Pennsylva-nia's program divides the state into six regions where up to 12 growers/processors will operate 27 dispensaries.[16] New Hampshire only allows four dispensaries in its medical program.

The structure varies in each of the 21 states that allow only medical mari-juana. Pointedly, no cannabis is available to nonstate residents. To buy can-nabis under a state's medical program, a patient must register with the state's department of health. Whereas recreational cannabis states have influxes of out-of-state customers, medical-only states negate it.

Some states set up their medical cannabis laws specifically to keep indus-trial interests from growing. Montana legalized medical marijuana in 2004, but the legislature didn't like the results. Advertisements and dispensaries sat uncomfortably close to churches and schools, some said. The medical busi-ness itself had become a cottage industry, with out-of-state physicians mov-ing in to essentially rubber-stamp prescriptions on a fee basis.[17] In 2011, the legislature passed an almost-repeal that limited dispensaries to three patients apiece—without any profit motive. Eventually, those laws themselves were repealed, and now Montana has some of the more relaxed marijuana laws in the country. Business owners don't even need to be state residents, unlike some recreational states and most medical states.

Some states lay out clearly what sicknesses and maladies are okay for pot use or how much exactly is the "adequate supply" for the patient and the over-all number of patients. This means some states can exclude entire groups of patients. In New Hampshire, chronic pain would not get a cannabis prescrip-tion originally[18] before a law change added moderate and severe chronic pain to the list of qualifying symptoms.

Earlier markets and western markets often have more lax laws than east-ern states. Arizona's market entry is more open than some East Coast states, and in some ways, guarantees larger businesses instead of smaller grows and dispensaries. The law allows licensed caregivers to grow cannabis for their medical card holder patients, but also allows dispensaries, which must have an Arizona-licensed physician as medical director. All Arizona pot grows must be attached to a dispensary, unlike recreational states where cultivators can exist on their own. Instead of a hard license cap, Arizona has a fluid license cap: there can be one cannabis dispensary per every 10 pharmacies.

Nonprofit Model

Compromises do not work sometimes. Some of the ways states control can-nabis companies backfire or simply allow a more insidious kind of gray mar-ket. Several states allow only nonprofits to be involved with medical cannabis, described as a good fix by RAND. Outside the confines of think tanks, though, the nonprofit model has proven a mixed bag in states that have it and is mostly reviled by industry policy experts.

John Hudak, a cannabis policy specialist at the Brookings Institution, crit-icized the RAND report in an interview specifically for its inclusion of the nonprofit model, which he calls a fantasy.[19] Other industry leaders agree, as in the case of attorney Larry Horowitz, who called the nonprofit model "abused" in states that have it.[20]

Indeed, cannabis nonprofits are both abused and ineffective. The trend first started partially at the suggestion of former California attorney general Jerry Brown. Brown wanted to cut down on the for-profit dispensaries with little oversight popping up throughout the state after the 1996 medical ballot. Years later, California authorities raided several shops and found some in posses-sion of more money than a nonprofit, cooperative, or collective should have,[21] an apparently statewide trend in the Golden State's nearly unregulated pre-2016 medical system.

Other nonprofit states show the same kind of behavior, as nonprofits sim-ply serve as a front for business opportunities. In New Mexico, the health department explicitly wanted to make sure the cannabis suppliers were in it for compassionate access reasons instead of profit motive—they wanted to keep prices low and ensure medical access. It hasn't yielded the desired result. For a variety of reasons, including heavy restrictions on how much the state can grow, New Mexico cannabis prices still exceed those of recreational states.[22] Furthermore, profit motive came into New Mexico's system anyway.

Nonprofit status doesn't mean there are no profits. In New Mexico, as men-tioned, the taxes, expenses, and salaries of licensed nonprofit producers (LLNPs) still came about $6 million short of the gross amount paid for medi-cal cannabis—and that in the first quarter of 2016 alone.[23] Furthermore, at least one nonprofit dispensary in New Mexico funneled money away[24] from its own operations and into an out-of-state, for-profit management company. Like everyone else in the industry, nonprofit leaders see the horizon of recreational legalization—many openly admit they want to gain a market foothold for when cannabis is recreationally legal.

To the extent nonprofits might work in theory, the federal/state gap gums it up anyway. The federal government itself is responsible in large part for the opacity of cannabis nonprofits and their openness to abuse. Because cannabis is federally illegal, the Internal Revenue Service does not require that cannabis nonprofits submit 990 tax reports—public financial records anyone can check on to ensure good management. Because cannabis businesses are cash businesses due to federally illegality, state officials can have a hard time tracing transaction history to prove wrongdoing.

Gateway Program

Studies are more and more debunking the theory that cannabis is a gateway drug, including studies from the Centers for Disease Control,[25] but medical cannabis is undeniably a gateway business. Most of the states that allow adult use had medical programs beforehand. This not only takes some pressure off the black market, but establishes the groundwork for a more well-oiled recreational machine further down the line (though some states and nations deny they have any interest). Having medical sets the tone and lets businesses set up supply chains and grows before going full-scale adult use.

South African officials specifically stated that the original legalizing proposal would have also legalized recreational weed, but they felt they had a better chance legalizing by starting with medical first.[26] Some U.S. states have taken the same approach—pass medical laws, then switch to full adult use at a later point. Of the eight states with recreational programs, all but one (Alaska) had a previously existing medical program. Ethan Nadelmann, former director of the Drug Policy Alliance, said this was indeed part of the entire strategy: get the ball rolling, then move on to other parts of the discussion focused around personal sovereignty or drug war policies:

> I and a few other key people (pass medical laws first) for two reasons. First, the belief that in the process of rolling back marijuana prohibition, those people who use it for medical (reasons) have a right to be first in line. Secondly, we have reason to believe, but no proof, that opening up medical will help to transform the broader dialogue about marijuana reform.[27]

Nadelmann's point about voter response seems bulletproof. Few medical states have not either expanded their programs in the last five years or gone fully recreationally legal. Aside from voter response, though, it simply makes a lot of business sense to legalize medical cannabis first. The states who try for a kind of agnostic cannabis system, where there are no distinctions in law between medical and recreational, do not fare well.

Alaska, for example, makes no distinction between medical and recreational use. This caused several problems for consumers, business, and the state itself. In states like Colorado, tax structures are in place that discount medical use. If a grow wants to produce medically oriented supplies, it has no tax incentive. Even though Alaska issues medical marijuana cards, it has no system through which medical users can buy. Medical dosage limits don't exist—a medical card holder is held to the same amount of tetrahydrocannabinol (THC) as a recreational user. Further, Alaska did not have any grows or dispensaries ready to sell when full legalization passed. Instead, the industry had to wait until the regulations were fully developed to even start applying for licenses. This plays a part in Alaska's slow industry start.

This trend may not be developed enough to glean anything useful, however. Alaska has a dozen other unique problems that pitch into its slow growth, and other states had different experiences. Washington State allowed medical marijuana use, but not production, before it legalized recreational, but its business mushroomed virtually overnight.

In-State Residents

All regulations in the cannabis industry change regularly as industry develops. In each of these states that have legalized marijuana, the structure prevents companies from economies of scale through one overarching regulation: with few exceptions, only state residents can own cannabis business licenses.

Colorado started this regulation trend. When it launched its recreational cannabis industry in 2014, it required all investors in cannabis licenses to be Colorado residents. This rule was intended to fulfill the Cole Memo's guidance, which wanted to make sure states did not let regulated cannabis serve as a vehicle for the black market. In theory, restricting businesses to state residents ensured the state could track each individual involved in the industry.

After a few years, however, laws started to change. Those watching the industry noted that the residency requirements had two unintended impacts. First, it created a capital crunch. Cannabis businesses already had little access to banks for funding. Residency rules pushed most financing into the hands of in-state private investors instead. In states with limited capital, like Alaska, this led to a very slow industry development. In better capitalized states Colorado, Washington, and Oregon, lawmakers and regulators eventually found that the residency restrictions weren't keeping outsiders out anyway. Real estate investors bought buildings to lease to cannabis companies and charged percentages of profit. Some companies founded out-of-state licensing agreements, in effect setting up franchises. Others simply started shell companies in the states where they planned to operate or found residents to serve as fronts. Second, it gave the industry to a handful of first movers in each state, who now control market share.

Though it creates a capital crunch, industry itself sometimes lobbies for these residency restrictions to keep bigger players out of their neighborhood. Alaska's Marijuana Control Board backtracked on an earlier decision and tightened its residency restrictions to some of the strictest in the country after backlash from industry leaders who wanted to avoid a Big Marijuana takeover.

The U.S. Pattern

Legalization movements start small and work their way up to the economic benefits of full recreational. Decriminalization is a quick and virtually painless way states can at least get rid of enforcement costs and legal system clogs, but it doesn't spur the same kind of economic development and doesn't destroy the black market. More often, it simply makes criminals of the people who supply the legal market.

The poster children for U.S. marijuana legalization, Colorado and Washington, follow the least restrictive model on the spectrum. They allow both medical and recreational cannabis, with full participation from "large, professionally operated suppliers that can realize economies of scale and promote a diverse range of products but also that those suppliers can be private companies who goal is profit maximization."[28] By 2016, the number of states that follow this model mushroomed to eight. These states are special specifically because they have taken the model that allows for American-style commerce to bloom—with all the taxes and booming businesses the next two chapters will outline.

Those laws were slow in the making, though. California is a clear example of what happens to the recreational industry if the lag between medical and recreational takes too long. It took the state of California over two decades to complete its medical cannabis laws. By then, the entire state was carved into fiefdoms with radically different rules. By the time it did complete them, a 2016 ballot initiative legalized recreational cannabis too. California will deal with the blowback for years. Instead of a clear state law, the country's most populous state has a patchwork of local laws that let businesses pick and choose where they have the most chance of controlling the local market. MedMen, one of Southern California's most powerful cannabis brands and venture capital firms, admits freely in interviews that its strategy is to locate areas with less competition and control as many licenses as possible.[29] Several California towns have already been bought entirely by cannabis companies to this end.

International

Colorado and Washington led the United States in commercializing pot, and other nations are catching up along the same lines. As the world's most popular drug, many countries have some experience toying with cannabis laws, but worldwide very few have officially legalized its production or sale. Very few have moved with the state-by-state pattern in America, either. Far more often, the federal government takes the lead.

That is not to say it never happens elsewhere as it has in the United States, where decriminalization slowly led to full recreational talks in a matter of years. Three of Australia's eight states decriminalized small amounts of cannabis possession before Victoria and New South Wales legalized medical cannabis in 2016, followed shortly afterwards by the Australian federal government. In India, several states have varying degrees of legal status even though the Indian government still declares it illegal. Certain provinces in Argentina have decriminalized possession, and Turkey allows medical cannabis growing in several provinces.

Those are the exceptions to a greater trend, however. Most nations change their laws at the federal level beginning with medical laws. Very few countries allow cannabis consumerism like Colorado.

Like the United States, many nations' federal governments restrict cannabis commerce but tolerate consumption. In Europe, this leads to cannabis tourism, but not business per se. Portugal decriminalized all drugs in 2001 but does not allow commercial sale or manufacture. The Netherlands has long been famous for its marijuana cafes, where patrons can buy a joint with their espresso. The nation's slackness brings in tourists, but not business: commercial-scale cannabis cultivation is still illegal. Spain has a similar system, where commercial sale is illegal but Spaniards can use cannabis for personal use—like the Netherlands, it has hundreds of private clubs specifically for cannabis. Belgium followed suit with decriminalizing small amounts in 2003. South America and Central America started with the same route. Columbia decriminalized small amounts of personally possessed cannabis in 1994, followed in later years by Chile, Jamaica, Mexico, Peru, and Paraguay. In the 2010s, nations like Chile, Germany, Australia, South Africa, Czech Republic, Mexico, and Israel started ramping up to medical research or medical use. Other countries like Ireland and Slovenia take the pharmaceutical route, legalizing only cannabis-based medicines but not the plant itself.

Apart from U.S. states, only a few countries are ready to open cannabis to the consumer. Canada, which already has a medical marijuana system, proposed recreational legalization only months after Germany's medical cannabis bill vote and will likely have its first sale by the summer of 2018. Uruguay made worldwide headlines when it legalized recreational cannabis in 2013 and began implementing it in 2015. Uruguay already had very lax drug laws, but the new law took it a step further. Uruguayans can carry as much cannabis as they want and grow up to six plants in their homes. Uruguayans can have growing clubs that have up to 100 plants to split between their members. In terms of business, though, Uruguay still falls short of the Colorado model. Instead of allowing total free market access, the state itself operates marijuana stores, the same way some U.S. states have state-controlled liquor stores.

Canada's medical model is also more tightly controlled than the even most U.S. states' models. As with alcohol, the Canadian government sets the prices and controls the distribution networks. As it shifts to recreational sales, this may or may not continue.

Whatever the rationale—crime, compassionate access, personal use—the developed world is moving away from outright cannabis prohibition in small steps, usually starting with the basic premise that a personal stash of cannabis should not equal jail time. If the United States is any indication, most national or state governments do not stop there and there is every incentive to legalize for the tax dollars.

CHAPTER SEVEN

Taxation and Ramifications

What are the states doing with their newfound income? What will it mean going forward, both as an economic driver and source of state revenue?

Taxes get pot laws passed as much as personal choice or reduction of incarceration rates or curative properties for illnesses—maybe more so. The lure of tax dollars is one of the most prominent differences between medical cannabis and recreational cannabis. Where the former appeals to science or to compassion, the promise of money is embedded into the campaigns of recreational cannabis. Drug Policy Alliance, arguably the group most directly responsible for U.S. cannabis legalization and in some cases abroad, had a strategy for recreational rhetoric. When states' ballot initiatives got two months away from voting day, advocates in the fight were to abandon all arguments except the terms *tax, regulate, control,* and *educate.*

"Wouldn't you have cops focus on real crime, and wouldn't you have the government tax and regulate instead of the gangsters running it? Those two arguments are hands down the strongest to sway swing voters," said former director Ethan Nadelmann.[1]

In most cases, the swing voters seem to know what they were doing. Colorado, Washington, and Oregon have funneled hundreds of millions from the pockets of recreational cannabis users into schools, health care programs, substance abuse initiatives, and more. At the local level, in some areas sales taxes have rejuvenated formerly stagnant public works. To this end, state governments are keen to keep the business running as smoothly as possible once the tax money starts rolling in and keener to get to the money chest—the explosive growth of congressional support for commercial cannabis, along with the defenses of governors and attorneys general from the Trump administration, is proof enough.

In some cases, though, there are fears states are too eager. If states intend to use cannabis taxes as a budget tool, this can lead to higher tax rates that critics argue will make legal pot prices too expensive to stamp out the black market, or potentially hook state governments on the new revenue source.[2]

For the industry itself, taxes are a hurdle. As with every other part of the cannabis trade, the federal/state gap causes problems. First and foremost, businesses cannot use the same kind of tax deduction strategies allowed to most businesses because of an obscure federal tax code, Section 280E, which is the industry's second-biggest federal foe. Next, cannabis businesses are simply dealing with the ugly reality of pay-to-play business in the United States.

How Much Money Can the State Make?

U.S. states with recreational pot are raking in cash. In most cases, cannabis taxes have simply become another feature of the budget in a time where state finances are thin in much of the country. Several of the states that legalized recreational cannabis, including Alaska, Colorado, Washington, and Oregon, have gone through cycles of state budget deficits that cannabis taxes have helped fill, or at least given another option for lawmakers to mull over.

The advocates and voters who imagine taxes as reason enough to legalize have every reason to expect a positive outcome. So far, states have collected billions in tax revenue. Colorado hit a milestone in the summer of 2017 when its cannabis tax receipts totaled over $500 million since legalization,[3] not including the countless local tax schemes in the state. Washington, which has a higher tax rate and larger population, has collected even more. Cannabis taxes yielded almost $472 million from 2016–2017, and for the 2017–2019 budget cycle alone the state government projects another $730 million.[4] After the first year of legal sales, Oregon brought in $75 million in cannabis taxes.[5] The only outlier to the large tax collections is Alaska, whose slow industry start and low population only collected $1 million in taxes after nine months of operational sales.[6]

The pie will only get bigger as states keep legalizing. The four states that legalized in 2016 have not yet harvested their cannabis taxes, but the projections put them in line with the big pots of the first mover states. Projections in California forecast an annual $1 billion in taxes.[7] Nevada collected half as much as Alaska in only the first four days of legal sales and predicts $60 million annually,[8] roughly the same as the $64 million the Massachusetts Department of Revenue forecasted in its state.[9] The Maine Center for Economic Policy forecasted $18 million from Maine's relatively small consumer base.[10]

Drawing from these states, the rest of the country would likely do as well. Because it is not federally legal, there are only projections as to how much cannabis could be worth in national tax dollars. However, the Tax Foundation's study laid out a projection for how much states could make from recreational cannabis sales tax. The numbers look promising for state coffers, based on sales trends from Colorado and Washington:

> If every state imposed a retail marijuana tax, total collections could range from $5.3 billion at a 15 percent rate to $8.8 billion at a 25 percent rate. Lower tax rates may capture more of the gray and black market than Colorado and Washington have to date, and state revenues in that circumstance could reach as much as $18 billion.[11]

In the experience of other states, even the Tax Foundation's forecast could prove lower than reality.

States that want to legalize can expect taxes not just to roll in, but after slow starts, they come in in bigger amounts than expected. In Washington, the state collected twice the forecasted amount, with $70 million during the first year of sales.[12] Oregon had collected $14.9 million in taxes by mid-2106, far more than the predicted $2 million to $3 million.[13]

This trend mirrors sales patterns themselves, which usually come in above forecast as well. Forecasts have many factors to contend with. Business simply moves too fast. The regulated market changes consumer spending. It makes cannabis a more sophisticated product than just flowers. The tax man cannot always predict how the market will shift according to consumer demands. The RAND Corporation projected this scenario:

> Both revenue and collateral consequences would depend on setting of tax levels, a task complicated by the possibility that increasing firm size and technological innovation would drive pretax production costs for basic product forms down substantially over time. The mix of product types could also evolve in ways that are difficult to foresee, e.g., with vaping gaining market share at the expense of traditional joints and bongs or the industry promoting products that contain both nicotine (tobacco) and THC (marijuana).

Indeed, this could be one of the reasons taxes come in over forecast. In Oregon,[14] revenue officials forecasted tens of millions less in tax dollars than what actually came into state coffers. One of the guesses for the inaccuracy is that value-added products like edibles and concentrates are less typically sold in the black market, so tax experts have no black market statistics on them to make any regulated predictions.

National Taxes

U.S. states are eager to reap the tax benefits of recreational cannabis, and the successes of Colorado and others in part shape the way foreign nations talk about the issue. International legalization advocates point to the untouched cannabis spoils as a carrot to legalize. However, proposals for foreign cannabis taxes are taking a different route than in the United States. If there is a lingering black market problem, some tie it to high taxes.

Internationally, governments typically heavily tax tobacco and alcohol. These "sin taxes" are a tempting model for cannabis. Most lawmakers' top concern is breeding a new generation of heavy cannabis users if they legalize. Sin taxes theoretically discourage use.

However, some, including *The Atlantic*, have argued sin taxes could backfire.[15] They may be a sound strategy for a long-legal market like tobacco, but could simply keep the black market alive with cannabis. Potentially, they make the retail product too expensive to compete with the already-embedded criminal cannabis. Instead of moving to the legal market, consumers will stick with their old dealers and their old prices if pot merchants cannot make a competitive price. Indeed, the taxation strategy when alcohol prohibition ended was to have extremely low costs of entry and low business taxes to coax black marketers into the light.

In the United States, this is an ongoing struggle. In a May 2016 report, Washington, D.C.–based think tank Tax Foundation authored a report that agreed with a Colorado state study—the lower the taxes, the better the chances of killing the black market.[16] So far, the United States is sticking with the high tax schedules they placed on cannabis to fund state governments.

Internationally, foreign governments seem less interested with funding their state than they are with killing the black market. Other nations keep taxes low or are proposing to keep taxes low.

Canada uses Nadelmann's tax-and-regulate rhetoric, but with a different take than American states—kill the gangsters first, shear the industry for taxes later. In Canada, Finance Minister Bill Morneau recommended that Canadian provinces keep their medical cannabis taxes low specifically to make sure the legal industry cuts into the black market with low, competitive prices.[17] Prime Minster Justin Trudeau's bill to legalize recreational cannabis does the same. Trudeau explicitly wants to focus on quashing the black market rather than hooking the Canadian government on cannabis taxes. Uruguay, which has a functioning national recreational industry, does not make cannabis producers pay either a production tax or a sales tax, though they do pay incomes taxes and licensing fees. Like in Canada, Uruguayan officials said the black market's death is the number-one goal—revenue generation is secondary.[18]

High taxes can also hurt the developing industry, which is already saddled with the startup costs, regulatory compliance costs, and licensing fees. In most states, the governing bodies for the cannabis industry draw their funding from those taxes and fees. If taxes trickle in slowly at first—and in most states with recreational cannabis, they have—the industry lags in a way that hurts the regulators.

This has led to at least one sticky situation related to one of the states that had not established a medical system before going full recreational. Washington and Alaska started their recreational programs in the similar manner, underfunded and understaffed for the workload ahead. In Alaska, the Marijuana Control Board was initially so severely understaffed that it could not process license applications in a speedy manner—hamstringing the exact industry whose tax dollars would fund more staffers. Legislators shoot themselves in the foot, regulating so heavily they stifle the tax income needed to fund their own regulations in a never-ending loop.

How They Use Them—Education and Budget Patches

Legalization advocates often shore up support by pointing out tax dollars to the state agencies that invariably seem to need more and more taxes every year. Most legalizing ballots or state legislatures direct cannabis taxes to education, law enforcement, and health care—just over half of Colorado's tax money has gone into education, according to a VS Strategies report.[19]

The heads of those agencies are usually all too happy to take cannabis taxes from the state legislature. Critics, though, point out that sin taxes have never been the most effective budget plug and have regressive tendencies to hurt the poor.[20] There is some evidence already springing up that those states with high cannabis taxes got themselves hooked. Each of the first four states to tax and regulate cannabis have gone through periods of budget woes, and the cannabis taxes look like a good patch.

Colorado was very eager to get the tax ball rolling, and over the years has come to rely on cannabis taxes as one more tool in the budget solution toolbox. In Colorado in 2012,[21] the legalizing ballot gave the first $40 million of pot taxes to the Building Excellent Schools Today Fund, which is not meant to build new schools, but "renew or replace deteriorating public schools" in largely rural areas. Originally, the ballot had agreed to leave Colorado's cannabis businesses untaxed for the first year to give them a head start. Instead, the legislature asked the people to let them start collecting early to get its $40 million. The people agreed, eager to put the theory into action that cannabis can help.

Anything beyond $40 million each year goes into a Marijuana Tax Cash Fund that spreads the money out to cannabis-related and later some miscellaneous expenses—behavioral health training, substance abuse prevention programs, public awareness campaigns to discourage or monitor youth cannabis use, the Marijuana Enforcement Division, and various health and homelessness funding in later years. Despite the cannabis money, though, Colorado still had trouble raising school money. To help patch up a $135 million budget gap in 2017, Gov. John Hickenlooper voted on a nearly unanimously lawmaker-approved spending bill that raised the cannabis industry's sales tax rate 5 percent—even though the tax was scheduled to go down that summer and Hickenlooper had already openly worried that high taxes could encourage the black market.

Similar scenarios played out in Washington State, where cannabis taxes are spent on the same kinds of programs as Colorado but are also eaten nearly in half by Medicaid.[22] In 2012, the state Supreme Court ruled that Washington State itself must pay for teacher salaries at public schools, and the state has been scrambling to find a way to pay. Gov. Jay Inslee proposed a suite of tax increases to pay for the resulting state budget need of $2.75 million, but in both 2015 and 2017 many state legislators wanted to talk about using cannabis taxes. The newer states where marijuana is legal had similar problems and discussed similar solutions.

Like Colorado, Oregon earmarks 40 percent of cannabis taxes for an educational fund, with the rest going towards law enforcement, health care, and substance abuse. In mid-2017, Oregon found itself in the middle of a nearly $2 billion budget deficit. Lawmakers began talking about the pot taxes.[23] In Alaska, the state has run a $3 billion to $5 billion deficit for years, but the state's $1 million in tax collections is meager.

In all these cases, though, state legislators looking to pay for more with more pot taxes must contend with the earmarks. None of them funnel their cannabis taxes back into the state's general fund and are not available for any old purpose. In each state, local governments get a share of the proceeds from state taxes, along with the option to levy their own.

Different Tax Models

No two states set up their markets the same way, and no two states tax their cannabis businesses the same way either. Just like the business regulations, mostly what states do to tax schemes is change them. In the few short years of legalization, most of the states with recreational cannabis have changed their tax schedules, sometimes even in the middle of the legalization process.

The first and biggest difference is usually between medical and recreational taxes. Many medical cannabis advocates argue that taxes should not be laid on the sufferers of illnesses. At the state revenue level, this can be a purely fiscal decision—the overwhelming majority of cannabis spending comes from recreational, not from medical, so making medical cannabis exempt from certain taxes does not affect the state's bottom line. Still, some states, like Oregon, exempt medical cannabis entirely. Colorado only applies one of several taxes to medical cannabis. Some of the states with both recreational and medical programs honor the thought by giving sales tax exemptions to customers who buy cannabis with a medical card. In Canada, medical cannabis patients can apply to the Canada Revenue Agency for a tax refund on what they spent for their prescription. So far Washington lays the biggest burden on medical users—they get only a small tax break.[24]

In each state, the most common tax schemes are a combination of excise taxes on producers and sales taxes on final retail sales. Arguments vary as to the relative strengths and weaknesses of either. Cannabis wholesale and retail prices continue to drop, meaning the state's take can grow less and less if it ties taxes directly to the price of goods sold. Colorado and Washington have both dealt with the impact of dropping prices on their tax incomes.

Concerns and Holdups with the IRS

Even though the taxes roll in, many lawmakers and policy experts have doubts that the bounty of pot taxes will outweigh whatever unknown consequences might happen from legalization. Kevin Sabet of Smart Approaches to Marijuana often points to taxes as a red herring, saying they do little to contribute to state coffers and more likely cost more that they produce.[25] The RAND Corporation has the same concerns:

> There are also many decisions about how exactly a government should tax marijuana. Taxes and fees are often thought of primarily as revenue-raising devices, but, in the case of marijuana, their collateral consequences (e.g., effects on youth consumption, heavy consumption, and the size of the black market) could outweigh revenue in importance.

So far, these fears have not found solid footing. The industry is still young, and data crunchers are still crunching the new national statistics on health, crime, and traffic, but as of 2017, RAND's question has a tentative answer: taxes are all gravy.

Many of the predictions opponents and advocates have made have not come true. Indeed, the only real measurable result of legalization has been that state treasuries end up stuffed, according to a mid-2016 study from the libertarian think tank the Cato Institute:

> Our conclusion is that state-level marijuana legalizations to date have been associated with, at most, modest changes in marijuana use and related outcomes. Our estimates cannot rule out small changes, and related literature finds some effects from earlier marijuana policy changes such as medicalization. But the strong claims about legalization made by both opponents and supporters are not apparent in the data.[26]

Crime, traffic fatality trends, and use have all stayed consistent with prelegalization patterns, according to this analysis and others. Even the positive impacts have little substance when economic trends are stretched out to a larger timeline than 2012 and forward.

Property values—which in Denver and Seattle have started to look like those of Manhattan or Los Angeles in terms of expense—are consistent with trends that were happening before legalization took place. Gross domestic product (GDP), the state's best measurement for increased economic output, stayed steady too. There are, of course, local themes that paint a rosy picture of local economies even if the state's GDP is not necessarily affected. Colorado's cannabis industry generates more local economic output than any other commercial sector except federal government employment.

Opposite the states, the industry has a different take. For all the new bridges and buildings and streets and schooling, the cannabis industry's experience with the U.S. tax system is far less merry than the states collecting the taxes. The industry's problem is not so much with the state taxes as the federal system that still draws on them despite their trade being federally illegal.

Apart from banking, industry leaders single out the Internal Revenue Service as the biggest issue facing them. Apart from the cash tax payments and the general burden of high tax rates, the federal tax system forces cannabis businesses to pay far more on their federal income statements than they would otherwise. This problem comes from an arcane part of the U.S. tax code that deals specifically with drugs. In 1982, just as the drug war launched into its 1980s heyday, Congress added Section 280E to the tax code.[27] Section 280E stops any traffickers of a Schedule I or II controlled substance from making business deductions to their federal income taxes, except cost of goods sold. The government made this rule to respond to a cocaine trafficker who wanted to claim business deductions on his income.

Even though it is federally illegal, cannabis businesses still must pay federal income taxes like anyone else—the IRS busted Al Capone for tax evasion, after all. Because it is federally illegal, though, cannabis businesses also fall under Section 280E. Instead of deducting their employment expenses, utilities, building expenses, or any of the other dozen deductions allowed in every other business, cannabis companies are taxed for nearly all their gross income.

Like the banking holdup, this bleeds down into the industry's operations in many ways. The National Cannabis Industry Association claims this raises the tax rate to roughly 70 percent instead of the 30 percent similar noncannabis businesses would pay.[28] In some cases, cannabis businesses end up paying more in taxes than they actually make in revenue.

The 280E tax issue also makes certain businesses foot the tax bill. Because only cost of goods sold is allowed as a deduction, retailers pick up the tab far more than growers or product manufacturers, who can deduct most, if not all, of their business expenses because the bulk of their expenses is with the product itself. It stops businesses from advertising in ways that would touch the Commercial Speech Doctrine. It also naturally set up an entire class of cannabis Certified Public Accountants (CPAs) who work with companies to find every loophole and deduction possible.

Like the cannabis industry's regulations, the banking issue, and the resulting high costs to entry, the tax code makes it harder for small businesses to stay afloat in the cannabis industry by sheer expense, while simultaneously setting up states with cash. In turn, this opens an entire multibillion dollar bonanza to those with the cash to invest.

CHAPTER EIGHT

Picks and Shovels—Ancillary and Support Industry

The tax burden, the nightmare of 280E, the daily drudges of regulatory compliance, and the expenses of licensing affect the producers and retailers. The real money is outside the difficulties, though, in an ancillary business community unchained by the federal/state gap or in many cases created by the federal/state gap.

While the cannabis industry grows, the money and spotlight attract security companies, public relations and promotional consultants, packaging and shipping companies, and media outlets looking to rise with the green tide. Many of the ancillary business leaders partner with, support, or are owned by each other, a trend most industry leaders chalk up to both the relatively small size of the cannabis industry and the constant paranoia of the federal/state gap.

Just a glance at the picks and shovels of cannabis shows that the industry already resembles the larger U.S. commercial world. Leading brands typically have leaders with noncannabis business experience and extensive ties to other leading brands. The market itself knows there is a store of money waiting and takes appropriate steps to support efforts to get more customers in more states. The ancillary industry section is arguably more a driving force for legalization efforts than cultivators and retailers are. Most leaders of each respective industry segment have ties both to media and to cannabis lobby leaders.

In most cases, the federal/state gap keeps these ancillary businesses from operating to full national scale. In others, the federal/state gap simply creates entire new industry segments.

As with other industries, much of the money in the cannabis industry isn't in the product itself but on the sidelines. Just as money is in shipping, not in corn, cannabis money is in support. Many industry leaders have nothing to do at all with businesses that touch the plant—the National Cannabis Industry Association's (NCIA's) board of directors has twice as many directors who represent ancillary businesses than it has cannabis producers.[1]

Simply dealing with information is a huge value proposition. Media outlets, tech ventures, and data analysts not only control the industry's tempo, but have an advantage over direct producers and retailers when it comes to dealing with the federal/state gap, because there are virtually no laws that affect information sharing.

Other industry segments spring up specifically because of the federal/state gap. In this way, the market ends up addressing most of the safety concerns lawmakers have about bringing this new product into the regulated world.

Security companies exist solely to protect the large cash stores on hand at retailers, because federal laws make banking and credit card transactions so difficult. Tracking systems spring up to ensure no cannabis leaves the tightly regulated framework and spills into the hands of children or the black market. Testing products like breathalyzers battle to be the first and foremost for law enforcement to test for drugged driving. Some existing industry sectors have simply folded their operations over into the cannabis space—business insurance companies, print shops for advertising, cannabis PR firms, gardening supplies, paraphernalia manufacturers, and any other business sector useful to a retail product.

Media

Motivations aside, the U.S. press is as important to the cannabis industry and as profiting from it as any other industry sector. For the last five years, media of all stripes—general news, business news, legal trade publications, etc.—have dived into cannabis head first. As a culturally momentous, lucrative, and politically important subject, cannabis deserves the depth and breadth of coverage it gets from the nation's media (see Chapter 9). However, media companies are money-making machines like any other and are cashing in on the conversation.

Ad revenue follows the endless sets of eyes hungry for all digital content even grazing the subject of cannabis, and newspapers familiar with the struggle are making hay while they can. The Cannabist, an offshoot of one of the largest newspapers in the country, the Denver Post, even has an e-merchandise store of its own and a line of Cannabist merchandise rivaling that of the companies it covers, partnered with Chiefton Supply Co, a Colorado-based, cannabis-focused apparel company[2]—despite the fact the Denver Post opposed the Amendment 64 ballot initiative.[3]

In a way, media has provided the only consistency the cannabis industry has. The cannabis industry is a patchwork development, not centralized by the federal government. To collaborate with or to imitate another state's laws, there needed to be communication. The industry itself, therefore, was largely shaped by newspapers, trade journals, and advocacy publications, rather than directly by industry or by lawmakers.

Of all the winners in the cannabis world, few match media, including this book. Since 2012, legacy publications have covered the fast-moving topic incessantly, and countless new digital and print publications popped up to write about the international and domestic implications, to gush over the new class of business owners cannabis is breeding, to tell now-outed cannabis users the best consumer news, or to crunch over the Trump administration's failures.

Media's division follows suit with many of the other industry segments, divided roughly into three camps: traditional cannabis, legacy-turned-cannabis, and cannabis originals. Former cannabis-centered publications like the venerable *High Times* still exist. Now, however, they compete with straight legacy media companies and startups looking to harness the countless page views and advertising dollars.

For newspapers and magazines, the cannabis industry has been a godsend. Journalism has had a rough decade since the Internet rearranged human society circa 2007. Newspapers had been steadily declining in circulation since the late 1980s,[4] but by 2007 the Internet popped any illusion of sustainability. Print advertising revenues shrank from $49 billion in 2006 to $22 billion in 2012.[5] Nationwide, newspaper jobs halved as companies struggled to make as much money in the digital world as the print world.

A casual glance at a state daily newspaper should reveal plainly how heated the media's interest in cannabis has grown and how necessary it has become to put a national movement into perspective. Entire documentaries have been devoted just to showing how cannabis coverage has helped dig struggling newsrooms out of dire straits.

Why So Much Coverage?

Uncomplicated events and issues don't need wide, deep coverage. Because of the federal/state gap, there are simply too many problems to talk about for cannabis to go uncovered. Legalization at the federal level has serious implications for the federal government. Among them, a loss of credibility is perhaps most concerning, considering an era where public attitudes are growing more and more hostile towards bureaucrats, policymakers, elected officials, and other society steerers.

There is definitely a coolness factor. The cannabis industry is soaking with millennial appeal. The data all agrees that youth are the heaviest pot users.

At the federal level, precious little takes place regarding cannabis except the occasional vague threats or denials from Attorney General Jeff Sessions or White House press secretary Sarah Huckabee Sanders. Action happens at the state level or the local level. State and local news, in an era searching for national context, has a new set of national, state, and local viewers as a result.

Regulations give daily publications as much fodder as they need. Every state has a different model of regulations to compare, as does every locality. A typical policy analysis article has several states to analyze and depends on sound reporting from each of them to make a national cohesive theme. Colorado and Washington warred in 2013 to figure out which regulatory schemes would work better, and the comparison continues as more and more states go online.

Flagship publications hint at the space cannabis occupied at the moment, straddling so many different coverage areas, from politics to justice to business to consumer reports to culture, that it needs its own section of the newspaper, called a "vertical" in newspaper industry. Two big city daily newspapers, the *Denver Post* and the *San Francisco Chronicle*, created an entirely new position to keep up with the demand for product news—cannabis editor. Like beer or wine coverage, the new vertical features whatever news would inform the reader about politics, positioning, product, or problems: strain profiles, company profiles, events calendars, cannabis-infused cookie recipes, listicles for the Top 10 High Hikes in Colorado, etc. The new demand unleashed a flood of reporters, freelance writers, and cannabis consumers.

Legacy media increasingly employ designated drug policy writers like Christopher Ingraham at the *Washington Post*. Established outlets like Politico and the *New York Times* frequently war with President Donald Trump's administration over statements made by Attorney General Jeff Sessions, press secretary Sarah Huckabee Sanders, and others.

In states where cannabis is legal, the smallest newsrooms have designated pot reporters, even in cities that ban commercial cannabis. Colorado Springs banned recreational cannabis, and yet both military town's papers, the *Colorado Springs Independent* and the *Colorado Springs Gazette*, have cannabis verticals.

Digital First Media

In the land of newspapers, MediaNews Group is king of cannabis coverage. Between Colorado and California—the first and largest cannabis markets, respectively—MediaNews Group controls one of the vastest swaths of polished cannabis reporting in the world. This new dominance began in 2013, the year after Colorado legalized. When Colorado legalized marijuana, the *Denver Post* was the last remaining daily paper in the state's capital city after the *Rocky Mountain News* folded in 2009. Since then, owner Digital First Media has refashioned itself into a weed coverage behemoth while dozens of both new and old industry-backed publications create their own spheres of influence.

MediaNews Group is known in the industry for its aggressive response to the post-2007 media world. It slashed newsroom budget and newsroom staff deeply and sold some of its larger properties, including the *Salt Lake Tribune*, which billionaire and former Utah governor John Huntsman subsequently bought and now controls in keeping with a new trend of billionaire newspaper owners, including Nevada's Sheldon Adelson and Jeff Bezos.

Like every other state in the United States and especially in the MediaNews Group family, the *Denver Post* hemorrhaged newsroom membership since 2007. Most recently, the *Post* bought out 20 of its newsroom staff in June 2016.[6] The buyouts didn't match the increased viewership and ad revenue from the Cannabist—the Cannabist's monthly viewership beat that of industry benchmark *High Times'* in 2016, though it lost to Marijuana.com.[7]

With the Cannabist as a success model, MediaNews Group attacked the next legalization wave with an even more finely tuned plan. Shortly after California legalized, MediaNews Group stitched together its nearly 30 California newspaper properties to form the *Cannifornian*. The *Cannifornian* draws from the lessons of the Cannabist, essentially serving as a California-only pot news aggregator. Like the Cannabist, it features advertising from the companies it covers and a prominent place for cannabis consumer news.

The Cannabist's role has been both to set the standard for industry and to set the example for other newspapers. The Cannabist was arguably the first paper to take the role seriously, not as a cannabis media source, but rather as a media source that happened to cover cannabis. It promoted old-school accountability journalism, using tried-and-true reportage to expose industry shortcomings alongside its successes, such as flaws in Colorado's potency testing system and irresponsible pesticide use by Colorado growers.

Regulators in other states refer to Colorado's, and to a lesser extent Washington's, example when crafting their own regulations. During Alaska's regulations process, the Marijuana Control Board argued endlessly over regulations that would either make their state more or less lenient than first mover Colorado. Without sharp-eyed reporting, this would not have been the case.

Trade Publications

In very real ways, media shaped the industry itself as it exists in 2017, not just the regulations. According to sources, including MJ Biz Daily founders,[8] in the early 2010s, companies in medical states and in Colorado had virtually no guidance from business or legal leaders and were largely left to stumble through a trial-and-error process. Trade publications and to a lesser extent consumer news stepped in to fill the role of message board, where industry best practices and best players and worst problems are crunched over.

Trade journals are one of the mainstays of commercial communication to solve these kinds of problems, and in the cannabis industry the first mover in this space was MJBiz Daily, an industry news publication. Like many industry leaders, MJBiz Daily was the product of noncannabis business experience that took on a life of its own once it entered the space.

Trade publication veterans Anne Holland and Cassandra Farrington started the venture in 2011 as a subscription-based trade publication for cultivators. By the time 2012 came around and Colorado legalized, they quickly learned that the industry was maturing. Readers were looking for market analysis, data points, and tips on how to avoid scam artists. Instead of an agricultural periodical as planned, MJBiz Daily started pulling the best examples of output, grow techniques, real estate practices, etc., in the process setting the industry performance benchmarks that for the most part remain.

Other trade publications have previous experience now tailored for cannabis coverage. *Cannabis Business Times* is owned by GIE Media, which owns a slew of agriculture trade publications. The trade publication niche is as full as any other—MJBiz Daily and *Cannabis Business Times* compete with *Marijuana Venture*, *Marijuana Business Magazine*, 420 Intel, THCbiz, Ganjapreneur .com, and countless other regional, state, and local publications that have a captive readership.

Industry-Owned Media and Industry-Media Connections

The Cannabist's accountability journalism and trade journals' hunt for business unity are two of three dominant media types. The third is directly owned by the industry or heavily sponsored. The most successful come from software, tech, or media in their pre-cannabis lives. Leafly, MJIC, MassRoots, and Marijuana.com, among others, each have a journalistic function. The sites not only produce their own news but also pull and aggregate information from legacy and trade publications.

Each of them has a vested interest in keeping the public, consumers, businesses, and public officials informed—each one is owned directly by industry, blurring the lines between commerce, advocacy, and journalism. Each also demonstrates the migration of experienced industry hands to fill spaces in the cannabis world.

Marijuana.com is owned by Weedmaps, which has even deeper connections to advocacy groups (see the section "Apps and Tech Companies"). Weedmaps founder Justin Hartfield is a board member of National Organization for the Reform of Marijuana Laws (NORML) and of the Marijuana Policy Project. Weedmaps began a partnership with NORML in 2011.

MJInews.com is a fairly straightforward news site. Sister sites Marijuana Index and Marijuana Investor news set themselves up to be a competitor to the MJBiz Daily's *Wall Street Journal* function, even posting stock graphs on its content page. All three sites are owned by Marijuana International Corporation, or MJIC, a California cannabis venture capital firm (see Chapter 4) or by Panther Media, MJIC's partner.

Publishing expertise, not cannabis knowledge, launched these companies. Kristin Fox, one of Panther Media's founders, worked as a director for Thompson Reuters and at several other hedge fund industry publications before starting Panther Media. Partner David Friedman previously worked as a limited partner at OCA Ventures, which focused on investing in tech businesses.

Leafly started in 2010 as a database where consumers could get strain information and find out where the nearest pot dispensary was. Founders Cy Scott, Brian Wansolich, and Scott Vickers, who met each other while working as software engineers for Kelley Blue Book, served as leadership until 2014, when they left to found Headset, a cannabis business intelligence company. The new CEO, Drew Reynolds, worked as chief technology officer of mywedding.com before Leafly. Big players took an interest in Leafly early. In 2011, Privateer Holdings bought Leafly and grew it into a news site, publishing much the same material as the Cannabist.

Even when industry doesn't directly own a media outlet, the realities of media revenue catch up to journalists in the form of corporate cannabis sponsorships. Ganajanpreneur.com is sponsored by testing equipment manufacturer Steep Hill Labs, the Marijuana Business Association, and EmeraldGold, an extract equipment manufacturer.

Just as in other areas of journalism, there is some crossover between those working directly for industry and those covering it. In at least one case, industry-owned journalism has spilled over into legacy journalism. Leafly, owned by one of the most dominant corporate interests in the cannabis industry, has now contributed to one of the definitive historical accounts of cannabis in the legacy media world.

Time produced a special issue on cannabis in mid-2017, combining the reportage of several journalists for a nationwide history. The hand steering the effort was as industry-connected as it gets. Bruce Barcott produced *Time*'s cannabis section. Barcott is an established journalist in his own right, with a cannabis-centered book to his credit and a lengthy history of publication in *The New York Times*, *Rolling Stone*, and other top-flight publications.

Barcott's reputation and book paid dividends professionally. As of the *Time* publication, Barcott worked as deputy editor at Leafly, an app owned wholly by international cannabis powerhouse Privateer Holdings. Far from the only *Time* connection at Leafly, Barcott is not even the highest ranking. Leafly's director of content, Samuel Martin, worked as an editor for *Time* before joining Leafly.

Editorial teams of other industry-owned news outlets are not reporters from traditional pathways, but came into journalism through advocacy. MassRoot's senior political writer, Tom Angell, is himself the chairman of the Marijuana Majority, an advocacy nonprofit that tries to get more celebrities and public policy officials to speak out in favor of legalization. Marijuana Majority's board members and advisory board include former and current members of NORML, the Marijuana Policy Project, and Drug Policy Alliance (DPA).

Drug Policy Alliance itself has a broad and deep pool of media personalities from both journalism and entertainment as backers and supporters. *Huffington Post* founder Arianna Huffington is an honorary DPA board member, along with Walter Cronkite.

AlterNet, an alternative news organization, has received several years' worth of $20,000 to $25,000 grants from Drug Policy Alliance to "continue their analysis and outreach efforts on behalf of drug reform—including their long-standing partnership with the Drug Policy Alliance—with a wide array of writers promoting articles featuring the most up to date, relevant news and analysis on the drug war and promoting it to their very large readership through social media."[9] Drug Policy Alliance acknowledges its media savvy in tax reports as its means to keep advertising and PR costs to a minimum:

> The Drug Policy Alliance initiates and shapes local, national, and international dialogue on drug policy reform, exposing the public to our messages and generating earned media each year equivalent in impact to what would cost millions of dollars in paid advertising. Our public relations efforts support our local and national programs and projects, help smaller organizations promote their own campaigns, and take advantage of breaking news to provoke debate framed by our mission and vision.[10]

Nor is industry/media crossover only the practice of cannabis advocates. The journalist/industry connection works the other way, too, sending reporters and editors to work directly for cannabis companies. Daniel Yi, a former *LA Times* reporter, now works as press relations coordinator for MedMen. Former *Denver Post* reporter Doug Brown does the same for BDS Analytics. The Cannabist's Ricardo Baca founded a cannabis content company, Grasslands. Veteran political and business reporters across the country have been peeling out of newsrooms to work for industry.

Even the flagship media outlet of cannabis, *High Times*, is very much a part of the new money-making standard. Investment firm Oreva Capital bought 60 percent of *High Times* in June 2017 along with Damian Marley, son of Bob Marley and the owner of one of cannabis's faster-growing brands. Together, Oreva Capital and Marley now run not only editorial content but the Cannabis Cup trade shows that *High Times* created a revenue generator.

Television is also making hay, with documentary after documentary on the ongoing industry struggles, including a Netflix series starring Kathy Bates.

Apps and Tech Companies

In the cannabis world, much of the media comes from apps. Apps inhabit a special place in the cannabis industry world, where nearly every other industry division deals with burdensome regulations of some kind. Their digital nature frees them from intrastate transport restrictions and the banking problems that keep most other parts of the cannabis industry from growing to national scale.

Because of their unique positioning, apps wield some of the cannabis industry's largest influence. They advertise and promote product lines and companies, list dispensaries and growers, connect capital-raising campaigns, and make sure cannabis-centric news and content get to the public, albeit through a pro-industry lens clearly intended for legalization assistance through their various partners in the lobbying, media, and corporate worlds. Apps in particular don't escape the pattern of experience migration that happens in most of the well-heeled cannabis operations.

What Kind and How Many?

Web industry leaders opened up the entire cannabis app market to competitors by not cornering it for themselves. Neither Facebook nor Google allows cannabis-related ads. Fear of having a grandmother see cannabis consumption on Facebook, in fact, led Isaac Dietrich to found MassRoots.[11]

Like any other part of the industry, software investors still have trouble buying into the new trend on a large scale until the federal government allows it on a large scale. Considering that even small companies need apps to compete in 2017, and considering that 18- to 24-year-olds spend the most time of any age group on mobile apps,[12] at 90 hours per month, and considering that this is the age group that consumes the most cannabis, it should be no surprise that there are literally thousands of cannabis-based apps.

Apps scale the entire landscape in purpose and scope. There are apps for casual cannabis sex, apps for medical cannabis information, apps for home cannabis delivery, apps for strain cataloguing, apps for growers, apps to hook up cannabis investors with seed money, apps to connect cannabis businesses to compliance experts in state government, and apps for cannabis news. Each has its own brand and focus, but in the mobile app world there are only a handful of basic buckets, including news content like BuzzFeed or Google News, games like Angry Birds, lifestyle (food, sex, travel, music, etc.) like Spotify or Uber, social media like Instagram and Facebook, utility like calculators and weight loss plans, and productivity like Google Calendar.

Nothing any of the cannabis apps do is unique—most incorporate similar technologies or similar formats of existing apps, simply geared towards cannabis users as a new market niche. There are thousands of cannabis apps, but Weedmaps, MassRoots, Leafly, HighThere! MyDx, PotBot, Cannacopia, Doobster, Duby, GrowBuddy, Eaze, Robinhood, MarijuanaStocks, and 420Friends are among the more heavily used and highly visible.

This categorization hints at the same thing as every other industry—the eventuality that existing corporate interests will absorb it. Buyouts are common in Silicon Valley. Where a key piece of an app's geolocation technology can help Facebook fine-tune its tagging algorithms, a key piece of Eaze could theoretically do the same for Uber or another delivery-based service.

Just like every other business segment touching cannabis, though, the subject is too new, too politically complex, too sexy, and too lucrative not to attract a crowd of cannabis-specific players who now dominate in their space, as well as celebrities. Damian Marley, son of reggae icon Bob Marley, is a co-owner of Weedmaps, alongside his stake in *High Times*. Snoop Dogg invests in Eaze through his own investment firm.

Despite the tech/cannabis crossover success, apps are still not without problems. Even though many are funded by Silicon Valley venture capital, the big investors won't have anything to do with cannabis companies, nor will the nation's big stock exchanges. MassRoots has tried and failed twice to go public and was rejected from being listed on the NASDAQ stock exchange.[13] Several app stores rejected them, and initial Silicon Valley investors turned them down for being cannabis-centric.

Further, employment contracts keep companies from developing software bugs. This happened in 2016, when Weedmaps discovered that over half of the Yelp-like reviews on its site were fake.[14]

In the digital realm, apps escape some oversight and sometimes end up propping up the black market or skirting in the gray one. Weedmaps advertises unlicensed sellers.[15] Eaze MD will connect a user with a doctor who can send you a prescription after a $30 fee—called a *recommendation*.

Partnerships

Rarely do tech firms offer only one service. App leaders like Leafly, MassRoots, Eaze, and Weedmaps play several roles for their users. Youth plays a factor here as much as anything, because none of the cannabis tech companies are more than half a decade old and have not narrowed down their core focuses. Still, the federal/state gap shapes their missions. These industry leaders can offer advertising channels and product partnerships, because neither e-commerce not traditional advertising channels are available to cannabis companies. They produce news and lifestyle content that help with legalization efforts. On occasion, they also prop up the black market.

The broad range of uses in a single app depends largely on cannabis being culturally and commercially abnormal. The owners of cannabis apps typically say they expect other apps or tech companies to absorb them once pot becomes federally legalized.

Tech companies were among the first to embrace this. The cannabis app story is every inch a Silicon Valley story already, built on acquisition—Leafly and Weedmaps both were startups-turned-megaliths by huge private buyouts.

There are lots of functions and users to absorb. MassRoots, which claims to have 1 million active members as of press time,[16] is the Facebook of cannabis where users connect and share content. Like Facebook, MassRoots serves as a critical focal point for its users' cannabis-related news and entertainment content. It even has a stable of cannabis reporters of its own.

Leafly started out as a store locator. Since then it has morphed into a cannabis content panacea similar to Yelp with a heavy news addition. Strain and shop reviews are the focus, but also an e-commerce function and an entire editorial team that both aggregates cannabis news and produces original cannabis news.

Weedmaps fills the same role, designed to showcase dispensaries, strains, and in general serve as a pro-cannabis information source. Instead of in-house news, though, Weedmaps owns marijuana.com, which also aggregates and produces original content. Weedmaps also launched Weedmaps TV, which has documentaries to go along with the booster videos.

Partnerships with cannabis industry interests are the rule, not the exception. Leafly partners with Steep Hill, an Arizona-based testing brand. It also partners with VaporNation, which makes vaporizers for cannabis extracts— part of the market development Brendan Kennedy of Privateer Holdings talks about.

Weedmaps partners with cannabis retail store software, Green Bits, which also integrates its software into Leafly's system. Weedmaps also partners with MJ Freeway, one of several available seed-to-sale tracking systems, to synch up store inventory with Weedmaps retail listings.

International Capabilities

If business is more forward-thinking than the federal government, then apps are some of the most forward-thinking industry sectors, particularly where international boundaries are concerned. One of the main advantages cannabis-based apps have over other companies is location. You can't ship cannabis across states lines, but the digital sphere is global and unhindered. This puts apps and tech endeavors ahead of virtually every industry sector, which must secure some kind of approval at the very least to operate outside their own nations. Like usual, the global cannabis players are either not from the United States or end up dividing their U.S. efforts to focus on more developed markets.

Successful apps capitalize on what the cannabis industry lacks. In the case of Global Cannabis Applications Co., the cannabis industry's well-known and well-despised lack of existing patient-driven data allows for international expansion. Consider GCAC, a Canadian-based app developer with over 25 countries' worth of users. In 2016, it partnered with Alfonzo Gonzales, creator of Cann Help Deck—flashcards on medical conditions, care methods, and strains for bud tenders in licensed Canadian medical shops. Because at this early stage there is little information about patient experience with cannabis, Gonzales's cards compile 10 years' worth of patient data, which will now be made available through GCAC's Citizen Green app to users in Europe and Australia.

Others simply look to where new regulations are developing and position themselves as authorities. Just as parent company Privateer Holdings works across international lines, app Leafly steps outside U.S. borders for content and readers. Leafly's editorial content keeps in close step with global cannabis developments. It hired a senior editor to focus on Canadian issues only a month after Canada decided to legalize. Shortly after Germany introduced legalization efforts in 2017, Leafly launched a German-language version.

The relative ease of operating a cannabis app underscores the realities of cannabis in more than the international space. Apps display the way the current regulatory framework overburdens the cannabis industry with more rules than it can absorb, overcome, or work around.

There is a risk factor at play here as in all areas—namely, that tech companies have little risk compared to the people who actually produce cannabis. Risk attaches itself to businesses that "touch the plant," hence why some of the best-performing and most lucrative cannabis companies are auxiliary, not primary. Farmers and retailers, who touch the product, participate in a less lucrative and more dangerous market.

Tech companies were the earliest movers and are the least likely to be accused of drug money laundering. Tech companies have nearly nothing to do with the regulations the rest of the cannabis industry deals with on a day-to-day basis. Tech companies have deep pockets and don't need the banking access most cannabis companies can't get to. They aren't involved in the production of anything, so they aren't tied by state residency requirements.

In short, apps and tech companies play heavily in cannabis not just because of the well-documented connection between them, but also because they are, for the most part, free of the regulatory hurdles and federal/state gap that plague every other industry sector.

Secured Transport

Sometimes the federal/state gap creates dangerous situations. As a result, entirely new industry segments that wouldn't be necessary otherwise spring up. Getting a product from one place to another or storing cash is a simple business transaction for most industries, but not for cannabis. The Controlled Substances Act creates a unique security risk that turns every cannabis grower, retailer, and broker into a cash-only business model ripe for theft or robbery.

As a result, security contractors specialize in hauling and storing cash, transporting cannabis between business licensees, and standing guard.

Opportunities open for noncannabis industry expertise in this area, as in other industry sectors. Security specialists from military and law enforcement have found a new demand for their services.

In response to the initial wave of reported crimes against cannabis businesses, a former Afghanistan veteran created Blue Line Protection Group, Inc., a publicly traded Colorado armed security company specializing in marijuana business guardianship. Companies from Alaska to the Southwest have followed suit, with former law enforcement and military personnel guarding the crop and cash their U.S.-employed counterparts are still paid to seize. Whether real or perceived, some states don't allow security for threats at all. Washington State doesn't allow armed security in cannabis retail shops whatsoever.

Even then, regulations still create demand for security contractors. Most state regulations require pot shops to have video surveillance and storage and as much personal security as possible. The specifics vary, but can be extreme. In Alaska, for instance, security requirements in Marijuana Control Board regulations[17] require a heavy investment for cannabis businesses. Cultivation operations must be out of the public view with extensive video monitoring and storage capacity, along with a coterie of requirements for door and window alarms, signs pointing out restricted access areas within the facility, and commercial-grade locks.

Not only does armed transport come because of regulations, but some states like Michigan require it. In Michigan, this led to tobacco and alcohol distributors vying for placement.[18]

Cannabis security firms are as much as part of the industry as the corporate cannabis counsel, but this depends as much on appearance as reality.

A goal of international legalization is to reduce black market–born violence. Studies dispute whether crimes in Denver or other cities have risen or fallen, but none of them make any link between cannabis legalization and increased crime. The data from Drug Policy Alliance, Colorado Department of Public Safety,[19] the city of Denver,[20] and the Metropolitan State University of Denver[21] all say much the same thing: there simply isn't a connection between crime increases in the Denver area and cannabis legalization.

In other areas, cannabis legalization preceded a drop in crime. In Washington State, violent crime rates decreased by 10 percent[22] from 2011 to 2014, and Portland, Oregon, saw crime rates drop since that state's legalization.[23] A study from the Cato Institute concluded that crime was on a downhill trend anyway. According to the study, Denver property crime and violent crime rates have stayed constant after 2012, when the state legalized adult use of marijuana, and 2014, when the first shops opened. Other Colorado cities, including Fort Collins, show the same trend. In Seattle, police data showed that property and violent crime rates have been dropping for the last two decades, without any changes in pattern either immediately before or after legalization. Oregon's crime rates stayed steady after the state's 2014 legalization.[24]

The Trump administration disputes all this data, even as federal laws create a violent situation for cannabis businesses in legal states. Attorney General Jeff Sessions said in 2017[25] that legal cannabis produces violence. In fact, federal banking laws have managed to produce some violence in the states where cannabis is legalized, though the amount from the banking glitch is clearly dwarfed by the old realities of the black market.

In Colorado, security firms insist cannabis business crimes are common, including gunpoint robbery, assault, and kidnapping, though some of this is marketing from security companies as much as reality. A 2014 report[26] detailed that 317 burglaries and seven robberies were directed at medical marijuana businesses in Colorado between 2011 and 2013. Recreational cannabis, however, was not legal in Colorado until 2014, and media reports on cannabis-related robberies and burglaries in Colorado declined somewhat afterward. Across the nation and in Canada, robberies are frequent; police state they may go underreported, as cannabis business owners still have a lingering fear of local and state police, and a legitimate fear of federal police.

Fatalities involving cannabis are not uncommon. In La Plata County, Colorado, three shooting deaths have occurred over cannabis since 2014, when it became commercially available. Twice as many armed robberies occurred in the same area and the same time frame.[27]

This safety issue has a silver lining for the cannabis industry, however. Politicians who didn't support legalization in the first place find themselves arguing for looser laws simply to cool down the threats of cannabis cash buildup. In the words of Alaska Republican Sen. Lisa Murkowski, who vocally opposed Alaska's cannabis Ballot Measure 2 in 2014:

> You have a product that, not too long ago, was run underground and is still a market where there's black marketing going on, and you know for a fact, or have to assume, that after the day's sale, you're going to have cash laying around. You're just setting yourself up for security issues, for a dangerous situation that is not right.[28]

Several bills linger in Congress designed to fix the banking issue, but none have had any hearings. Until they do, cannabis businesses will continue to ease a government-bred security threat with private firms.

Data and Analytics

In 2017, the age of social media–driven Big Data, data is as important as a storefront, and firms that can provide useful statistics are in high demand. The federal/state gap makes that data hard to come by, even though industry-funded firms continue to produce statistics for a growing market.

Data firms, most of which have previous experience in government, finance, and consulting, will aggregate, analyze, and visualize employment and consumer data. Cannabis businesspeople of all stripes need this data to improve performance and capture market share—the same kind of in-depth regional market analysis, market sizing, opportunity assessment, price bench-marking analysis, product trend evaluation, predictive modeling, and scenario analysis that other industries need to stay on top of the competition.

In most other areas, data is easy to find, but cannabis business statistics are scarcer than other areas because of the Controlled Substances Act (CSA) listing. Typically, analysts can get consumer and employment data from many sources—state databases because of census operations and state records keeping, equivalent federal databases, international studies, etc. Because cannabis is an illegal substance, though, companies don't have nearly the same amount of labor, finance, or consumer data available as do other industries. International data is scarce, as is data from places like Nevada and California, which don't have enough sales history to know demographics. In this case, the law actively keeps the regulations from doing what they are supposed to do.

In the cannabis industry, 30 states each have their own unequal reporting systems and their own ways of gathering data. Across all 30 states, none of the reporting systems have the same product code. A store in Colorado might ring up a single prerolled joint and classify the transaction the same as a pack of three prerolled joints, confounding the entire concept of inventory control and the retail metrics gleaned from it.

This complicates several goals. Regulators don't know if businesses are following the regulations. Most states have limits on how much product they can sell to a single customer. On the business front, it stops entrepreneurs from being as efficient as they can. Without decent metrics, businesses don't know what their revenue and cost are like. The federal/state gap's problem-causing tendencies tend to bleed into each other.

Banking realities also put a kink in data gathering. Analysts often take consumer data from credit card companies—which for the most part don't allow cannabis purchases. The cash-only standard means data companies can't get important information like age, locality, and other data points that tell retailers where to market their goods. Still, data crunchers find ways. BDS Analytics, one of the leaders in the cannabis data space, started using point-of-sale software in 2017 to track purchasing habits, as did cannabis data firm New Frontier.

Like other industry leaders, they learned best practices in the noncannabis world. New Frontier founder Giadha DeCarcer worked for JPMorgan Chase & Co. as an industry analyst, as a government analyst following 9/11, and as the founder of two data-gathering technologies before founding New Frontier in 2014. Before founder and CEO Roy Bingham started BDS Analytics, he worked in the financial industry and invested in a data service that catered specifically to the natural foods market, which continues to brush against the cannabis marketing demographic.

In a data-driven economy and with a data-driven political world, it's little surprise that some of the most influential and well-positioned cannabis companies were founded by former financial analysts. Privateer Holdings, founded by Brendan Kennedy, Christian Groh, and Michael Blue, was built on this experience—both Kennedy and Groh formerly worked for SVB Analytics, or Silicon Valley Bank Analytics, before moving into cannabis.

Apart from cannabis-specific data firms, legacy analysts have started paying more attention to the industry as it keeps racking up higher and higher sales. Bloomberg and Cowen & Company, both Wall Street mainstays, have released basic cannabis market reports.

Plant Tracking Software and Tech Companies

Regulations create their own business sectors. Even companies that actively make business difficult for the cannabis industry can make money. Most states require what's called "seed to sale" tracking systems as a safeguard against black market activity. States award contracts for a single piece of tracking software that charts a cannabis plant all the way from a seedling to the final bud and flower or wax or shatter on the counter. Plants have little metal tags that work as cannabis barcodes for the state's inventory system. State inspectors come by for inspections to make sure a cultivator or retailer only has what the system says they should have, in keeping with the anti–black market commandment in the Cole Memo.

Predictably, companies used previous expertise to fill the new demand not only for the states to track companies, but also for cannabis cultivators to have their own systems for scheduling, labor, point-of-sale tracking, and other general business uses.

Aficionados and former black marketers pop up in most industry segments, but tech-reliant industry segments draw from other experience. Both data analytics and tracking software are rare areas of the cannabis industry that rely almost entirely on noncannabis experts. Most, if not all, of the largest players in the tracking software space have wide experience in a related field. Franwell, a Florida-based company, provides cannabis-tracking services for Alaska, Colorado, and Oregon. As a piece of equipment, the METRC gun resembles a graphing calculator glued to a Glock. This isn't a coincidence. Franwell has made these kinds of guns since 1993 for fresh food and cargo tracking.

State governments in Delaware, Hawaii, Illinois, New Mexico, New York, and Washington use BioTrackTHC, another Florida-based company that formerly tracked pharmaceuticals. MJ Freeway is in use in several countries as well as most legal states—the brainchild of Jessica Billingsley and Amy Poinsett, IT and web development experts, respectively.

The regulatory complexity and the general industry newness present problems. The regulations differ from state to state, so each system must be calibrated differently and used differently. Furthermore, at least two systems favored by legal states—METRC and BioTrackTHC—are notoriously buggy and almost universally loathed by the industry as ineffective, needless complications.[29] Washington farmers even started a petition asking for a swatch of changes to BioTrackTHC in 2016.[30]

When METRC developers had to craft an entirely new system for Alaska, entire crops' worth of information was overlooked. Cultivators had no way to enter either seeds or waste into the system and had to keep detailed physical records of seeds, waste, and growing plants in the meantime. The METRC gun read through the facility's metal walls into adjoining rooms at one point.

Other tracking systems are industry driven instead of state driven. MJ Freeway is a Denver-based tracking system that also incorporates analytics and data to point-of-sale systems. MJ Freeway partners with Weedmaps and with Marijuana Policy Project (MPP), NCIA, and California Cannabis Industry Association (CCIA—that state's NCIA chapter).

Unlike most areas, big industry is already cutting itself a slice of the tracking system pie. Before Washington decided on BioTrackTHC, computer company Xerox bid for the tracking system. In June 2016, Microsoft and KIND Financial announced a partnership to mine for government regulation compliance contracts, including seed to sale tracking using the system Agrisoft.[31]

Insurance

Insurance companies see dollar signs like everyone else. And like everyone else, full-scale acceptance will depend on federal legalization. In the meantime, cannabis insurers will have to deal with bundles of issues that make cannabis businesses uniquely expensive to insure.

As per usual, personal attitudes are far more accepting than businesses. In private life, cannabis use doesn't affect life insurance rates substantially, even if pot users were denied coverage during the height of the War on Drugs, though the heavier the user, the greater the cost increases. A 2015 survey of 150 insurance underwriters proved they care far more about nicotine use than cannabis use—almost one-third don't even classify cannabis smokers as "smokers."[32]

The business world hasn't caught up. Regulations can create a kind of spiral effect for ancillary cannabis industries—the federal/state gap causes the banking dilemma, which causes security issues from cash buildup, which creates a need for armed guards, etc.

Insurance follows this pattern. Because of the risks and the stigma attached to the industry and caused by yet other stigmas and risks, cannabis businesses often face enormous premiums for business insurance. Because of regulations, they can't make the smart fiscal move and go without it, either.

Cannabis companies didn't start out thinking about insurance, but as the industry has matured, so have the business owners. After a short intro period to commercialism, the risks started looking risky. Product, property, or general liability insurance are a fine way to cope with the federal-born risks of robbery or the standard agriculture risks of crop failure for large-scale outdoor cultivators, along with the run-of-the-mill business worries most companies want coverage for.

It doesn't all boil to risk and maturation, however. Risk is a moot point in some states where cannabis companies don't have a choice and are required to hold insurance. This trend started in Washington, where regulations force recreational cannabis licensees to carry general liability insurance of $1 million or more. Alaska follows suit, though it doesn't specify the amount of coverage like Washington does.

Most cannabis companies are glad for the insurance, but also know they wouldn't have to pay the same coverage rate as they do in the pot trade. A history of prohibition and the current federal/state gap play a role in how insurers charge. High premiums and deductibles are the rule, not the exception.

Some industry segments are shameless gougers, but insurers back up their high prices with the same kind of risk aversion that bankers do. The industry is both too young to know much about and too hairy. The cyclone of problems caused in other areas creates risk for insurers. Insurers have very little information about loss risk without the decades or centuries of information most other industries have.

But insurers are right to be cautious. Major banks won't underwrite cannabis companies, so finances are often sketchier than would normally be advisable. If there is a public health risk, it is unknown, because public health reports on cannabis are unbacked by the force of a federal approval stamp. The banking issue creates a higher risk for theft, complicating general liability and cargo insurance. Best practices for cannabis lab equipment aren't set, so equipment breakdown insurance is confounded. Workers compensation, which usually figures into an insurer's rates, is more complicated than usual.

Reluctance in the insurance industry can even spill over into personal lives, much like banking. Derek Peterson of Terra Tech had his life insurance policy abruptly canceled on him when his carrier found out his involvement in the cannabis industry.

As usual, many of the chief mainstream companies don't involve themselves, so a small cadre of experienced insurers reaps the high deductibles in the cannabis industry. Insurance being the complex industry it is, the industry leaders invariably migrated from more standard insurance markets. There was enough toe-wetting to know that the field is lucrative. Some businesses dabbled in the cannabis trade, then reconsidered. Lloyds of London, one of the largest international insurance providers, was very friendly to the emerging cannabis industry at first and underwrote many cannabis companies. The tune changed with little warning. In May 2015, company leadership sent a memo around to colleagues explaining that Lloyd's of London would discontinue all its cannabis business underwriting until the federal/state gap disappears, and with it, the risk of drawing a stiff federal penalty for federal money laundering. This left a sizable gap that other insurance brokers have filled in the meantime by smaller insurers.

Next Wave Insurance quickly filled the vacuum left by Lloyd's of London, and in fact subsumed some of the same market share. Next Wave offered everything from commercial to travel insurance before it bought MMD Insurance Services in 2014. MMD Insurance Services formerly underwrote medical cannabis business through Lloyd's of London before they left the market.

Specialized cannabis sections of insurance companies are common. Insurers like Cannarisk are divisions of larger, more established companies. BIM Agency is a construction insurance broker in Washington. When the market opened in 2014 it started the Cannarisk division to take care of the new recreational businesses.

Other companies used former experience to branch off into standalone, cannabis-specific firms. The similarly themed Cannasure had two big advantages, following the path of other industry leaders. The company acted quickly, forming in 2010 before the cannabis boom sunk in with Colorado and Washington's recreational legalization. The company also had generations of experience on its side. Before 2010, founder Patrick McManamon was yet another son of the McManamon family to accept the position of company president at McManamon Insurance. Previous industry experience guided McManamon's hand to the Beltway honeypot. Like many other ancillary cannabis industry leaders, Cannasure also backs the D.C. pot lobby as one of the sponsors of the National Cannabis Industry Association.

Compared to State Farm, of course, cannabis insurance companies are small time, but there is wiggle room. Major firms won't deal directly with cannabis, but that doesn't stop many smaller subsidiaries and general managers from doing so. A kind of trickle-up play is at work where other big international players are concerned—they may be more involved than they think. Smaller regional operations attached to big conglomerates will underwrite cannabis even if the larger industry leaders don't acknowledge it.

On its face, Allen Financial Insurance Group would seem like a perfect fit to underwrite cannabis companies for insurance. Before it started doing so, it specialized in areas that would have touched black market cannabis—entertainment and events insurance, tattoo shops insurance, and bar and liquor store insurance. But there is another connection. Allen also focuses on agribusinesses like farms and ranches. It's a requirement as the management arm of ACE Agriculture, one of the world's larger insurers and a co-defendant in the widely publicized 2004 New York investigation against insurers including AIG. ACE Agriculture is the rural insurance arm of Chubb, a multibillion-dollar international insurance firm.

Packaging and Labeling

Packaging is another area like security, where well-intentioned regulations at the state level create more opportunities for profit. This brings the industry one step closer to the kind of distinctive branding found in other consumables packaging, but can take chunks from the bottom line in the process.

Most states model cannabis packaging requirements on alcohol, but can beef them up substantially until they reach the safety features on cleaning chemicals. The packaging regulations started in Colorado, where most of the initial concerns centered around child safety.[33] Even where public attitudes are pro-cannabis, voters and lawmakers have serious concerns when it comes to the identifiability of cannabis, the ease of access to cannabis packages, and edibles. As each state legalized, it adopted variations of the same rules.

Regulations are invariably strict. Most require cannabis purchases to leave the store in resealable, childproof, opaque bags. Most require warning labels about cannabis's known effects and possible health effects. All require labeling for tetrahydrocannabinol (THC) content. In the case of edibles, recreational states like Colorado must include a suggested serving size in their packaging, ranging as low as 5 milligrams of THC to 10 milligrams. Some states require that the edibles themselves be marked off in breakable portions corresponding to the suggested serving size.

Everything from national brands to local manufacturers fill the demand for both packaging and labeling. Kush Bottles, one of the cannabis industry's publicly owned companies, has much of the market share on compliance-fulfilling packaging and claims to be the largest wholesale distributor of cannabis packaging in the nation. Kush Bottles demonstrates the kind of cross-pollination in other business segments. The company was built on a stream of acquisition. It bought Kim International Corporation, a Colorado packaging manufacturer called Dank Bottles,[34] and vape-manufacturing company CMP Wellness, which makes a line of vaporizers under the brand name MEDePEN.

It also has similar connections to venture capital. At the end of 2016, Kush Bottle elected Eric Baum to its board of directors. Baum is a founding partner of real estate investing firm Summit Capital and is affiliated with Acquis Capital and its subsidiary Solidea Capital, some of the bigger names in California pot venture capital.

Other companies developed a cannabis focus in response to consumer demand. MMC Depot, another NCIA member and supporter, is only the most recent branch of a century-old company, Denver-based Central Bag & Burlap Company.

Packaging even brings in other industry segments. Chicago's Perimeter Architects designed special boxes for Illinois's medical dispensaries.[35]

International companies are already in the game of providing compliant packaging. Alibaba, the Asian Amazon equivalent, sells bulk Chinese-made packaging bags that conform to most states' opacity standards. Like other industry segments, packaging has to morph according to lawmakers. Cannabis regulations are in a constant state of flux in every state where it is legal. Because of this, companies must pivot to satisfy new demands, often at great cost to the bottom line.

In the fall of 2016, Colorado changed its labeling rules for edibles in further response to safety concerns. Poison control received more calls of children accidentally eating cannabis than in the years before legalization, although a Colorado Department of Revenue work group clarified that the number of children who accidentally ingested cannabis was far lower than other toxins or chemicals.[36] Because edibles sales nearly doubled in Colorado from 2014 to 2015,[37] Colorado updated its rules in 2016 to make edibles manufacturers include a THC stamp on all their products. For some, this cost upwards of $100,000 in equipment upgrades.[38]

Apart from day-to-day difficulties in keeping up with regulations, the federal/state gap creeps into unexpected areas. Benign packaging still runs the risk of seizure for being drug related, which means companies can't use the economic benefits of overseas manufactures that every other U.S. company has available to them. In a way, this satisfies a kind of U.S.-made mentality in the cannabis industry, as federal officials seize cannabis-related paraphernalia that China makes more cheaply than the United States does.

In June 2017, federal officials seized 1,000 bags made by Colorado company Stashlogix.[39] The bags resemble soft lunch boxes, but are designed with pot in mind, one of several lines of odor-eliminating products designed to allow consumers to carry cannabis without anyone smelling it. Federal authorities treat this cannabis-specific carrier as a more dangerous product than most of the paraphernalia used for smoking bud and flower. Whereas bongs, vape pens, and pipes come into the country unimpeded from China and other manufacturing hubs, the cannabis-only use of the Stashlogix boxes make it suspect enough to be seized. Instead of leaving their product to be more cheaply made in China, Stashlogix will move its operations entirely to the United States—though it does plan to export as much as possible to other countries where cannabis is nationally legal.

This list is not exhaustive by any stretch. Virtually any support industry that exists in the noncannabis world has a cannabis equivalent, and the federal/state gap creates entire webs of businesses that would be unnecessary in a federally legal business—and making it a federally legal business will be more difficult than reformers hope.

CHAPTER NINE

The Future of Cannabis

The industry will only grow, and as states continue to legalize one at a time, the federal government will eventually catch up. What will it take, and what could it look like?

To a person, the leaders of the cannabis industry believe the federal government will eventually do something about cannabis. There is less of a consensus on the timeline. In interviews, leaders said anything from the next two years to a decade.

There is a range of options for how federal law could change. John Hudak at the Brookings Institution, one of the country's foremost authorities on cannabis policy, laid out the process by which the federal government might change laws—neither option looks promising in the next few years.[1] In practice, either the president or Congress would have to change the Controlled Substances Act (CSA) itself. The goal of cannabis reform is either to pull cannabis from the Controlled Substances Act altogether—deschedule it—or knock it down to a less restrictive category on the Controlled Substances Act—reschedule it.

To reschedule cannabis would not fix every issue with recreational cannabis. It would only make cannabis another scheduled drug, no easier to get for a consumer than cocaine, which is itself a Schedule II controlled substance. Reformers therefore argue in favor of descheduling cannabis, which would allow for medical use but also keep the recreational state network.

Presidential Action

The decades-old stoners' presidential call to arms, "legalize it," is not as simple an action as advocates might want—and it involves one of the federal government's most vocally anti-cannabis officials, Attorney General Jeff Sessions, as the gatekeeper.

The U.S. Drug Enforcement Agency (DEA) is an executive agency and so answers to the president. In theory, Trump could issue an executive order to halt any drug enforcement related to cannabis whatsoever. Whether this would stand up to the Republican Party's, U.S. Supreme Court's, or Congress's scrutiny is another story. Furthermore, it would only patch the wounds of the federal/state gap, not heal them. To fix the issue entirely, the administration would have to either deschedule or reschedule cannabis.

A petition to reschedule or deschedule cannabis from either the secretary of the U.S. Department of Health and Human Services or an interested outside party, including the president, would start the process. The petition's first stop would be to the attorney general, who would then kick the petition back to the Department of Health and Human Services (DHHS) for review. The U.S. Food and Drug Administration is responsible for reviewing the scientific evidence and potential for abuse. DHHS then returns the petition to the attorney general with a recommendation either to deschedule or reschedule. If there is "sufficient evidence," the attorney general starts the steps to make a new rule under the Administrative Procedures Act, during which the White House can conduct its own review.

People have tried versions of this route before, and each has failed. Filers have submitted similar petitions directly to the DEA almost since the CSA was written, including in 1972, 1995, 2002, 2009, and 2011, the last of which was filed by former Washington Gov. Christine Gregoire. The DEA has remained adamant that until the Food and Drug Administration (FDA) approves medical use of cannabis, it will continue treating it as the Schedule I drug it is.

The FDA is unlikely to change anything now of its own volition, either. There are simply not enough federally accepted studies for the FDA to make the change, stemming from the fact that it is federally illegal in the first place and difficult to secure for testing. Even opponents of cannabis legalization like Kevin Sabet are now advocating for increased access to federal testing, but as of press time none have amounted to much.

Any presidential administrative action seems almost laughable, too, considering Sessions' stances on cannabis and Trump's lack of action or speech on the issue. Neither he nor Obama were shy about wielding executive power, but even former president Barack Obama told CNN that cannabis and the CSA was a job for Congress, not for the president.[2]

Congressional Action

With presidential action looking less likely in the current term, the 2018 midterm appears a quicker route. Both California's and Canada's recreational sales will have begun by that point, and cannabis-friendly Democrats could potentially take one or both houses of the legislature.

Congress could potentially change cannabis's status by simply passing a law to direct the attorney general or the FDA to reschedule or deschedule cannabis. With Jeff Sessions as attorney general and an increasingly receptive Republican Party, it would seem a quicker route than direct federal petitions or a presidential administrative action.

Historically, Congress and especially Republicans have not welcomed chances to change cannabis laws, and there have been many. Each dies in committee before Congress can vote on it. Following the 2012 ballots of Colorado and Washington, lawmakers have stepped up attempts to pass cannabis legislation, but bills die there the same as before.

There are currently a dozen cannabis-legalizing measures in Congress. Sen. Cory Booker introduced The Compassionate Access, Research Expansion, and Respect States Act of 2015, or CARERS Act. The House version was kicked to a handful of subcommittees. Californian Republican Rep. Dana Rohrabacher introduced the Respect State Marijuana Laws Act of 2015 in April of that year, only to have it stagnate in subcommittees.

Growth of Congressional Support and Current Bills

Still, there are several cannabis-related bills in Congress as of press time, each dealing with a different part of the federal/state gap. Since 2012, members of Congress have been hurtling to support cannabis-related policies as popular and political support broadens.

Along with California Democrat Rep. Barbara Lee, who has long supported legalization efforts, reformers highlight the most important lawmakers as the co-chairs of the Congressional Cannabis Caucus, a bipartisan group formed in early 2017 to push friendly legislation. As of press time, the caucus only has four members: Reps. Don Young (R-AK), Jared Polis (D-CO), Earl Blumenauer (D-OR), and Dana Rohrabacher (R-CA). Among them, the four have introduced, co-sponsored, or signed handfuls of bills that would have opened banking access, stripped funding from federal drug enforcement, and rescheduled or descheduled cannabis.

In early 2017, Democrats Sen. Ron Wyden and Rep. Earl Blumenauer from Oregon introduced the Path to Marijuana Reform, a package of several bills aimed at removing cannabis from the Controlled Substances Act entirely or putting in protections for the banking industry. Other measures like that introduced by Sen. Cory Booker in August 2017 would deschedule cannabis. Colorado Democrat Rep. Jared Polis again introduced the Regulate Marijuana Like Alcohol Act, which would deschedule cannabis. The Path to Marijuana Reform pulls in Republican supporters. Sen. Rand Paul, R-Kentucky, is co-sponsoring Wyden's bill, and Florida Republican Rep. Carlos Curbelo is sponsoring companion legislation in the House.

When it comes to actually getting this legislation through Congress, reformers point mainly to two key committee leaders: Sen. Chuck Grassley (R-IA) and Rep. Bob Goodlatte (R-VA). Grassley and Goodlatte are chairs of the Senate and House judiciary committees. Moving cannabis reform legislation through Congress depends on whether each passes a bill from their committees. Neither has a friendly record concerning cannabis. Grassley has long been a thorn in the side of cannabis reformers—in previous conversations, National Organization for the Reform of Marijuana Laws (NORML) deputy director Paul Armentano pinpointed Grassley as one of the more problematic Congress members. He has a long history of anti-cannabis actions and is chairman of the Senate's International Narcotics Control Caucus, which is specifically created to keep the United States in compliance with international drug treaties.

In the House, Goodlatte could be friendlier than Grassley due to his home turf. Goodlatte is a district neighbor in Virginia to Rep. Tom Garrett (R-VA), who has put himself firmly in the states' rights camp where marijuana is concerned, but to date Goodlatte has opposed pro-cannabis bills.

The Senate does not have as broad a base, but still has growing levels of support for cannabis. In the Senate, notable pro-cannabis politicians include Sens. Cory Booker (D-NJ), Rand Paul (R-KY), Kirsten Gillibrand (D-NY), Jeff Merkley (D-OR), Ron Wyden (D-WA), Elizabeth Warren (D-MA), and Lisa Murkowski (R-AK).

Members of Congress can also keep the cannabis industry safe through appropriation by denying funding for the Drug Enforcement Agency's cannabis efforts in states where marijuana is legal. So far, these are the only congressional actions related to cannabis that get a vote of any kind.

Republicans and States' Rights

Representatives from the four cannabis lobbying groups are up front that they will court Republicans more in the future. They'll have to. Democrats are not the impediment, though several notable Democrats like Feinstein have opposed cannabis legalization measures. The Democratic Party itself put cannabis reform as a goal in its 2016 party platform.[3]

Congressional Republicans, whether from changing attitudes or desire for taxes or pro-business stances, are changing tune with the times. In the White House and in GOP leadership, though, drug war attitudes die hard.

Through Trump has said he supports medical cannabis and states' rights and legalizing cannabis would gain him political support from the exact segment of the public that despises him, he seemed hell-bent on stacking his Cabinet with what Armentano called a "murderer's row"[4] of stalwart anti-cannabis voices. These included New Jersey Gov. Chris Christie and former New York

Mayor Rudy Giuliani, both vocally anti-cannabis and both once on the nominee list for Trump's attorney general, where Sessions now sits.

Trump also seems to follow his attorney general's lead. A 2017 appropriations bill stripped funding from the Department of Justice to enforce cannabis laws. Sessions, in turn, wrote letters to Congress asking them to keep the funding in. In a White House statement on the bill, Trump dialed back on his states' rights platform, writing he will "treat this provision consistently with [his] constitutional responsibility to take care that the laws be faithfully executed."[5]

Trump's and Sessions' actions coincide with the attitudes of Republican leadership, if not of the entire party. Indeed, though Trump has spent his first presidential year alienating himself from the GOP,[6] cannabis policy seems one of the few things they agree on and another item showing a schism in Republican ranks.

In 2014, a similar cannabis enforcement–denying appropriations bill passed in the House of Representatives with a surprisingly bipartisan vote. Republicans from states both with and without legal cannabis voted in favor, including Reps. Dana Rohrabacher (R-CA), Don Young (R-AK), Tom McClintock (R-CA), Paul Broun (R-GA), Steve Stockman (R-TX), Barbara Lee (D-CA), and Justin Amash, (R-MI).

High-ranking Republicans, though, opposed it, including then-Majority Leader Eric Cantor (R-VA), then-Majority Whip Kevin McCarthy (R-CA), and Republican Conference Chairwoman Cathy McMorris Rodgers (R-WA) and assorted committee chairmen including Robert Goodlatte (R-VA) and Paul Ryan (R-WI).

The vote is unsurprising. Anti-cannabis attitudes are the rule in GOP leadership. McCarthy, now the GOP House Majority Leader and a notable defender of some of Trump's gaffes, has voted against several bills that would have somehow prohibited cannabis enforcement. Conference Chairman McMorris Rodgers disagrees that it is a states' rights issue and has declared publicly she wants Congress to act on cannabis.[7] Senate Majority Leader Mitch McConnell (R-KY) has stated clearly that he is against legalizing cannabis.[8] Only Ryan, the Senate Speaker of the House and Trump's biggest intraparty political opponent, said he accepts it as a states' rights issue, though he has voted against medical cannabis appropriations every time they have come up.

Even when cannabis opponents loosen their stances, it is in small steps and not towards recreational business. Grassley and ranking committee member and storied cannabis opponent Sen. Diane Feinstein (D-CA) introduced a bill that would have expanded opportunities for medical research.

Despite conservative opposition, though, reformers targeting Republicans say their values do coincide with some of the cannabis industry's and are hopeful for change.

Morgan Fox, communications manager for the Marijuana Policy Project, said he isn't particularly worried about a newly Republican-dominated Washington:

> This is a bipartisan issue, and while support has always been a little less strong with Republicans, we also have a lot of Republican support in a lot of states as well as certain people in the legislature.[9]

Fox, Armentano, Drug Policy Alliance's (DPA's) Michael Collins, and NORML's Justin Strekal believe there is more common ground showing through. Both the GOP and cannabis industry ostensibly value personal freedoms, both value robust American business and economic development, and both value the importance of states' rights. A Republican's best government is one that governs least in the name of protecting personal freedoms and fostering business and economic development.

Despite GOP leadership attitudes, more Republicans are supporting cannabis legalization. Of the dozen bills in Congress, half are sponsored, co-sponsored, or supported by Republicans like Curbelo, Young, Rohrabacher, Paul, Murkowski, and McClintock.

Republican voters are changing attitudes as well. In a Gallup poll, more than 42 percent of polled Republicans support legalizing cannabis, double what the Republican support was only 10 years ago.[10] The fact that most cannabis laws are passed by ballot is helpful in showing this support. Red states are just as likely as blue states to legalize. West Coast blue states and New England blue states Maine and Massachusetts each have recreational marijuana, along with swing state Colorado and deep red Alaska. Red states like Arizona, Florida, Montana, Arkansas, and North Dakota have legal medical cannabis, and red states like Mississippi, Missouri, North Carolina and Nebraska have decriminalized small possession.

In short, a congressional bill to reschedule or deschedule cannabis will depend on an open party rebellion against both congressional and White House leadership.

Industry Itself

Given U.S. performance with associated industries like agriculture, alcohol, and pharmaceuticals, it is reasonable to expect the cannabis industry to develop along established industry patterns and to potentially use some of the same political channels.

Some in the cannabis industry don't like to speculate too far as to what the future holds. The federal government hasn't legalized cannabis yet, and there is no telling what a potential regulatory scheme could look like. Others are more up front. Industry leaders, including Brendan Kennedy and Steven

DeAngelo, along with cannabis wealth managers and attorneys, have readily admitted in interviews that their respective companies' strategy is to set their businesses up to fold them into Big Industry when cannabis becomes federally legal.

Far from being a stoner conspiracy theory or an anti-cannabis scare tactic, there is evidence that several industries have had their eyes on commercial cannabis either as a competitor or potential product for decades. There is no way to know of an impending takeover, but the connections exist all the same.

Because cannabis has missed a century of industry development, its products could fall into several categories and several industries. Seeing how any or all could overtake the cannabis industry is no stretch—each dwarfs cannabis in terms of sales, scope, respectability, and lobbying muscle.

Opinions differ as to the effects the inevitable corporate takeover of cannabis interests would have. Small operators denounce it, whereas policy experts embrace it. John Hudak, in a paper funded by the Koch Brothers, argues that the effects of corporatization will mostly benefit the public. Both he and NORML deputy director Paul Armentano argue that the country has learned from the damaging mistakes of Big Tobacco, the phantom menace of Kevin Sabet and Project SAM. Big corporate interests, he argues, are easier to regulate and tax, bring in reputable businesspeople who are better at responding to market and government, better and cheaper and more consistent product for the consumer, and a more stable supply side[11]—simply put, American big business is good business when it comes to addressing touchy issues like cannabis.

Big Agriculture

As with other potential takeovers, most well-capitalized industry leaders, including Steve DeAngelo, say it's only a matter of time before Big Agriculture steps in. Agricultural interests are some of Washington, D.C.'s most powerful in terms of lobbying. Agribusinesses, which include crop growers, meat and dairy producers, timber companies, and food manufacturers, spent $127.5 million in lobbying in 2016.[12]

While American pot farmers are being slowly strangled by regulation and cost, international producers are beefing up at breakneck speed. Cannabis farming already has its share of dominant players, most of whom have international partnerships and subsidiaries, and most of whom are vertically integrated businesses with full product ranges. As covered in Chapter 1, these companies are already hard at work making international shipments for research, medicine, and recreation.

As of mid-2017, Canada leads the world in cannabis cultivation output. Canada's Canopy Growth is arguably the world's largest legal cannabis supplier, traded on the Toronto exchange under the stock symbol WEED. Among the company's holdings are hundreds of thousands of grow acreage. Canopy

Growth owns Tweed, the single largest cannabis greenhouse in the world. It also owns Bedrocan Canada, a partnership with the Netherlands brand of the same name focusing on standardizing crop output through genetics.

Despite the United States' laws, licensing agreements can play across borders for these farms. Some of Canada's larger growers even have U.S. partnerships. Aphria, Inc., another Canadian company, has interest in Copperstate Farms LLC, which owns a 40-acre greenhouse in Arizona.

Other Canadian producers have agreements with destination countries where cannabis is legal nationally. Aurora Cannabis will complete construction on what will be one of the world's largest cannabis production farms in the first half of 2018.[13] The project, a Dutch-designed greenhouse called Aurora Sky, will give Aurora just under 1 million square feet of cultivation space. Aurora Sky's location at the Edmonton International Airport is no coincidence—Aurora owns Pedanios, one of Germany's cannabis importers and distributors, and invests in Canna Group Limited, an Australian cannabis cultivator.

Some of the world's largest grows are owned by pharmaceutical companies. UK-based GW Pharmaceuticals is in the process of building an English facility of just under 2 million square feet of space.

Apart from Canada, international producers are cropping up in most nations where cannabis is legal. International Cannabis Corp. (ICC), a Uruguayan company, has more than 100 acres of growth and processing space. Because Uruguay's market is tightly controlled by the state, ICC is one of only two national licenses. Smaller farms are flooding into Israel pending approval from that country's Health Ministry, juniors to Israeli cannabis research magnate Tikun Olam, which itself has grow partnerships with U.S. cannabis companies in four different states.[14]

Despite the Controlled Substances Act and the assorted problems with national cannabis growth, mass-scale farms are starting to emerge in the industry alongside the McDonald's- and Starbuck's-style retail chains dotting many western states. Terra Tech, one of cannabis' better-performing American stocks and biggest companies, has been eyeing farmland in New Jersey in anticipation of the drug's potential legalization there in addition to its many dispensary licenses in Nevada.

Colorado's AmeriCann is not only one of the western states' largest growers, but has expansion goals. It started building the country's largest grow facility in Massachusetts in 2017, along with massive greenhouses in both Denver and Illinois. The combined growing capacity of all three, once the Massachusetts facility is complete, will be over half a million square feet. Like Terra Tech, AmeriCann does not stop with cultivation. The company's facilities include testing and research labs, as well as corporate offices.

The plant will likely catch up to modern agricultural practices, as well. Cannabis growth is rapidly entering the world of genetic engineering. In the United States, this is a somewhat moot point from a marketing standpoint, because cannabis companies cannot use the federal organic label. However, there is some evidence pointing to the building blocks of corporate genetic cannabis in the works in the United States, following an international trend to do the same. That being said, American agricultural conglomerates deny they have anything cooking with cannabis because it isn't legal at the federal level.

In other countries, major producers are already using genetics. But a few connections hint that the agricultural industry could be laying groundwork for the same kind of seed patent holding seen with corn, soy, and other commodity crops. Until federally legal, however, this won't be an issue.

There are already several links between U.S. Big Agricultural interests and the cannabis industry, namely through pharmaceutical companies and major cannabis legalization controller George Soros. As of 2017, some media outlets have speculated about George Soros' connections in Uruguay, where Monsanto and other genetically modified (GM) crop engineers could potentially become involved in cannabis.

Through a series of agricultural and pharmaceutical connections, genetically modified seed conglomerate Monsanto has access to some of the world's deepest pools of cannabis research. Monsanto signed an agreement in 2007 with Bayer AG, which gives it access to all the research on cannabis Bayer itself has through its relationship with GW Pharmaceuticals. GM Pharmaceuticals has the right to use HortaPharm B.V. cannabis for its research. Hortapharm, a Dutch company, is one of the only companies the DEA allows to import cannabis extracts. David Watson, the company's CEO, has created what is arguably the world's largest database of cannabis seed varieties for patent. Big Agriculture's entry into cannabis could eventually put the industry at odds with the small-scale norm of the industry's early days. For cultivators, cannabis is often seen as a new cash crop that allows entry into heavily dominated agriculture. However, the new industry may have to bear through until larger agricultural reforms push through.

Hudak argues regulations designed to help small farmers would most likely fail as they have elsewhere:

> Those attracted to the use of marijuana regulation as an industrial policy favoring small or local cannabis operators might do well to remember that heroic efforts to protect small-scale farms for other crops in the United States have performed miserably, transferring countless billions of taxpayer dollars to the wealthy without materially impeding agribusiness consolidation.[15]

Big Tobacco

The counterculturally born cannabis industry has nursed paranoia about a Big Tobacco takeover for years. Some industry leaders and anti-legalization advocates say the takeover is inevitable. Smart Approaches to Marijuana, a leading anti-legalization concern, paints the cannabis industry as Big Tobacco 2.0, worrying the past could repeat itself in terms of public health.

Big Tobacco has displayed interest in the past, but so far there are no smoking guns. Officials deny they have any interest in getting into cannabis. Still, there is some evidence that points to possible future involvement from the tobacco industry.

In several ways, cannabis would be a natural fit for Big Tobacco's market, methods, and connections. They both produce inhalable products. Market demographics are already swinging in favor of cannabis over tobacco. Whereas cannabis use and acceptance are increasing, there are fewer and fewer tobacco smokers every year. Further, cannabis and tobacco use go hand in hand with young populations.[16] Tobacco companies could easily fold in most of the manufacturing, marketing, agricultural, and distribution elements of its operations for cannabis, to say nothing of tobacco companies' lobbying power and deep experience picking through federal and state regulations.

As of publication date, tobacco companies have stayed quiet about cannabis legalization, but this does not mean they are not involved. Some of the world's leading tobacco companies started considering cannabis production the same decade it was placed on the Controlled Substances Act. In 1969, Phillip Morris began researching cannabis as both a potential product and as a potential business threat at the urging of a University of Virginia professor spearheading the company's university research collaborations.[17] According to documents gathered by Milbank Quarterly, a health policy publication, Phillip Morris applied for and received a permit from the Department of Justice to produce cannabis extract in 1970. RJ Reynolds and British American Tobacco conducted similar market studies.

These companies have connections to cannabis legalization campaigns. George Soros's wealth management fund owns half a million shares of Reynolds American, the country's second-largest tobacco company, as well as shares in Phillip Morris International.

None of the available information either advocated for or against legalization, but subsequent studies from each company looked closely at market demographics, financial impacts of legalization, and possible products.

Tobacco companies are also eyeing the exact smoking methodology cannabis manufacturers are getting into with e-cigarettes and vape pens.[18] Phillips Morris parent company Altria now owns the domains for AltriaCannabis .com and AltriaMarijuana.com.

Big Alcohol

Inhaled cannabis does not share the same relationship to alcohol as to the tobacco industry, but infused cannabis drinks are a new potential competitor.

If the federal government legalizes cannabis, small manufacturers could be snapped up by Constellation Brands, the alcohol conglomerate behind Corona beer and Svedka vodka. At the end of 2016, CEO Rob Sands admitted his company was considering a cannabis-infused product line.[19]

The $107.6 billion a year alcohol industry has had a strained relationship with cannabis. It competes in the same recreational intoxication market, which also affects the carefully constructed drunk driving and distribution laws the alcohol industry wants to stay unchanged.

Reports give a conflicting image of how cannabis affects alcohol sales. Some studies, including those by DPA, show consumers substituting alcohol for cannabis. In first-mover states Colorado, Oregon, and Washington, both domestic and craft beer underperformed in sales following legalization, according to a 2016 Cowen and Company analysis of Nielsen data. However, tax data from 2015[20] shows Colorado's collections from alcohol sales increased. Both Boston Beer and Brown-Forman, the makers of Sam Adams and Jack Daniels, respectively, have acknowledged to their investors that cannabis sales are a potential threat. Whether fears are justified is a moot point. Big Alcohol has acted as though such fears are true.

Beer companies and alcohol distribution companies have funded anti-legalization in several states, including in the failed 2016 adult use legalization initiative in Arizona. The Arizona Wine and Spirits Wholesale Association became the campaign's largest funder. Wine and Spirit Wholesalers of Massachusetts and Beer Distributors of Massachusetts did the same in their state.[21]

Alcohol groups lobby at the federal level too. Wine and Spirits Wholesalers of America implored Congress in 2016 to fund an appropriation that would pour more money into Department of Transportation studies on drugged driving and impairment standards, as well as determine tetrahydrocannabinol (THC) detection methods.[22]

There are instances where Big Alcohol supports legalization, but that support depends on getting its own take of the business. In Nevada, alcohol distributors donated towards the state's successful legalization campaign because the regulations would give liquor distributors exclusive rights to move cannabis. In California, union-backed liquor distributors are lobbying for the same thing.

The cannabis lobby itself is uncomfortable with the idea of Big Cannabis, but some leaders acknowledge it was a knee-jerk reaction. In a Vice interview, former NORML executive director Allen St. Pierre said he envisioned a "Dionysus lobby" of cannabis, tobacco, and alcohol.[23] The actions of Rob Kampia, former executive director of Marijuana Policy Project, seem to agree with St. Pierre. In 2017, Kampia admitted to soliciting campaign donations from several tobacco organizations in Michigan—and even ended up taking $50,000 in contributions from a Michigan tobacco chain.[24]

Big Pharmaceuticals

Legalization advocates have argued in favor of cannabis for medicinal uses for decades. Unfortunately for small growers and retailers, there are few medical substances that are either controlled by small businesses or allowed to be sold recreationally.

Of the cannabis industry's biggest takeover possibilities, the $333 billion[25] U.S. pharmaceutical market is most poised. It is the world's largest pharmaceutical market—three times larger than that of China, its closest competitor, and 35 percent of the world's total demand. Pharmaceutical Research and Manufacturers of America has extensive lobbying power, spending nearly $20 million in 2016,[26] and has as much knowledge navigating FDA and DEA regulations as any industry interest.

Cannabis will indeed cut into pharmaceutical market share. Several studies have linked medical cannabis to a decrease in opioid use and to a general decrease in the demand for other drugs. A University of Georgia study[27] found physicians in medical marijuana states prescribed nearly 2,000 fewer painkillers than in nonmedical states. This is a blessing to a nation in the grips of an opioid overdose epidemic, as it presents cannabis as an alternative to prescription painkillers. New Frontier analysis found that pharmaceutical sales for the top nine most-prescribed illnesses would fall by $18.5 billion in three years if cannabis were federally legalized.[28] Drug companies know this and are both trying to get the jump on medical designs and impede adult use campaigns.

Axim Biotechnologies, Inc., Nemus Bioscience, Inc., Corbus Pharmaceuticals, and Intec Pharma Ltd. are each developing cannabis-based painkillers. Arena Pharmaceuticals and Cara Therapeutics each have pre-clinical trial interest in cannabis. UK-based GW Pharmaceuticals has been in the cannabis sphere for 20 years, receiving a license to grow medical cannabis in the United Kingdom in 1998. In 2010, GW Pharmaceuticals licensed the world's first cannabis-derived drug, Sativex, which is approved widely as a multiple sclerosis treatment in the European Union but not in the United States. Currently, the company is seeking approval from the FDA for a drug called Epidiolex, an epilepsy treatment based on cannabidiol. The FDA seems willing—it gave Epidiolex Fast Track approval status in 2015. GW Pharmaceuticals has every reason to secure the market for its drugs. Though valued at $3 billion, the company has been bleeding money developing these products.

Pharmaceutical companies are some of anti-legalization efforts' biggest funders. The Community Anti-Drug Coalition of America's donors include Purdue Pharma, the manufacturer of OxyContin; Abbott Laboratories, the manufacturer of Vicodin; Alkermes, Johnson & Johnson subsidiary Janssen Pharmaceutical; and Pfizer.[29] Several academics who served as advisors to many of these companies are among the most virulent anti-legalization supporters.

In concert with alcohol, drug manufacturers were in part responsible for the failure of Arizona's 2016 adult use campaign. Insys Therapeutics gave half a million dollars to anti-legalization efforts in Arizona. Insys developed Syndros, an oral liquid used for nausea and anorexia treatment that the DEA approved in 2016.[30] Syndros is based on dronabinol, a THC synthetic the DEA lists as a Schedule II substance. Apart from Syndros, Insys's only other drug is a synthetic opioid.

United States Would Take Point on Global Conversation and Trade

Whichever industry interests subsume the current cannabis industry, if cannabis were descheduled it would inevitably become a global concern. Internationally, the United States is the top agricultural exporter, pharmaceutical developer, and consumer goods producer, and the globe is changing rapidly into a massive new marketplace.

States with legal cannabis are already used to federal regulations in that the federal/state gap forces them to overcompensate. Nevada uses Environmental Protection Agency (EPA) limits for pesticides. Every recreational state but Alaska follows the federal standard for Drug Free school zones. Cannabis testing labs are adopting international best practices and seeking the approval of the same national body that oversees blood banks. Private equity firms and industry lobbying organizations are already raising money for businesses and for their favorite politicians. States already have a loose framework of how to take tax dollars from cannabis businesspeople. Through the pores of the four lobbying organizations and their associated business lawyers, regulations are getting more and more similar across states.

Conceivably, the industry would morph into a version of what followed Prohibition. The United States would allow states to opt out, just as states allow localities to opt out from alcohol, creating a patchwork of laws and regulations that vary dramatically from region to region.

Industry Changes

Speculation runs rampant, but one thing industry leaders agree on is that their businesses will end up subsumed into the greater U.S. commercial machine if cannabis were federally legal. Many freely admit their strategy is to secure market share beforehand so they become an appealing buyout option. To the extent there is a Big Marijuana now, it is not the growers or the retailers, either.

The cannabis industry as it currently stands is a big, monetized coping mechanism. It does not thrive on cannabis itself, but on the legal troubles the federal/state gap presents. Business attorneys and cannabis media profit from the complexities of the laws; security companies and cryptocurrencies and financial solutions and private equity firms profit from the banking problem;

specialized CPAs profit from the 280E problem; apps profit from the industry's novelty and inability to advertise through traditional channels; tourism companies profit from the disparity among state laws; and so on.

Even the businesses that touch the plant profit in some ways from their biggest problem. Brick-and-mortar retail stores exist in their present form against all consumer trends because cannabis cannot be shipped. Cultivation still has no access to the economies of scale that other aspects of agriculture do.

If the federal government were to deschedule or reschedule cannabis, it is not unthinkable that most cannabis businesses will change dramatically, sell to competitors, or evaporate once their services are no longer necessary for the industry to navigate the federal/state gap. All that will be left is supply, demand, and cost efficiency—the kind of thing that the big companies currently waiting on the sidelines are prepared to handle with swift, brutal American corporate effectiveness. In a warped way, the Controlled Substances Act made the current incarnation of the cannabis industry—dominated by startup private equity firms, advocates-turned-businesspeople, lawyers, and ancillary businesses—dependent on it.

If cannabis were descheduled, the industry would be open to a cataclysmic round of creative destruction. Federal legalization would open opportunities to the average businessperson and to the most massive banking systems alike. Entrepreneurs could find loans more easily. Companies could go public and move product across state lines.

Big Cannabis would happen.

However, the world will not have to wait for federal legalization to see this happening. Price plummeting, license consolidation, and franchising are already happening, just on a statewide level that excludes most of the U.S. business community. Once that risk-averse attitude is out of the equation, whatever free market trends happening now would accelerate with the full force of the total U.S. market and become a business truly international and truly American.

Businesses are already becoming more obsolete in the face of increasing commercial normalization. Security companies, darlings the media once anointed as saviors of the cash-stacked cannabis company, are beginning to go under. Hypur, the cannabis financial company run by a former DOJ employee, had to bail out Blue Line Protection Group in 2016 after Blue Line's finances and stock prices started to plummet from their 2014 high.[31] Meanwhile, investment analysts point out that the plethora of business popping up to handle cannabis finances—like Hypur—will evaporate once the federal government acts and makes their services unnecessary.[32]

If it looks anything like most other U.S. consumer industries, the fully federalized cannabis industry will be a souped-up version of the Colorado market. Most of the market is controlled by several well-politicized, mass-producing conglomerates who offer more choice, lower price, and more convenient delivery than small-scale competitors by economies of scale and savvy legislation and regulation. In doing so, it will open smaller shards of the market for the crowd of people who want organically grown, farm-to-table, small batch nutraceuticals or those who want to grow their own.

Consumer Patterns and Preferences

Just like the suppliers will adapt to modern industry standards, consumers will fold cannabis into a network of behaviors and preferences. The consumption of cannabis will become more sophisticated, following other consumer luxuries. The alcohol industry shifted in the 2000s as alcohol consumers exploded in their knowledge. Microbrews and home brewing became fashionable, and former Bud Light drinkers started boring into the minutiae of IBU, color, mash bill, hops profile, yeast strains, etc. Whiskey drinkers stopped taking shots and started profiling the different barrels and bouquets of small-batch bourbon. Wine tasting tours, once a bourgeois affectation, became as accessible and acceptable as amusement parks.

Cannabis is taking a similar route for a variety of reasons. When the black market supplied Mexican cartel ditchweed, consumers took what they could. As choices expand, so will tastes not just in what cannabis strain but in why strains act the way they do. Smoking cannabis flower is by far the most popular method, but not the most effective. Smoked cannabis only delivers roughly 20 percent of the total contained cannabis into a user's bloodstream. As consumers become more educated, they will shift to more efficient delivery means, along with the plethora of candies and cookies and concentrates and oils increasingly available on the market.

Market statistics bear this out. Consumers tend towards value-added products rather than whole products. New Frontier data shows consumers spending more and more on vape oils and edibles than on bud and flower,[33] and the range of nonflower products continues to expand.

As use expands into the market, culture will normalize. Without fear of federal law enforcement, cannabis social clubs and cafes would likely sprout up. Employers and athletic organizations may drop their drug testing requirements. The voters of the statewide ballot initiatives would have the fully normalized version of their vote—the opportunity to consume cheap, quality product, in the comfort of their own homes or in an appropriate public venue, free from the fear of arrest, job termination, or social exclusion.

Notes

Introduction

1. "Should Legalizing Marijuana Be on the Ballot in Maryland?" *Baltimore Sun.* http://www.baltimoresun.com/news/maryland/politics/bs-md-cannabis-vote -20170130-story.html

Chapter 1

1. Anderson Economic Group. "Executive Summary: The Market for Legal Cannabis Products in the 50 United States, November 2015." *Issue.* n.p., 1969. Web. 30 Sept. 2016.

2. "Cannabis Industry Expected to Be Worth $50 Billion by 2026." *Bloomberg .com.* Bloomberg, n.d. Web. 30 Sept. 2016.

3. Smith, Aaron. "Market for Legal Pot Could Pass $20 Billion." *CNN*, Nov. 11, 2016.

4. "Silicon Valley Investors Are Starting to Warm Up to Weed." *The Cannabist.* n.p., n.d. Web. 30 Sept. 2016.

5. Borchardt, Debora. "Here Are the Top 2017 Predictions for the Marijuana Industry." *Forbes*, Dec. 26, 2016. https://www.forbes.com/sites/debraborchardt /2016/12/26/here-are-the-top-2017-predictions-for-the-marijuana-industry/#75ee 3b262ad8

6. "Cannabis." World Health Organization, last modified 2017. http://www.who .int/substance_abuse/facts/cannabis/en/

7. National Academies of Sciences, Engineering, and Medicine. 2017. *The Health Effects of Cannabis and Cannabinoids: The Current State of Evidence and Recommendations for Research.* Washington, D.C.: The National Academies Press. https://doi .org/10.17226/24625

8. Thompson, Amy E. Medical Marijuana. *JAMA.* 2015; 313(24):2508. doi:10.1001/jama.2015.6676

9. National Academies of Sciences, Engineering, and Medicine. 2017. *The Health Effects of Cannabis and Cannabinoids: The Current State of Evidence and Recommendations for Research.* Washington, D.C.: The National Academies Press. https://doi.org/10.17226/24625

10. "Recent Research on Medical Marijuana." National Organization for the Reform of Marijuana Laws, 2017. http://norml.org/component/zoo/category/recent-research-on-medical-marijuana

11. "Cannabis Research." National Center for Natural Products Research, University of Mississippi, 2017. https://pharmacy.olemiss.edu/ncnpr/research-programs/cannabis-research/

12. "The White House Drug Czar on Fighting Addictions—Including His Own." Politico Pulse Check, Soundcloud, 2016. https://soundcloud.com/politico-pulsecheck/michael-botticelli

13. Hall, Wayne. "The Mental Health Risks of Adolescent Cannabis Use." *PLoS Med* 3(2):e39. https://doi.org/10.1371/journal.pmed.0030039

14. Caulkins, Jonathan P., Kilmer, Beau., Kleiman, Mark A. R., MacCoun, Robert J., Midgette, Gregory., Oglesby, Pat., . . . Reuter, Peter H. "Considering Marijuana Legalization: Insights for Vermont and Other Jurisdictions." 2015. https://www.rand.org/pubs/research_reports/RR864.readonline.html

15. Hesson, Ted. "To Sanjay Gupta: We Need a Scientific Approach to All Drugs, Not Just Pot." *ABC News*, Aug. 8, 2013. http://abcnews.go.com/ABC_Univision/News/sanjay-gupta-scientific-approach-drugs-pot/story?id=19904395

16. "The DEA: Four Decades of Impeding and Rejecting Science." Drug Policy Alliance. https://www.drugpolicy.org/sites/default/files/DPA-MAPS_DEA_Science_Final.pdf

17. "World Drug Report." United Nations, 2016. http://www.unodc.org/doc/wdr2016/WORLD_DRUG_REPORT_2016_web.pdf

18. "Cannabis and Cannabinoids." National Cancer Institute, last modified April 7, 2017. https://www.cancer.gov/about-cancer/treatment/cam/hp/cannabis-pdq#section/_11

19. Innes, Emma. "Smoking Cannabis CAN Kill You: German researchers Identify Two Men Who Died Purely as a Result of Using the Drug." Feb. 24, 2014. http://www.dailymail.co.uk/health/article-2568326/Smoking-cannabis-CAN-kill-German-researchers-identify-two-men-died-purely-result-using-drug.html

20. "The DEA Position on Marijuana." U.S. Drug Enforcement Agency, dea.gov, 2011. https://www.dea.gov/docs/marijuana_position_2011.pdf

21. "AMA Policy: Medical Marijuana." American Medical Association, 2009. https://medicalmarijuana.procon.org/sourcefiles/AMA09policy.pdf

22. "Medical Marijuana Patient Numbers." Marijuana Policy Project, last modified 2017. https://www.mpp.org/issues/medical-marijuana/state-by-state-medical-marijuana-laws/medical-marijuana-patient-numbers/

23. McCarthy, Justin. "One in Eight U.S. Adults Say They Smoke Marijuana." Gallup, Aug. 8, 2016. http://www.gallup.com/poll/194195/adults-say-smoke-marijuana.aspx

24. "Cannabis." World Drug Report, United Nations Office on Drugs and Crime, 2016. http://www.unodc.org/wdr2016/en/cannabis.html

25. Pacula, Rosalie. L., Powell, David., Heaton, Paul., & Sevigny, Eric L. Assessing the Effects of Medical Marijuana Laws on Marijuana Use: The Devil is in the Details. *Journal of policy analysis and management : [the journal of the Association for Public Policy Analysis and Management]*. 2015; 34(1):7–31.

26. "Marijuana Use Among Youth in Colorado." Colorado Department of Public Health and Environment, 2015. https://www.colorado.gov/pacific/sites/default /files/PF_Youth_MJ-Infographic-Digital.pdf

27. "2016 Washington State Healthy Youth Survey." Washington State Department of Social and Health Services, 2016. http://www.doh.wa.gov/Portals/1 /Documents/8350/160-NonDOH-DB-MJ.pdf

28. "World Drug Report 2016." United Nations, 2016. http://www.unodc.org /wdr2016/

29. Interview, Brendan Kennedy, May 27, 2017.

30. "Global 500." Fortune, 2016. http://fortune.com/global500/exxon-mobil/

31. "World Drug Report 2016." United Nations, 2016. http://www.unodc.org /wdr2016/

32. "World Drug Report 2016." United Nations, 2016. http://www.unodc.org /wdr2016/

33. Wootliff, Raoul. "Getting Baked on Passover Not Just for Matzah, Rabbi Rules." *Times of Israel*. April 19, 2016. https://www.timesofisrael.com/getting-baked -on-passover-not-just-for-matzah-rabbi-rules/

34. Miroff, Nick. "Losing Marijuana Business, Mexican Cartels Push Heroin and Meth." *Washington Post*, Jan. 11, 2015.

35. Light, Miles, Orens, Adams, Rowberry, Jacob, & Saloga, Clinton. "The Economic Impact of Marijuana Legalization in Colorado." Marijuana Policy Group, Oct. 2016. http://www.mjpolicygroup.com/pubs/MPG%20Impact%20of%20Mar ijuana%20on%20Colorado-Final.pdf

36. James, Tom. "The Failed Promise of Legal Pot." *The Atlantic*, May 9, 2016.

37. Light, Miles, Orens, Adams, Rowberry, Jacob, & Saloga, Clinton. "The Economic Impact of Marijuana Legalization in Colorado." Marijuana Policy Group, Oct. 2016.

38. "2015 Annual Drug Report." Alaska State Troopers, 2015. http://www.dps .alaska.gov/AST/ABI/docs/SDEUreports/2015%20Annual%20Drug%20Report.pdf

Chapter 2

1. Gaming Revenue Information, Nevada Gaming Commission. http://gaming .nv.gov/index.aspx?page=149

2. Dickinson, Tom. "Obama's War on Pot." *Rolling Stone*. Feb. 12, 2012. http:// www.rollingstone.com/politics/news/obamas-war-on-pot-20120216

3. "Memorandum for Selected United State Attorneys on Investigations and Prosecutions in States Authorizing the Medical Use of Marijuana." United States

Department of Justice. Oct. 19, 2009. https://www.justice.gov/archives/opa/blog/mem
orandum-selected-united-state-attorneys-investigations-and-prosecutions-states

4. Riggs, Mike. "Obama's War on Pot." *The Nation*. Oct. 30, 2013. https://www
.thenation.com/article/obamas-war-pot/

5. Cole, James. "Guidance Regarding Marijuana Enforcement." Aug. 29, 2013.
https://www.justice.gov/iso/opa/resources/3052013829132756857467.pdf

6. Ibid.

7. Johnson, Jenna. "Trump Softens Position on Legal Marijuana." *The Washington Post*. Oct. 29, 2015. https://www.washingtonpost.com/news/post-politics
/wp/2015/10/29/trump-wants-marijuana-legalization-decided-at-the-state-level
/?utm_term=.53a84887ae4c&wpisrc=nl_daily202&wpmm=1

8. Statement by President Donald J. Trump on Signing H.R. 244 into Law. The
White House. May 5, 2017. https://www.whitehouse.gov/the-press-office/2017/05
/05/statement-president-donald-j-trump-signing-hr-244-law

9. Wagner, John, & Zapotsky, Matt. "Spicer: Feds Could Step Up Anti-Pot
Enforcement in States Where Recreation Marijuana Is Legal." *The Washington Post*.
Feb. 23, 2017. https://www.washingtonpost.com/news/post-politics/wp/2017/02
/23/spicer-feds-could-step-up-anti-pot-enforcement-in-states-where-recreational
-marijuana-is-legal/?utm_term=.f9dd9a0fb540

10. Sen. Jeff Sessions Clip: "Good People Don't Smoke Marijuana." Caucus on
International Narcotics Control. https://www.washingtonpost.com/video/c/embed
/bab3b09a-add8-11e6-8f19-21a1c65d2043

11. "Attorney General Jeff Sessions Delivers Remarks on Efforts to Combat Violent Crime and Restore Public Safety Before Federal, State and Local Law
Enforcement." U.S. Department of Justice. March 15, 2017. https://www.justice
.gov/opa/speech/attorney-general-jeff-sessions-delivers-remarks-efforts-combat
-violent-crime-and-restore

12. Moreno, Ivan. "Sessions: Drug Overdoses 'The Top Lethal Issue' in the U.S."
Associated Press. Aug. 29, 2017. http://www.pbs.org/newshour/rundown/sessions
-drug-overdoses-top-lethal-issue-u-s/

13. "Yahoo News/Marist Poll: Weed and the American Family." Marist College Institute for Public Opinion. April 17, 2017. http://maristpoll.marist.edu/wp
-content/misc/Yahoo%20News/20170417_Summary%20Yahoo%20News
-Marist%20Poll_Weed%20and%20The%20American%20Family.pdf

14. "Alcohol Facts and Statistics." National Institute on Alcohol Abuse and
Alcoholism. Updated Feb. 2017. https://www.niaaa.nih.gov/alcohol-facts-and
-statistics

15. Krouse, William J. "Gun Control Legislation." Congressional Research Service. Nov. 14, 2012. https://fas.org/sgp/crs/misc/RL32842.pdf

16. Herbert, Arthur. "Open Letter to All Federal Firearms Licensees." Bureau
of Alcohol, Tobacco, Firearms and Explosives. Sept. 21, 2011. https://www.atf.gov
/file/60211/download

17. U.S. Court of Appeals for the Ninth Circuit, No. 14-15700 D.C.
No. 2:11-CV-01679-GMN-PAL. https://cdn.ca9.uscourts.gov/datastore/opinions
/2016/08/31/14-15700.pdf

18. "Access to Clinical Programs for Veterans Participating in State-Approved Marijuana Programs." Veterans' Health Administration. Jan. 31, 2011. https://www.va.gov/vhapublications/ViewPublication.asp?pub_ID=2362

19. Anzuoni, Mario. "War on Weed: Veterans' Access to Medical Marijuana Blocked by Republicans." *Reuters.* July 29, 2017. https://www.rt.com/usa/397958-veterans-medical-marijuana-amendment-rep/

20. "Data, Analysis, and Documentation." Office of Personnel Management. Updated 2014. https://www.opm.gov/policy-data-oversight/data-analysis-documentation/federal-employment-reports/historical-tables/executive-branch-civilian-employment-since-1940/

21. Archuleta, Katherine. Memo. United States Office of Personnel Management. May 26, 2015. https://www.chcoc.gov/content/federal-laws-and-policies-prohibiting-marijuana-use

22. Memorandum for Selected United States Attorneys. U.S. Department of Justice, Office of the Deputy Attorney General. Oct. 19, 2009. https://www.justice.gov/sites/default/files/opa/legacy/2009/10/19/medical-marijuana.pdf

23. Bohrer, Becky, & Thiessen, Mark. "Alaska Marijuana Board Rejects Onsite Use at Retail Shops." Associated Press. Feb. 2, 2017. http://www.thecannabist.co/2017/02/02/alaska-marijuana-onsite-consumption/72905/

24. "Colorado Lawmakers Wash Hands of Regulating Pot Clubs." Associated Press. April 13, 2017. http://www.thecannabist.co/2017/04/13/colorado-pot-clubs-legislation/77304/

25. "Cannabis Consumption Licenses." Business Licensing Center. https://www.denvergov.org/content/denvergov/en/denver-business-licensing-center/marijuana-licenses/social-consumption-advisory-committee.html

26. McVey, Eli. "Chart of the Week: 100,000+ Workers Employed by Marijuana Companies." *Marijuana Business Daily.* July 25, 2016. https://mjbizdaily.com/chart-week-100000-workers-employed-cannabis-companies/

27. Jarrett, Tracy. "Six Reasons African Americans Aren't Breaking into the Cannabis Industry." *NBC News.* April 19, 2015. https://www.nbcnews.com/news/nbcblk/6-reasons-african-americans-cant-break-cannabis-industry-n344486

28 Leff, Lisa. "California Localities Rush to Issue Bans on Growing Marijuana." Associated Press. Jan. 25, 2016. http://www.thecannabist.co/2016/01/25/california-marijuana-growing-laws-local-bans/47103

29. "Record of Cities/Counties Prohibiting Licensed Recreational Marijuana Facilities." Oregon Liquor Control Commission. http://www.oregon.gov/olcc/marijuana/Documents/Cities_Counties_RMJOptOut.pdf

30. Summers, D. J. "Marijuana Board Chair Gathers Signatures for Borough Ban." *Alaska Journal of Commerce.* July 27, 2016. http://www.alaskajournal.com/2016-07-27/marijuana-board-chair-gathers-signatures-borough-ban

31. Rothenberg, Jill. "Welcome to Pueblo, Colorado: The 'Pot Rush' Town for the Marijuana Industry." *The Guardian.* Oct. 19, 2015. https://www.theguardian.com/society/2015/oct/19/pueblo-colorado-legal-marijuana-industry-migration

32. "Memorandum. Policy Statement Regarding Marijuana Issues in Indian Country." U.S. Department of Justice. Oct. 28, 2014. https://www.justice.gov/sites

/default/files/tribal/pages/attachments/2014/12/11/policystatementregardingma rijuanaissuesinindiancountry2.pdf

33. "Frequently Asked Questions." Bureau of Indian Affairs. https://www.bia .gov/frequently-asked-questions

34. "Political Map." National Indian Cannabis Commission. http://niccunited .org/political-map/

35. Nord, James. "S.D. Sioux Tribe's Cannabis Resort Consultant Faces Trial on Drug Charges." Associated Press. May 18, 2017. http://www.thecannabist.co/2017 /05/18/south-dakota-cannabis-native-american-resort-trial/79726/

36. Armitage, Lynn. "Pot Raid Has Pit River Tribe Fuming." *Indian Country Today.* July 17, 2015. https://indiancountrymedianetwork.com/news/politics/pot -raid-has-pit-river-tribe-fuming-rips-bia/

37. "Marijuana Manufacturing Operation on Moapa Indian Reservation." U.S. Department of Justice. Feb. 23, 2017. https://assets.documentcloud.org/documents /3476575/NV-US-Attorney.pdf

38. Adi News Services. "Navajo Nation Council Committee Approves Production of Cannabis, Hemp." *Arizona Daily Independent.* July 1, 2017. https://arizona dailyindependent.com/2017/07/01/navajo-nation-council-committee-approves -economic-development-through-production-of-cannabis-hemp/

39. Adi News Services. "Navajo Nation Oppose Marijuana Legalization." *Arizona Daily Independent.* April 6, 2015. https://arizonadailyindependent.com/2015 /04/06/navajo-nation-reaffirms-opposition-to-marijuana-legalization/

40. Selsky, Andrew. "Busts in the US Highlight Pot Smuggling from Legal States." Associated Press. Aug. 14, 2017. https://www.usnews.com/news/best-states /texas/articles/2017-08-14/busts-in-the-us-highlight-pot-smuggling-from-legal-states

41. Nelson, Steven. "Drug Mail Drops After Pot Stores Open." *U.S. News & World Report.* March 14, 2016. https://www.usnews.com/news/articles/2016-03 -14/drug-mail-drops-after-pot-stores-open

42. Blevins, Jason. "Only 4% of Colorado Tourists Came for the Legal Weed in 2015, Survey Says." *The Denver Post.* July 20, 2016. http://www.denverpost.com /2016/07/20/colorado-tourism-legal-marijuana-2015/

43. Pickton, Todd, Lewandowski, Brian, Orens, Adam, & Light, Miles. "Market Size and Demand for Marijuana in Colorado." Colorado Department of Revenue. 2014. https://www.colorado.gov/pacific/sites/default/files/Market%20Size %20and%20Demand%20Study,%20July%209,%202014%5B1%5D.pdf

44. Coughlin-Bogue, Tobias. "Why Seattle Is Failing at Pot Tourism." *The Stranger.* June 22, 2016. http://www.thestranger.com/news/2016/06/22/24238128 /why-seattle-is-failing-at-pot-tourism

Chapter 3

1. White, Liz Essley. "The Pot Industry Is Taking Over Pro-Pot Efforts." Slate. Aug. 12, 2016. http://www.slate.com/articles/news_and_politics/politics/2016/08 /big_weed_is_throwing_some_of_its_new_money_into_politics.html

2. The DEA Position on Marijuana. U.S. Department of Justice. April 2013. https://www.dea.gov/docs/marijuana_position_2011.pdf

3. Swift, Art. "Support for Legal Marijuana Use Up to 60% in U.S." Gallup. Oct. 19, 2016. http://www.gallup.com/poll/196550/support-legal-marijuana.aspx

4. Chapters. National Organization for the Reform of Marijuana Laws. http://norml.org/chapters

5. http://norml.org/chapters?map=all

6. National Organization for the Reform of Marijuana Laws Political Action Committee. Federal Election Commission. 2017. http://docquery.fec.gov/cgi-bin/fecimg/?C00383604

7. http://docquery.fec.gov/cgi-bin/fecimg/?C00383604

8. Ibid.

9. Drug Policy Alliance. Open Secrets. 2016. https://www.opensecrets.org/orgs/summary.php?id=D000033289&cycle=2016

10. https://www.opensecrets.org/orgs/totals.php?id=D000033289&cycle=2016

11. https://www.opensecrets.org/orgs/summary.php?id=D000033289&cycle=2016

12. Ibid.

13. Drug Policy Alliance. Tax Form 990. 2015. http://www.drugpolicy.org/sites/default/files/FYE_2016-2015_DRUG_POLICY_ALLIANCE_FORM_990.pdf

14. Sorvino, Chloe. "An Inside Look at the Biggest Drug Reformer in the Country: George Soros." *Forbes.* Oct. 2, 2014. https://www.forbes.com/sites/chloesorvino/2014/10/02/an-inside-look-at-the-biggest-drug-reformer-in-the-country-george-soros/#11007e5a1e29

15. Hickley, Walter. "The Five People Who Are Leading the Fight to Legalize Marijuana." *Business Insider.* April 15, 2013. http://www.businessinsider.com/legal-marijuana-norml-dpa-weedmaps-2013-4

16. U.S. Programs, Drug Policy Alliance. Open Society Foundations. 2012. https://www.opensocietyfoundations.org/about/programs/us-programs/grantees/drug-policy-alliance-0

17. O'Connor Davies Accountants and Advisors. Drug Policy Alliance Financial Statements. May 31, 2016. http://www.drugpolicy.org/sites/default/files/Drug%20Policy%20Alliance%202016%20Audited%20Statements.pdf

18. http://www.drugpolicy.org/sites/default/files/FYE_2016-2015_DRUG_POLICY_ALLIANCE_FORM_990.pdf

19. Bonnie, Joe. "U.S. MA: Column: You Down with MPP?" Media Awareness Project. Feb. 11, 2003. http://www.mapinc.org/drugnews/v03/n237/a06.html?127

20. Marijuana Policy Project. Open Secrets. 2016. https://www.opensecrets.org/orgs/totals.php?id=D000027382&cycle=2016

21. Marijuana Policy Project. Open Secrets. 2016. https://www.opensecrets.org/pacs/lookup2.php?cycle=2016&strID=C00389882

22. Mission and Values. National Cannabis Industry Association. 2017. https://thecannabisindustry.org/mission-and-values/

23. Ibid.

24. National Cannabis Industry Association. Propublica. 2016. https://projects .propublica.org/nonprofits/organizations/273484449

25. Corasaniti, Nick. "Marijuana Industry Gears Up After N.J. Candidate Backs Legislation." *The New York Times*. July 7, 2017. https://www.nytimes.com/2017/07 /07/nyregion/new-jersey-marijuana-industry.html

26. NCV Newswire. "Doug Francis Succeeds Justin Hartfield as Weedmaps CEO." New Cannabis Ventures. Feb. 23, 2016. https://www.newcannabisventures .com/doug-francis-succeeds-justin-hartfield-as-weedmaps-ceo/

27. Israel Hayom staff. "Watch: Israel Hayom Inside on Cannabis Legalization in Israel." Israel Hayom. Feb. 11, 2014. http://www.israelhayom.com/site/newsletter _article.php?id=15411

28. Kennedy, Patrick. Open Secrets. 2016. https://www.opensecrets.org /overview/topindivs.php

29. Kennedy, Patrick. Open Secrets. 2016. https://www.opensecrets.org /politicians/industries.php?cycle=Career&cid=N00000360&type=I

30. Armstrong, David. "Mystery Solved: Addiction Medicine Maker Is Secret Funder of Kennedy-Gingrich Group." The Boston Globe. March 3, 2017. https:// www.bostonglobe.com/business/2017/03/05/backer-opioid-treatment-group -drug-maker/MygT6BfgVdlUTTTGdC4TlL/story.html

31. Kennedy, Patrick and Gingrich, Newt. "Congress Should Ignore CBO and Increase Access to Opioid Addiction Medication." The Hill. July 7, 2016. http:// thehill.com/blogs/pundits-blog/healthcare/286796-congress-should-ignore-the -cbo-and-increase-access-to-recovery

32. Warner, Joel. "Kevin Sabet Is the Marijuana Movement's Biggest Threat, But Can He Really Stop 'Big Pot'?" *IBTimes*. Dec. 9, 2015. http://www.ibtimes.com/kevin -sabet-marijuana-movements-biggest-threat-can-he-really-stop-big-pot-2214390

33. Sabet, Kevin. "The ICSDP Published Misleading Report on Marijuana." Florida Drug Policy Institute. Aug. 2015. https://com-psychiatry-dpi.sites.medinfo .ufl.edu/files/2015/08/UF-RESPONSE-TO-ICSDP.pdf

34. The Science. Smart Approaches to Marijuana. https://learnaboutsam.org /science/

35. McGreevy, Patrick. "Anti-Pot Group Faces Campaign Finance Violations from Its Work Opposing Marijuana Legalization in California." *Los Angeles Times*. April 10, 2017. http://www.latimes.com/politics/essential/la-pol-ca-essential-politics -updates-national-anti-pot-group-faces-fines-for-1491849434-htmlstory.html

36. Californians for Drug Free Youth. IRS tax form 990. 2013. http://990s.foun dationcenter.org/990_pdf_archive/770/770202396/770202396_201312_990.pdf

37. Sullum, Jacob. "Jumping Ahead of Evidence, Prohibitionists Claim Legalizing Pot Boosts Underage Consumption." *Forbes*. April 7, 2016. https://www.forbes .com/sites/jacobsullum/2016/04/07/jumping-ahead-of-evidence-prohibitionists -claim-legalizing-pot-boosts-underage-consumption/#1c26a40e239c

38. Chappell, Bill. "Side Effect of Legal Pot: Police Budgets Take a Hit." *NPR*. Jan. 13, 2014. http://www.npr.org/sections/thetwo-way/2014/01/10/261476346 /side-effect-of-legal-pot-police-budgets-take-a-hit

39. Fang, Lee. "Police and Prison Guard Groups Fight Marijuana Legalization in California." The Intercept. May 18, 2016. https://theintercept.com/2016/05/18/ca-marijuana-measure/

40. Interview, Larry Horowitz.

41. Interview, Ryan Hurley.

42. Rule 1.2: Scope of Representation & Allocation of Authority Between Client & Lawyer. American Bar Association. 2017. https://www.americanbar.org/groups/professional_responsibility/publications/model_rules_of_professional_conduct/rule_1_2_scope_of_representation_allocation_of_authority_between_client_lawyer.html

43. Ethics Opinions. State Bar of Arizona. 2017. http://www.azbar.org/Ethics/EthicsOpinions/ViewEthicsOpinion?id=710

44. Colo. Bar Assn Ethics Comm., Formal Opinion 125—The Extent to Which Lawyers May Represent Clients Regarding Marijuana—Related Activities, 42 COLO. LAW. NO. 12, 19 (adopted Oct. 21, 2013). http://www.cba.cobar.org/tcl/tcl_articles.cfm?articleid=8370

45. 1 Colo. Rules of Professional Conduct, Rule 1.2 of Representation and Allocation of Authority Between Client and Lawyer, Amended and Adopted by the Court, En Banc (March 24, 2014). https://www.courts.state.co.us/userfiles/file/court_Probation/Supreme_Court/Rule_Changes/2014/2014%2805%29%20redlined.pdf

46. Davis, Christopher. "The Ethics of Cannabis Representation in California." National Cannabis Bar Association. April 10, 2016. http://www.canbar.org/newsworthy/2016/3/17/the-ethics-of-cannabis-representation-in-california

47. Interview, CBS, May 22, 2017.

48. Report of the Task Force of the Independent Lawyer. "Lawyers Doing Business with Their Clients: Identifying and Avoiding Legal and Ethical Dangers." American Bar Association. 2011. https://www.americanbar.org/content/dam/aba/publications/litigation_news/lawyers-avoid-ethical-dangers.authcheckdam.pdf

49. Jaywork, Casey. "A Pioneer Square Startup Is Using Bitcoin to Let People Buy Pot with a Credit Card." *Seattle Weekly.* March 22, 2017. http://www.seattleweekly.com/news/you-can-now-buy-pot-with-a-credit-card-in-washington-state-because-technically-youre-not/

50. Reuters and Israel Hayom staff. "Israel Works to Lead $50 Billion Medical Marijuana Market." Israel Hayom. March 24, 2017. http://www.israelhayom.com/site/newsletter_article.php?id=41297

Chapter 4

1. Swann, Kristen. "Eagle River Couple Has High Hopes for Anchorage Pot Business." *Chugiak-Eagle River Star.* April 27, 2017. http://www.alaskastar.com/2017-04-19/eagle-river-couple-has-high-hopes-anchorage-pot-business#.Wa84x8iGNPY

2. Gelles, David. "A Real Estate Boom, Powered by Pot." *The New York Times.* April 1, 2017. https://www.nytimes.com/2017/04/01/business/a-real-estate-boom -powered-by-pot.html?mcubz=0

3. Mosendz, Polly, & Clark, Patrick. "Weed Votes Are Already Boosting Ware-house Rents." *Bloomberg.* Nov. 30, 2016. https://www.bloomberg.com/news /articles/2016-11-30/weed-votes-are-already-boosting-warehouse-rents

4. Rusch, Emilie. "Marijuana Industry Drives Denver Metro Area's Real Estate Recovery." *The Denver Post.* Oct. 19, 2015. http://www.denverpost.com/2015/10 /19/marijuana-industry-drives-denver-metro-areas-real-estate-recovery/

5. Martin, Jonathan. "Opening a Legal Marijuana Store in Seattle? Prepare to Get Gouged." *The Seattle Times.* Feb. 25, 2013. http://www.seattletimes.com /opinion/opening-a-legal-marijuana-store-in-seattle-prepare-to-get-gouged/

6. Summers, D. J. "Marijuana Industry Faces Steep Lease Rates in Tight Mar-ket." *Alaska Journal of Commerce.* Feb. 17, 2016. http://www.alaskajournal.com /2016-02-17/marijuana-industry-faces-steep-lease-rates-tight-market

7. Bush, Evan. "Legal Pot by the Numbers: 99 Stores Licensed, $64 Million in Sales." *The Seattle Times.* Dec. 31, 2014. http://blogs.seattletimes.com/pot/2014 /12/31/legal-pot-by-the-numbers-99-stores-licensed-64-million-in-sales/

8. Summers, D. J. "Cultivation Licenses Dominate Marijuana Applications." *Alaska Journal of Commerce.* March 21, 2016. http://www.alaskajournal.com/2016 -03-21/cultivation-licenses-dominate-marijuana-applications

9. "Small and Mid-Sized Farmer Resources." U.S. Department of Agriculture. 2017. https://www.usda.gov/topics/farming/resources-small-and-mid-sized -farmers

10. "Crop Insurance." Report to Congressional Requesters. U.S. Government Accountability Office. March 2015. https://www.gao.gov/assets/670/669062.pdf

11. Carah, Jennifer, Howard, Jeanette, Thompson, Sally, Gianotti, Anne, Bauer, Scott, Carlson, Stephanie, . . . Hulette, Lisa. "High Time for Conservation: Add-ing the Environment to the Debate on Marijuana Liberalization." *BioScience,* 2015; 65(8):822–829. https://academic.oup.com/bioscience/article-lookup/doi/10 .1093/biosci/biv083

12. Gabriel, Mourad W., Woods, Leslie W., Poppenga, Robert, Sweitzer, Rick A., Thompson, Craig, Matthews, Stefan M., . . . Clifford, Deana. "Anticoagulant Rodenticides on Our Public and Community Lands: Spatial Distribution of Expo-sure and Poisoning of a Rare Forest Carnivore." *PLoS ONE* 2012; 7(7):e40163. https://doi.org/10.1371/journal.pone.0040163

13. Butsic, Van, & Brenner, Jacob. "Cannabis (*Cannabis sativa or C. indica*) Agri-culture and the Environment: A Systematic, Spatially-Explicit Survey and Poten-tial Impacts." *Environmental Research Letters.* April 21, 2016. http://iopscience.iop .org/article/10.1088/1748-9326/11/4/044023/meta;jsessionid=71328E25E39F5 859C4F6C61FA425C4BD.c1.iopscience.cld.iop.org

14. Mills, Evan. "The Carbon Footprint of Indoor Cannabis Production." http:// www.sciencedirect.com/science/article/pii/S0301421512002285?via%3Dihub

15. Schroyer, John. "Industry Snapshot: Testing Labs." *Marijuana Business Daily.* Jan. 2016. https://mjbizmagazine.com/industry-snapshot-testing-labs/

16. "Licensees—Marijuana Enforcement Division." Colorado Department of Revenue. 2017. https://www.colorado.gov/pacific/enforcement/licensees-marijuana -enforcement-division

17. Interview, Robert Martin, June 7, 2017.

18. License renewals. Alaska Marijuana Control Board. 2017. https://www .commerce.alaska.gov/web/Portals/9/pub/MCB/MJRenewals/LicensesRenewa l2017.pdf

19. Miyoga, David, & Baca, Ricardo. "Denver Issues Two More Recalls of Pot Containing Unapproved Pesticides." *The Denver Post.* Oct. 2, 2016. http://www .denverpost.com/2015/09/18/denver-issues-two-more-recalls-of-pot-containing -unapproved-pesticides/

20. "Pesticide List." Nevada Department of Agriculture. Jan. 9, 2017. http://agri .nv.gov/uploadedFiles/agrinvgov/Content/Plant/Environmental_Compliance /MME%20Pesticide%20list-%2001-09-2017%20Updated.pdf

21. "Bureau of Marijuana Control Proposed Text of Regulations." State of California. 2016. http://bmcr.ca.gov/laws_regs/mcrsa_lab_ptor.pdf

22. Interview, Robert Martin, June 7, 2017.

23. Baca, Ricardo. "Tests Show THC Content in Marijuana Edibles Is Inconsistent." *The Denver Post.* March 8, 2014. http://www.denverpost.com/2014/03/08 /tests-show-thc-content-in-marijuana-edibles-is-inconsistent/

24. NCV Newswire. "More Washington Cannabis Testing Lab Cheating Alleged." New Cannabis Ventures. April 30, 2017. https://www.newcannabisven tures.com/more-washington-cannabis-testing-lab-cheating-alleged/

25. Washington State Liquor Control Board. April 2013. http://lcb.wa.gov /publications/Marijuana/I-502/I-502—BOTEC%20Summary%20II—4-18-13 .pdf

26. "Licensees—Marijuana Enforcement Division." Colorado Department of Revenue. 2017. https://www.colorado.gov/pacific/enforcement/licensees-marij uana-enforcement-division

27. Sullum, Jacob. "The Lurking Law that Turns Marijuana Ads into Felonies." *Forbes.* March 31, 206. https://www.forbes.com/sites/jacobsullum/2016/03/31/the -lurking-law-that-turns-marijuana-ads-into-felonies/#7ab756054a58

28. McGreevy, Patrick. "California Initiative Draws Fire for Opening the Door to TV Ads that Promote Pot Smoking." *Los Angeles Times.* July 31, 2016. http:// www.latimes.com/politics/la-pol-ca-california-pot-ads-20160731-snap-story .html

29. *Green Solution Retail v. United States,* No. 16-1281 (10th Cir. 2017) http:// law.justia.com/cases/federal/appellate-courts/ca10/16-1281/16-1281-2017-05-02 .html

30. Flores v. LivWell, Inc. District Court, Denver County, Case no. 2015-CV-33528. https://mjbizdaily.com/wp-content/uploads/2015/10/2015-10-05-04-49 -31-Flores-v.-LiveWell-Complaint-FINAL.pdf

31. Summers, D. J. "At Long Last Alaskans Can Buy Legal Weed." *Alaska Journal of Commerce.* Oct. 29, 2016. http://www.alaskajournal.com/2016-10-29/long -last-alaskans-can-buy-legal-marijuana#.Wa89psiGNPY

32. Borchardt, Debra. "Marijuana Prices Fall in 2016 as Growers Flood the Market." *Forbes.* Jan. 31, 2017. https://www.forbes.com/sites/debraborchardt/2017/01/31/marijuana-prices-fall-in-2016-as-growers-flood-the-market-with-pot/#7228e9f12f7f;

33. Miyoga, David, & Baca, Ricardo. "Special Report: The Behemoths of Denver's Marijuana Industry." *The Cannabist.* May 8, 2016. http://www.thecannabist.co/2016/05/08/denver-top-marijuana-business-owners/53816/

34. Grieog, Tina. "Inside Colorado's Flourishing Black Market for Pot." *The Washington Post.* July 30, 2014. https://www.washingtonpost.com/news/storyline/wp/2014/07/30/inside-colorados-flourishing-segregated-black-market-for-pot/?utm_term=.c5753a62aa99

Chapter 5

1. Olson, Becky. "Chart of the Week: 60% of Cannabis Companies Don't Have Bank Accounts." *Marijuana Business Daily.* n.p., 2015. Web. 30 Sept. 2016.

2. Ibid.

3. Merkley, Jeff. "Bipartisan Group of Senators Presses Federal Regulator for Clear Guidance on Banking Services for Vendors Working with Legal Marijuana Businesses." Dec. 14, 2016. https://www.merkley.senate.gov/news/press-releases/bipartisan-group-of-senators-presses-federal-regulator-for-clear-guidance-on-banking-services-for-vendors-working-with-legal-marijuana-businesses

4. Migoya, David. "Judge Tosses Denver Cannabis Credit Union's Suit for Federal Approval." *The Denver Post.* n.p., 2016. Web. 30 Sept. 2016.

5. http://www.denverpost.com/2016/01/05/judge-tosses-denver-marijuana-credit-unions-suit-for-federal-approval/

6. U.S. Department of the Treasury Financial Crimes Enforcement Network. BSA Expectations Regarding Marijuana-Related Businesses. Feb. 14, 2014. https://www.fincen.gov/resources/statutes-regulations/guidance/bsa-expectations-regarding-marijuana-related-businesses

7. Sidel, Robin. "Card Conundrum Develops in Colorado Over Cannabis Sales." *Wall Street Journal.* n.p. 2014. Web. 28 Sept. 2016

8. "Visa for Pot: The Credit Card Smokescreen." *FOX31 Denver.* n.p., 2015. Web. 30 Sept. 2016.

9. Walsh, Chris. "Chart of the Week: Huge Spike in Number of Banks, Credit Unions Serving Cannabis Companies." *Cannabis Business Daily.* n.p., 2016. Web. 30 Sept. 2016.

10. "History of Anti-Money Laundering Laws." *United States Department of the Treasury Financial Crimes Enforcement Network.* n.p., n.d. Web. 30 Sept. 2016.

11. Blake, Andrew. "Cannabis Sales in Washington State Top $1 Billion: Report." *The Washington Times.* n.d. Web. 30 Sept. 2016.

12. Colorado. Legislature. "Concerning the Provisions of Financial Services to Licenses Cannabis Businesses. HB 1398. 2013–2014." Colorado Legislature. Web. Sept. 22, 2016.

13. "Oregon. Legislature. Relating to Cannabis; and Declaring an Emergency. (HB 4094)." 2016. Reg. Sess. *Oregon State Legislature*. Web. Sept. 23, 2016.

14. Sliwoski, Vince. "Canna Law Blog." *Canna Law Blog*. n.p., n.d. Web. 30 Sept. 2016.

15. "Home." *RSS*. n.p., n.d. Web. 30 Sept. 2016.

16. "Home." *RSS*. n.p., n.d. Web. 30 Sept. 2016.

17. Chang, Ellen. "How to Invest in Nasdaq-Traded Cannabis Stocks and Private Pot Companies." *TheStreet*. n.p., 2016. Web. 30 Sept. 2016.

18. Securities and Exchange Commission 17 CFR Parts 200, 227, 232, 239, 240, 249, 269, and 274 [Release Nos. 33-9974; 34-76324; File No. S7-09-13] RIN 3235-AL37

19. "S.683 - 114th Congress (2015–2016): Compassionate Access, Research Expansion, and Respect States Act of 2015." Congress.gov. n.p., n.d. Web. 30 Sept. 2016.

20. "H.R.1538 - 114th Congress (2015–2016): CARERS Act of 2015." Congress .gov. n.p., n.d. Web. 30 Sept. 2016.

21. "S.1726 - 114th Congress (2015–2016): Cannabis Businesses Access to Banking Act of 2015." Congress.gov. n.p., n.d. Web. 30 Sept. 2016.

22. "DEA.gov / Headquarters News Releases, 08/11/16." DEA.gov / Headquarters News Releases, 08/11/16. n.p., n.d. Web. 30 Sept. 2016.

23. "DEA.gov / Headquarters News Releases, 08/11/16." DEA.gov / Headquarters News Releases, 08/11/16. n.p., n.d. Web. 30 Sept. 2016.

Chapter 6

1. Caulkins, Jonathan P., Beau Kilmer, Mark A. R. Kleiman, Robert J. Mac-Coun, Greg Midgette, Pat Oglesby, Rosalie Liccardo Pacula and Peter H. Reuter. Considering Marijuana Legalization: Insights for Vermont and Other Jurisdictions. Santa Monica, CA: RAND Corporation, 2015. https://www.rand.org/pubs /research_reports/RR864.html.

2. "Senate Bill No. 491." 97th General Assembly, Missouri Senate. 2014. http:// www.senate.mo.gov/14info/pdf-bill/tat/SB491.pdf

3. "Mississippi Laws and Penalties." National Organization for the Reform of Marijuana Laws. 2017. http://norml.org/laws/item/mississippi-penalties-2

4. Kelley, Bill. "How Tough Is Nebraska on Pot Possession? Depends on the County." *NET News*. Sept. 18, 2014. http://netnebraska.org/article/news/938774 /how-tough-nebraska-pot-possession-depends-county

5. "Illinois Laws and Penalties." National Organization for the Reform of Marijuana Laws. 2017. http://norml.org/laws/item/illinois-penalties

6. "Ohio Laws and Penalties." National Organization for the Reform of Marijuana Laws. 2017. http://norml.org/laws/item/ohio-penalties-2

7. "North Carolina Laws and Penalties." National Organization for the Reform of Marijuana Laws. 2017. http://norml.org/laws/item/north-carolina-penalties-2

8. Roes, Thijs. "Trouble in Europe's Pot Paradise." Vice. April 19, 2016. https:// news.vice.com/article/trouble-in-europes-pot-paradise-a-bloody-gang-war-is -raging-in-amsterdam

9. "The Success of Portugal's Decriminalization Policy." Transform: Getting Drugs Under Control. July 14, 2014. http://www.tdpf.org.uk/blog/success-portu gal%E2%80%99s-decriminalisation-policy-%E2%80%93-seven-charts

10. "Alaska State Troopers." Alaska Bureau of Investigation Statewide Drug Enforcement Unit. 2015. http://www.dps.state.ak.us/ast/abi/docs/SDEUreports /2015%20Annual%20Drug%20Report.pdf

11. "Contractor Chosen for Louisiana Medial Marijuana Production." Associ- ated Press. June 17, 2017. https://www.usnews.com/news/best-states/louisiana /articles/2017-06-17/contractor-chosen-for-louisiana-medical-marijuana-production

12. "Medical Marijuana FAQ." Hawaii Department of Health. 2016. http:// health.hawaii.gov/medicalmarijuana/wp-content/blogs.dir/93/files/2016/02 /FAQs-for-Drafting-Rules-for-MMJ-Dispensary-licensing-program-002.pdf

13. "General Information about the Minnesota Medical Cannabis Program." 2017. http://www.health.state.mn.us/topics/cannabis/about/factsheet.html

14. "Arkansas Medical Marijuana Dispensary Zones." Arkansas Medical Mari- juana Commission. 2017. http://www.mmc.arkansas.gov/Websites/mmsar/images /8Zonemap.pdf

15. "Medical Cannabis Pilot Program Licenses." Illinois Department of Finan- cial and Professional Regulation. 2017. https://www.idfpr.com/Forms/MC /ListofLicensedDispensaries.pdf

16. "Pennsylvania Medical Marijuana Program." Pennsylvania Department of Health. 2017. http://www.health.pa.gov/My%20Health/Diseases%20and%20Con- ditions/M-P/MedicalMarijuana/Pages/FAQ.aspx#.Wa97RciGNPY

17. Cochran, Diane. "Once-Supportive Doctors Angered by Mass Clinics." *Mis- soulian.* June 1, 2010. http://missoulian.com/news/local/medical-marijuana-once -supportive-doctors-angered-by-mass-clinics/article_c82327c6-6d37-11df-bcdc -001cc4c03286.html

18. Wallstin, Brian. "Why New Hampshire's Medical Marijuana Law Shuts Out People with Chronic Pain." *NHPR.* July 19, 2016. http://nhpr.org/post/why-new -hampshires-medical-marijuana-law-shuts-out-people-chronic-pain

19. Interview, John Hudak, July 26, 2017.

20. Interview, Larry Horowitz, May 19, 2017.

21. Hernandez, Salvador. "'Nonprofit' Key to Medical Marijuana Sales." *Orange County Register.* Dec. 4, 2009. http://www.ocregister.com/2009/12/04/nonprofit -key-to-medical-marijuana-sales/

22. "New Mexico Medical Cannabis Sales Soar 86 Percent in First Quarter." Ultra Health. May 3, 2017. https://ultrahealth.com/2017/05/03/new-mexico -medical-cannabis-sales-soar-86-percent-first-quarter/

23. Groggel, Ken. "2016 First Quarter Report Summary." New Mexico Depart- ment of Health. https://nmhealth.org/publication/view/report/3080/

24. St. Cyr, Peter. "Growing Pains: How Money Flows from a Nonprofit Can- nabis Product in Santa Fe to a For-Profit Arizona Company." *Santa Fe Reporter.* April 6, 2016. http://www.sfreporter.com/santafe/article-11802-growing-pains .html

25. Azofeifa, A., Mattson, M. E., Schauer, G., McAfee, T., Grant, A., & Lyerla, R. "National Estimates of Marijuana Use and Related Indicators—National Survey on Drug Use and Health, United States, 2002–2014." *MMWR Surveill Summ* 2016; 65(No. SS-11):1–25. doi: https://www.cdc.gov/mmwr/volumes/65/ss/ss6511a1.htm

26. Newsroom. "Medical Cannabis Gets the Go-Ahead." *IOL*. Feb. 20, 2017. http://www.iol.co.za/news/politics/medicinal-cannabis-gets-the-go-ahead-7842750

27. Interview, Ethan Nadelmann, Aug. 29, 2017.

28. "Options and Issues Regarding Marijuana Legalization." https://www.rand.org/content/dam/rand/pubs/perspectives/PE100/PE149/RAND_PE149.pdf

29. Interview, Daniel Yi, May 23, 2017.

Chapter 7

1. Interview, Ethan Nadelmann, Aug, 29, 2017.

2. Borchardt, Debra. "$1 Billion in Marijuana Taxes Is Addicting to State Governors." *Forbes*. April 11, 2017. https://www.forbes.com/sites/debraborchardt/2017/04/11/1-billion-in-marijuana-taxes-is-addicting-to-state-governors/#18f26602c3bc

3. VS Strategies. "Special Report: Colorado Exceeds $500 Million in Cannabis Revenue Since Legalization." July 19, 2017. http://vsstrategies.com/wp-content/uploads/VSS-CO-MJ-Revenue-Report-July-2017.pdf

4. Gutman, David. "Is Marijuana Money the Answer to Fund Washington Schools?" *The Seattle Times*. Jan. 21, 2017. http://www.seattletimes.com/seattle-news/politics/state-weighs-using-pot-revenue-to-plug-school-funding-gap/

5. "Oregon Marijuana Tax Statistics." Oregon Department of Revenue. 2016. http://www.oregon.gov/DOR/programs/gov-research/Pages/research-marijuana.aspx

6. Brooks, James. "Alaska Marijuana Taxes Top $1 Million." *Juneau Empire*. July 3, 2017. http://juneauempire.com/state/2017-07-03/alaska-marijuana-taxes-top-1-million

7. "Proposition 64: Frequently Asked Questions." Drug Policy Alliance. 2016. https://d3n8a8pro7vhmx.cloudfront.net/responsiblemarijuanareform/pages/31/attachments/original/1468260214/Drug_Policy_Action_Fact_sheet_Prop_64_FAQs.pdf?1468260214

8. O'Neal, Nathan. "$60 Million in Tax Revenue Projected as Nevada Preps for Recreational Marijuana." KSVN 3News Las Vegas. http://news3lv.com/news/marijuana-in-nevada/60m-in-tax-revenue-projected-as-nevada-preps-for-recreational-marijuana

9. Bartlett, Jessica. "State Taxes on Recreational Marijuana Estimated at $64M in First Year." *Boston Business Journal*. March 20, 2017. https://www.bizjournals.com/boston/news/2017/03/20/state-taxes-on-recreational-marijuana-estimated-at.html

10. Portland Press Herald. "Pot Tax Debated in Maine." *New Hampshire Union Leader.* July 14, 2017. http://www.unionleader.com/article/20170713/NEWS06/170719579/-1/mobile?template=mobileart

11. Scarborough, Morgan, & Henchman, Joseph. "Marijuana Legalization and Taxes: Lessons for Other States from Colorado and Washington." Tax Foundation. May 12, 2016. https://taxfoundation.org/marijuana-taxes-lessons-colorado-washington/

12. Johnson, Gene. "Washington State Has Brought in $70 Million in Tax Revenue from Legal Marijuana Sales." Associated Press. July 4, 2017. http://www.businessinsider.com/recreational-marijuana-washington-state-tax-revenue-2015-7

13. "So Far, So Good." Drug Policy Alliance. Oct. 13, 2016. http://www.drugpolicy.org/sites/default/files/Marijuana_Legalization_Status_Report_101316.pdf

14. Darling, Dylan. "Pot Revenue Higher Than Anticipated." *The Register Guard.* Jan. 21, 2017. http://projects.registerguard.com/rg/news/local/35198483-75/oregon-rakes-in-60-million-in-state-sales-taxes-from-marijuana.html.csp

15. James, Tom. "The Failed Promise of Legal Pot." *The Atlantic.* May 9, 2016. https://www.theatlantic.com/politics/archive/2016/05/legal-pot-and-the-black-market/481506/

16. Scarborough, Morgan, & Henchman, Joseph. "Marijuana Legalization and Taxes: Lessons for Other States from Colorado and Washington." Tax Foundation. May 12, 2016.

17. Postmedia Network. "Federal Government to Push Provinces to Keep Marijuana Taxation Rates Low: Report." *Toronto Sun.* June 19, 2017. http://www.torontosun.com/2017/06/19/federal-government-to-push-provinces-to-keep-marijuana-taxation-rates-low-report

18. Castaldi, Malena. "Uruguay to Sell Marijuana Tax-Free to Undercut Drug Traffickers." *Reuters.* May 19, 2014. http://www.reuters.com/article/us-uruguay-marijuana-idUSBREA4I0CJ20140519

19. VS Strategies. "Special Report: Colorado Exceeds $500 Million in Cannabis Revenue Since Legalization." July 19, 2017. http://vsstrategies.com/wp-content/uploads/VSS-CO-MJ-Revenue-Report-July-2017.pdf

20. Hoffer, Adam, Shughart, William II, & Thomas, Michael. "Sin Taxes: Size, Growth, and Creation of the Sindustry." Mercatus Center, George Mason University. Feb. 2013. https://www.mercatus.org/publication/sin-taxes-size-growth-and-creation-sindustry

21. https://leg.colorado.gov/sites/default/files/15-10_distribution_of_marijuana_tax_revenue_issue_brief_1.pdf

22. Gutman, David. "Is Marijuana Money the Answer to Fund Washington Schools?" *The Seattle Times.* Jan. 21, 2017. http://www.seattletimes.com/seattle-news/politics/state-weighs-using-pot-revenue-to-plug-school-funding-gap/

23. Tierney, John. "State of Oregon Has Yet to Distribute Any Marijuana Money." *KGW.* May 5, 2017. http://www.kgw.com/news/verify-what-is-the-status-of-oregons-millions-in-tax-revenue/437143713

24. "Taxes Due on Marijuana," Washington State Department of Revenue. 2017. http://dor.wa.gov/Content/FindTaxesAndRates/marijuana/Default.aspx

25. Sabet, Kevin. "Legal Weed Isn't Living Up to All of Its Promises. We Need to Shut It Down." *CNBC.* July 27, 2017. https://www.cnbc.com/2017/07/27/trump -should-crackdown-on-legal-weed-commentary.html

26. Dills, Angela, Goffard, Sietse, & Miron, Jeffrey. "Dose of Reality: The Effects of State Marijuana Legalization." Sept. 16, 2016. https://www.cato.org/publications /policy-analysis/dose-reality-effect-state-marijuana-legalizations

27. U.S. Code 280E. Internal Revenue Service. Cornell Law School. https://www .law.cornell.edu/uscode/text/26/280E

28. 280E. National Cannabis Industry Association. 2015. https://thecanna- bisindustry.org/uploads/2015-280E-White-Paper.pdfx

Chapter 8

1. Board members. National Cannabis Industry Association. 2017. https:// thecannabisindustry.org/board-members/

2. "Cannabist Shop." *The Cannabist.* 2017. http://www.thecannabist.co/shop/

3. Editorial. "Amendment 64 Is the Wrong Way to Legalize Marijuana." The Denver Post. Oct. 12, 2014. http://www.denverpost.com/2012/10/12/editorial -amendment-64-is-the-wrong-way-to-legalize-marijuana/

4. "U.S. Daily Newspaper Circulation." Pew Research Center. Aug. 1, 2007. http://www.journalism.org/numbers/u-s-daily-newspaper-circulation/

5. "State of the News Media 2013, An Annual Report on American Journal- ism." Pew Research Center's Project for Excellence in Journalism. 2013. http:// www.stateofthemedia.org/2013/newspapers-stabilizing-but-still-threatened/1 -print-advertising-fall-online-grows-copy-5/

6. Avery, Greg. "Denver Post Cutting Staff in the Newsroom, Again." *Denver Business Journal.* June 4, 2015. http://www.bizjournals.com/denver/blog/boosters _bits/2015/06/denver-post-cutting-staff-in-the-newsroom-again.html

7. Petty, Daniel. "Humble Brag: Cannabist Surpasses High Times in Unique Visitors for First Time." *The Cannabist.* Oct. 12, 2016. http://www.thecannabist .co/2016/10/12/cannabist-visitors-surpasses-high-times/65123/

8. Interview, Cassandra Farrington, May 12, 2017.

9. "2016 Annual Report." Drug Policy Alliance. 2016. http://www.drugpolicy .org/sites/default/files/DPA-Annual-Report_2016.pdf

10. "IRS Tax Form 990." Drug Policy Alliance. 2011. http://www.drugpolicy .org/sites/default/files/DOC032613.pdf

11. Woolf, Nicky. "Marijuana Social Network MassRoots Enjoys Natural High of Success." *The Guardian.* Nov. 16, 2015. https://www.theguardian.com/society /2015/nov/16/marijuana-social-network-massroots-ceo-isaac-dietrich

12. Dogtiev, Artyam. "App Download and Usage Statistics 2017." Business of Apps. Sept. 5, 2017. http://www.businessofapps.com/app-usage-statistics-2015/

13. Kavilanz, Parija. "Nasdaq Rejects Pot Startup MassRoots." *CNN Money.* May 24, 2016. http://money.cnn.com/2016/05/24/smallbusiness/massroots -nasdaq/index.html

14. Paresh, Dave. "Weedmaps—a Yelp for Pot—Is Riddled with Suspicious Reviews." *Los Angeles Times.* Aug. 24, 2016. http://www.latimes.com/business /technology/la-fi-tn-weedmaps-data-breach-20160817-snap-story.html

15. Staggs, Brook Edwards. "Dispensaries Are Already—Illegally—Selling Recreational Marijuana under the Guise of Prop. 64." The Cannifornian. Jan. 6, 2017. http://www.thecannifornian.com/cannabis-news/california-news/dispen saries-already-illegally-selling-recreational-marijuana-guise-prop-64/

16. "Investors." MassRoots. 2017. https://www.massroots.com/investors

17. "Regulation of Marijuana Industry." Alaska Department of Commerce. https://www.commerce.alaska.gov/web/Portals/9/pub/MCB/StatutesAndRegula tions/MarijuanaRegulations.pdf

18. Schroyer, John. "Alcohol, Tobacco Interests Eyeing Michigan Marijuana Market." *Marijuana Business Daily.* April 27, 2017. https://mjbizdaily.com/alcohol -tobacco-interests-eyeing-michigan-marijuana-market/

19. Reed, Jack. "Regulation of Marijuana Industry. Alaska Department of Commerce. 2015." Colorado Office of Research and Statistics. March 2016. http:// cdpsdocs.state.co.us/ors/docs/reports/2016-SB13-283-Rpt.pdf

20. "Open Data Catalog." City and County of Denver. 2017. https://www .denvergov.org/opendata

21. "Students Explore Impact of Marijuana Legalization." Metropolitan State University. June 30, 2015. https://www.msudenver.edu/newsroom/news/2015 /june/30-marijuana-studies.shtml

22. "Marijuana Legalization in Washington After 1 Year of Retail Sales and 2.5 Years of Legal Possession." Drug Policy Institute. July 2015. https://www .drugpolicy.org/sites/default/files/Drug_Policy_Alliance_Status_Report _Marijuana_Legalization_in_Washington_July2015.pdf

23. https://object.cato.org/sites/cato.org/files/pubs/pdf/pa799.pdf

24. Ibid.

25. Reilly, Ryan, & Ferner, Matt. "Jeff Sessions Issues Ominous Warning on State Marijuana Legalization." *Huffington Post.* Feb. 27, 2017. http://www.huffing tonpost.com/entry/jeff-sessions-marijuana-comments_us_58b4b189e4b0780b ac2c9fd8

26. "High Crimes: Robber Gangs Terrorize Colorado Pot Shops." *NBC News.* Feb. 5, 2014. http://www.nbcnews.com/storyline/legal-pot/high-crimes-robber -gangs-terrorize-colorado-pot-shops-n20111

27. "Fatal Shooting Near Durango Allegedly Part of Pot Robbery." Associated Press. June 12, 2017. http://www.denverpost.com/2017/06/12/durango-fatal-shoot ing-pot-robbery/

28. Summers, D. J. "Security Service Pot Businesses Latest to Enter State Market." *Alaska Journal of Commerce.* Aug. 19, 2017. http://www.alaskajournal.com /business-and-finance/2015-08-19/security-service-pot-businesses-latest-enter -state-market

29. Schroyer, John. "Washington State Cannabis Growers Upset with Inventory Tracking System, Urge Fixes." *Marijuana Business Daily*. March 25, 2016. https://mjbizdaily.com/washington-state-growers-upset-inventory-tracking-system-urge-fixes/

30. "Cannabis Farmers Council Petition." Washington State. https://www.petitions24.com/cfc_petition_on_behalf_of_i-502_cannabis_farmers

31. "KIND Financial Launches Government Division Targeting Cannabis Contracts." *PR Newswire*. June 16, 2016. http://www.prnewswire.com/news-releases/kind-financial-launches-government-division-targeting-government-cannabis-contracts-300285881.html

32. "Nearly One-Third of Life Insurance Companies Classify Marijuana Users as Non-Smokers, Finds Munich Re Survey." *PR Newswire*. June 2, 2015. http://www.prnewswire.com/news-releases/nearly-one-third-of-life-insurance-companies-classify-marijuana-users-as-non-smokers-finds-munich-re-survey-300091071.html

33. "Senate Bill 15-136." First Regular Session, 70th General Assembly, State of Colorado. http://www.leg.state.co.us/clics/clics2015a/csl.nsf/fsbillcont/A41536D017AEC63687257DBD005D918C?Open&file=136_01.pdf

34. Kush Bottles. "Form 10-Q. U.S. Securities and Exchange Commission." Feb. 2017. https://www.sec.gov/Archives/edgar/data/1604627/000151116417000183/kush2281710qv1.htm

35. Dalheim, Robert. "Wooden Marijuana Packaging Saves Dispensary $50,000 a Year." Woodworking Network. June 5, 2017. http://www.woodworkingnetwork.com/wood/panel-supply/wooden-marijuana-packaging-saves-dispensary-50000-year

36. Brohl, Barbara. "House Bill 1366 Marijuana Edibles Work Group Report." Colorado Department of Revenue. Jan. 30, 2015. https://www.colorado.gov/pacific/sites/default/files/HB%201366%20Work%20Group%20Report_FINAL.pdf

37. Brohl, Barbara. "Report to House and Senate Finance Committees." Colorado Department of Revenue. April 1, 2016. https://www.colorado.gov/pacific/sites/default/files/DOR%20MED%20April%201%202016%20Report%20to%20the%20JBC.pdf

38. Borchardt, Debra. "Edible Marijuana Company Ready for New Rules." *Forbes*. June 6, 2016. https://www.forbes.com/sites/debraborchardt/2016/06/06/edible-marijuana-company-ready-for-new-rules/#3bbed5dd479a

39. Castle, Shay. "Boulder's Stashlogix, Maker of Pot Carrying Cases, Under Fire as Feds Confiscate Product." *Boulder Daily Camera*. June 8, 2017. http://www.dailycamera.com/boulder-business/ci_31048759/boulder-pot-case-maker-under-fire-feds-confiscate

Chapter 9

1. Hudak, John, & Wallack, Grace. "How to Reschedule Marijuana and Why It's Unlikely to Happen Anytime Soon." Brookings Institute. Feb. 13, 2015.

https://www.brookings.edu/blog/fixgov/2015/02/13/how-to-reschedule
-marijuana-and-why-its-unlikely-anytime-soon/

2. Tapper, Jake. "Jake Tapper: Exclusive Interview with President Obama."
CNN. Jan. 30, 2014. http://cnnpressroom.blogs.cnn.com/2014/01/30/just-released
-cnns-jake-tapper-exclusive-interview-with-president-obama/

3. Adams, Mike. "Democratic Party Officially Incudes Marijuana Reform
in Its 2016 Platform." *High Times.* June 27, 2016. http://hightimes.com/news
/politics/democratic-party-officially-includes-marijuana-reform-in-its-2016
-platform/

4. Summers, D. J. "The Great Cannabis Divide." *Alaska Journal of Commerce.*
Nov. 17, 2016. http://www.alaskajournal.com/2016-11-17/great-cannabis-divide#
.Wi7E68anFPY

5. "Statement by President Donald J. Trump on Signing H.R. 244 into Law."
White House. May 5, 2017. https://www.whitehouse.gov/the-press-office/2017/05
/05/statement-president-donald-j-trump-signing-hr-244-law

6. Bennett, John. "Trump Is Quickly Running Out of GOP Factions to Alien-
ate." *Roll Call.* Aug. 18, 2017. https://www.rollcall.com/news/politics/trump-gop
-factions-alienate

7. Camden, Jim. "Rep. Cathy McMorris Rodgers: Putin Is Trying to Undermine
the U.S." *The Spokesman Review.* Feb. 26, 2017. http://www.spokesman.com/stories
/2017/feb/26/rep-cathy-mcmorris-rodgers-putin-is-trying-to-unde/

8. Berg, Rebecca. "Mitch McConnell: 'I'm Against Legalizing Marijuana." *Washington Examiner.* Sept. 27, 2014. http://www.washingtonexaminer.com/mitch
-mcconnell-im-against-legalizing-marijuana/article/2554052#!

9. Interview, Morgan Fox, April 22, 2017.

10. Swift, Art. "Support for Legal Marijuana Use Up to 60% in U.S." Gallup. Oct. 19, 2016. http://www.gallup.com/poll/196550/support-legal-marijuana
.aspx

11. Hudak, John, & Rauch, Jonathan. "Worry About Bad Marijuana—Not Big
Marijuana." Center for Effective Public Management at Brookings. June 2016.
https://www.brookings.edu/wp-content/uploads/2016/07/big-marijuana-1.pdf

12. "Agribusiness." Open Secrets. https://www.opensecrets.org/lobby/indus
.php?id=A

13. Schiller, Melissa. "Aurora Cannabis Breaks Ground on Production Facility
at Edmonton International Airport Amidst Canada's Expanding Industry." July 10,
2017. http://www.cannabisbusinesstimes.com/article/aurora-cannabis-facility
-edmonton-airport/

14. Lubell, Maayan, & Back, Lianne. "Israel Looks to Leverage Tech in $50
Billion Medical Marijuana Market." *Reuters.* March 23, 2017. http://www.reuters
.com/article/us-israel-cannabis-idUSKBN16U1PZ

15. Hudak, John, & Rauch, Jonathan. "Worry About Bad Marijuana—Not Big
Marijuana." Center for Effective Public Management at Brookings. https://www
.brookings.edu/wp-content/uploads/2016/07/big-marijuana-1.pdf

16. Ramo, Danielle E., Delucchi, Kevin L., Hall, Sharon M., Liu, Howard., Pro-
chaska, Judith J. "Marijuana and Tobacco Co-Use in Young Adults: Patterns and

Thoughts About Use." *Journal of Studies on Alcohol and* Drugs 2013; 74(2): 301–310. https://www.ncbi.nlm.nih.gov/pmc/articles/PMC3568169/

17. http://onlinelibrary.wiley.com/doi/10.1111/1468-0009.12055/abstract;jsessi onid=1A32F2BDE81D175B2D4A22DBC8A94B38.f03t02

18. Mickle, Tripp. "Japan Tobacco to Acquire U.S. Electronic Cigarette Company Logic Technology Development." *Wall Street Journal.* April 30, 2015. https:// www.wsj.com/articles/japan-tobacco-to-acquire-u-s-electronic-cigarette-company -logic-technology-development-1430423065

19. Ad Age. "Cannabis Could Be Added to the Mix by Alcohol Giants as Laws Ease." AdvertisingAge. Nov. 10, 2016. http://adage.com/article/cmo-strategy /cannabis-added-alcohol-giant-laws-ease/306722/

20. "Colorado Liquor Excise Taxes." Colorado Department of Revenue. May 2015. https://www.colorado.gov/pacific/sites/default/files/Liquor%20Excise %20Tax%200515.pdf

21. "2016 60th Day Preceding Election Report." Massachusetts Office of Campaign and Political Finance. http://www.ocpf.us/Reports/DisplayReport?menu Hidden=true&id=584060#schedule-a

22. "POLITICO Huddle." Wikileaks. https://wikileaks.org/dnc-emails/email id/393

23. "Vice Wars: Tobacco, Alcohol, and the Rise of Big Marijuana." *NBC News.* Nov. 24, 2014. http://www.nbcnews.com/storyline/legal-pot/vice-wars-tobacco -alcohol-rise-big-marijuana-n253801

24. "MPP Chief Ready to Barter for Marijuana Campaign Donations." *Marijuana Business Daily.* April 28, 2017. https://mjbizdaily.com/mpp-chief-ready -barter-marijuana-campaign-donations/

25. "2016 Top Markets Report: Pharmaceuticals." International Trade Administration, U.S. Department of Commerce. 2016. http://trade.gov/topmarkets/pdf /Pharmaceuticals_Executive_Summary.pdf

26. "Pharmaceutical Research and Manufacturers of America." Open Secrets. 2017. https://www.opensecrets.org/lobby/clientsum.php?id=D000000504&year =2017

27. Bradford, Ashley, & Bradford, David. "Medical Marijuana Laws Reduce Prescription Medication Use in Medicare." Health Affairs. http://content.healthaffairs .org/content/35/7/1230

28. "Medical Cannabis Poised to Cannibalize to Pharmaceutical Industry." New Frontier Data. May 24, 2017. https://newfrontierdata.com/marijuana-insights /medical-cannabis-poised-cannibalize-pharmaceutical-industry/

29. Fang, Lee. "The Real Reason Pot Is Still Illegal." *The Nation.* July 2, 2014. https://www.thenation.com/article/anti-pot-lobbys-big-bankroll/

30. "Schedules of Controlled Substances: Placement of FDA-Approved Products of Oral Solutions Containing Dronabinol [(-)-delta-9-trans-tetrahydrocannabi nol (delta-9-THC)] in Schedule II." Drug Enforcement Administration. March 3, 2017. https://www.federalregister.gov/documents/2017/03/23/2017-05809/schedules -of-controlled-substances-placement-of-fda-approved-products-of-oral-solutions -containing

31. Brochstein, Alan. "Bail Out for Blue Line Protection Group." New Cannabis Ventures. May 18, 2016. https://www.newcannabisventures.com/bail-out-for-blue-line-protection-group/

32. Brochstein, Alan. "Entrepreneurs Working to Solve Cannabis Banking Issues Could Be Wasting Time." New Cannabis Ventures. May 23, 2017. https://www.newcannabis ventures.com/entrepreneurs-working-to-solve-cannabis -banking-issues-could-be-wasting-time/

33. "Report: Even If Trump Cracks Down, Legal Marijuana Industry's 27% Annual Growth Rate Through 2021 Remains Unchanged." BDS Analytics. March 23, 2017. http://www.bdsanalytics.com/arcview-market-research-marijuana -industry-report/

Index

About the Author

D. J. Summers is a freelance journalist working in Colorado, covering developments in the cannabis industry. Formerly he was a business and investigative reporter for the *Alaska Journal of Commerce*, covering Alaska's recreational marijuana industry since it began in 2015. In addition to cannabis, he has covered health care, banking, politics, and telecommunications, with numerous articles picked up by the Associated Press for national distribution. Previously, he covered cyber security for *Fortune* and worked as a general assignment reporter for the *Salt Lake Tribune* in addition to other publications. Summers earned a master's degree in journalism from Syracuse University in 2014.